# TRADER VIC'S
# PACIFIC ISLAND COOKBOOK

# TRADER VIC'S
# PACIFIC ISLAND
# COOKBOOK

With Side Trips to Hong Kong,
Southeast Asia, Mexico and Texas
300 Food and Drink Recipes
from 18 Different Places

PHOTOGRAPHY BY BRUCE HARLOW

ILLUSTRATIONS BY WING LOW

*1968*

DOUBLEDAY & COMPANY, INC.

GARDEN CITY, NEW YORK

# CONTENTS

*Recipes for items that are capitalized in the text can be located by consulting the Index*

# PHOTOGRAPHS IN COLOR

# INTRODUCTION

MY PURPOSE in writing this book is twofold. First, I want to tell you about the foods I have encountered during my travels the past few years. Second, I want to suggest ways in which you can adapt these recipes from other lands to your own use; give you some ideas for making everyday meals festive; tell you how to give successful parties that let you have fun, too.

The history of foods and cooking has always fascinated me. I have been intrigued by the history of bread-making, the foods of the early Greeks and Romans, as well as the foods of primitive peoples. No matter how far back you delve, one fact stands out: man's social structure has always revolved around food and its presentation. The basis of hospitality, yesterday and today, is the sharing of food and drink with friends and acquaintances.

The success of entertaining depends upon three factors: how well you coordinate your food with your decor; how attractively you present food and drink to your guests; but most important of all, how you welcome your guests and how comfortable you make them feel.

The pleasure of entertaining is doing something you have created and planned, and it isn't necessary to spend days or weeks doing this. Some people make cooking a project and take hours to prepare a dish or meal. That's goofy. You are too busy nowadays to make cooking the drudgery it was in the past. Most recipes, excluding those for cakes, breads and certain classical sauces, need not be followed exactly. They can be altered or varied. That's all most recipes really are—just guidelines. The most fun in cooking is improvising and experimenting.

In this wonderful country of ours, we are blessed with the greatest array of fresh, frozen, canned and prepared foods in the world. There are spices, condiments and imported specialties on your grocer's shelves to let you cook in any language and with imagination. There are all kinds of prepared foods which you can mix together to achieve a close facsimile to any foreign dish you may care to try. Why do it the hard way?

Food and its related products is our country's second largest industry. Millions of dollars are spent annually to influence our eating habits. Every woman's magazine has a recipe section. Every newspaper has a weekly food section. Even such men's magazines as *Playboy* and *Esquire* have succumbed. With all of the foods and information at our disposal, there is no reason for any meal to be ordinary or for you to spend hours in the kitchen.

Every country, every island has at least one outstanding dish worth adding to your collection, so expand you culinary repertoire. Try out new dishes on your family. For example, find a curry recipe you and your family enjoy. Work out the accompaniments, or sambals, you like best. Experiment until you find your favorite chutney. Then plan special table decorations, special linens and dishes for your curry dinner and have a party.

Mexican food is fun for family and guests. Work out a Mexican menu that appeals to your family and then add a few extras, like guacamole, small cocktail tacos, tiny cheese enchiladas or tamalitas for a festive evening with friends. Shop for special serving dishes, glassware and table decorations. With import outlets springing up all over the country you should be able to find some effective table appointments without too much cash outlay.

Special dishes and table decorations make a family dinner a treat, too. Do the unusual for birthdays, anniversaries or any important event in your lives. Dinner by candlelight with table decorations shouldn't be reserved just for guests.

Some of the recipes in this book are just the way I got them. If the dish turned out all right, tasted good and had appeal, no changes were made. Some of them, however, have been worked over and adapted to American tastes. Many so-called authentic dishes have little appeal to the average American. Chinese dishes are very popular in this country but there are many which, if served exactly as they were originally created, simply wouldn't be accepted.

Most people enjoy the familiar Japanese dishes such as sukiyaki, tempura or teriyaki, and even these dishes are often changed to appeal to American preferences. Very few people care for sashimi, which is very fresh raw fish, such as sea bream or tuna, sliced paper thin and served with wasabi or horseradish mixed with soy sauce. I am addicted to it. Sushi, which is rice boiled in vinegared water and seasoned with salt and sugar, is shaped around sashimi, cooked shrimp or topped with cucumber slices and some form of seafood. This is a favorite Japanese tidbit but is a seldom acquired taste with Americans.

As more and more people travel, foreign foods become more enjoyable. Often it is simply a matter of exposure. But I still find that most Americans do not appreciate food which is too far out. It takes time, and the willingness to taste everything, to educate your taste buds to the point where you can appreciate many foreign flavors and textures.

Cooking and entertaining can be an adventure, a source of great satisfaction, a means of self-expression, to say nothing about promoting friendships. Like golf, bridge, tennis or dancing, they are to be enjoyed and shared. Fun and food go together, and I hope this book will provide some fun for you and your family.

# TRADER VIC'S
# PACIFIC ISLAND COOKBOOK

# Polynesia

POLYNESIA starts with the Hawaiian Islands and includes the islands east of Melanesia and Micronesia, extending from the Hawaiian Islands south to New Zealand. Polynesians, described as a brown-skinned people, speaking a closely related Austronesian language, include the Maoris of New Zealand, the Tahitians Samoans, Hawaiians and the natives of Easter Island.

Many anthropologists believe that Polynesians paddled over from the Malay peninsula many centuries ago, to the South Pacific Islands, and hence to Hawaii. But there are still many questions to be answered and many differences of opinion on the subject among the experts. The Kon Tiki expedition proved that the Polynesians could have arrived in the South Pacific from the coast of Peru, but not that they did.

Throughout the islands of the mid- and South Pacific the primitive cooking methods of the Hawaiians, Tahitians, Samoans and other island groups were basically the same. Food was roasted over an open fire, steamed underground or simply eaten in its natural state. The native diet was practically the same everywhere, consisting of fish, pork, chicken, bananas, coconuts, sweet potatoes, breadfruit and taro.

For some reason, never explained satisfactorily, the Hawaiians are the only group that hanker for poi, the cooked and pounded root of the taro. Most of the other groups use the taro root in much the same way as we do potatoes.

The old ways are still clung to in some parts of the Society Islands, like Riatea, Bora Bora and Mooréa, and out of the way islands, but in Papeete, capital of Tahiti, and of French

Polynesia, where the French influence on island cooking is strongest, many of the old ways have been discarded in favor of Western utensils and methods. Civilization, so-called, has changed the native cooking until today's recipes are a nice blend of Tahitian and French cuisine. The underground oven, or ahimaa, is used only for the Tahitian feast called a tamaaraa, the equivalent to the Hawaiian luau.

Only in the Hawaiian Islands have modern ways really taken hold.

# Hawaii

SINCE World War II there has been an ever increasing interest in the culture and foods of the South Pacific and the Far East. Countless books and plays have been written about Hawaii, the South Pacific Islands and countries in the Pacific Theater of War. James Michener hit pay dirt with *Tales of the South Pacific,* *Sayonara* and *Hawaii.* Thor Heyerdahl wrote his account of the Kon Tiki raft expedition which left Peru in 1947 to prove that the forefathers of Polynesians could have originated in the Americas. Again in 1955 he led an expedition to Easter Island and published the results of his findings in *Aku-Aku* three years later. Meantime Carrie Guild wrote *Rainbow in Tahiti,* the late Eugene Burns wrote *The Last King of Paradise,* a lusty, rollicking tale of Hawaiian royalty, and the late Eugene Burdick contributed *Blue of Capricorn.*

Many GIs, fresh from Midwest farms, found themselves on the receiving end of warm island hospitality. They took home tales of pikake leis, luaus and lovely hula hands in little grass shacks. The occupation forces in post-war Japan learned to appreciate the Japanese, their way of life, customs, art and culture. They brought home wonderful descriptions of the Japanese countryside, its lakes and mountains, and sometimes brought home Japanese brides.

As the years passed, and memories of Pearl Harbor, Hiroshima and Nagasaki gradually faded, the ensuring hurts and hates faded too. The Americas, the South Pacific and the Far East were brought sharply into focus and travelers, forsaking European haunts, toured the Orient by plane and ship, with Honolulu the first stop.

But the years between 1941 and 1968 have brought progress, statehood and skyscrapers to the Hawaiian Islands. Waikiki Beach is hemmed in by tall, modern hotels; high-rise apartment buildings and condominiums are springing up all over Honolulu. The old Hawaiian customs, long on the wane, have retreated to the outer islands.

Today, Polynesians, assorted Caucasians, Chinese, Japanese and Koreans, people from all over, are contributing to the cultural, industrial and domestic welfare of Hawaii, the fiftieth state of the Union. Men and women of all races compete for state and national political positions, all working for a better and more prosperous community.

Inter-marriage has produced some handsome, intelligent people. Nowhere else do you find so many different races, with different religions, languages and customs, living together with such tolerance and understanding. The Hawaiians are proud of their state, proud to be Americans. Some of our mainland states could take a long, long lesson from them.

It is to be expected that every facet of island life—homes, furnishings, clothes and foods—has been affected by the various peoples who have migrated to Hawaii. The Americans arrived first and introduced pineapples and sugar to the islands. The British came next, and then the Chinese, to work in the sugar fields.

Everywhere you find the Chinese influence: the cheongsams, the mandarin collar, frog closings in clothes; teak furniture, carved jades; and the symbols of Longevity, Double Happiness and Good Luck. Noodles and long rice, silver noodles, bean threads, ginger, star anise, black fermented beans, water chestnuts, bean sprouts and Chinese pea pods or snow peas, originally from China, are a part of the daily island fare. But most of all is the evidence of Chinese energy and know-how.

The Japanese came next, bringing with them the cult of cleanliness, the love of natural beauty and serenity, brush painting, and the zori, inspiration for the countless types of sandals or go-aheads worn by both men and women in Hawaii. With the Japanese came the hibachi, sashimi, sushi, tempura, sukiyaki and sake.

The Portuguese, the first Europeans to migrate to Hawaii, contributed their native spicy dishes seasoned with tomatoes, onions and green pepper; and the steel guitar. Then through the years, in small groups or individually, Spaniards, Filipinos, Italians, Puerto Ricans, Scandinavians and peoples from all parts of the world came to Hawaii and contributed to her culture.

But the greatest influence of all still remains that of the original Polynesians. Much of the charm of the Hawaiian Islands can be traced to the good nature, simple dignity, friendliness, love of fun and bounteous hospitality of those original citizens who somehow managed to impart this spirit to all who live in the Hawaiian Islands. May it never change.

## HAWAIIAN LUAU

Symbol of island hospitality is the luau, the celebration feast of the Polynesians, given in honor of birthdays, weddings, holidays, visiting dignitaries and Aloha Week. Tradition demanded that the star of this feast be the Kalua pig, baked underground in the imu, along with fish wrapped in ti leaves, yams, breadfruit, bananas and laulaus.

In bygone days, the preparation took days and everyone helped. Some dug the underground oven. Others gathered wood to heat the special stones for the oven. Fish were caught; shellfish, fruit and flowers were gathered. Ti leaves were cut in abundance for use in cooking and for the native tablecloth. Woven mats were spread on the ground and the ti leaves so arranged that guests might sit on the mats on either side. Down the center of the ti leaves were piled the fruits and flowers. Shells and bowls were filled with such goodies as poi, opihis, roasted kukui nuts and red salt.

While the feast cooked underground, there was singing, chants and ceremonial hulas, along with a bit of imbibing. When the pit was dug open, the steaming food was taken from the imu, the meat was cut up in chunks and rushed, in large wooden bowls, to the waiting guests. Everyone ate with his fingers from banana leaves and drank from coconut cups.

Originally, the partaking of fermented libations was confined to the priests and chiefs, as part of their rituals, a custom which appears to have prevailed in all early civilizations. In later years a fermented sweet potato juice was used during festival times by the common folk. Apparently there was no particular ceremony connected with its use, but the early Hawaiians reserved it for special occasions.

It wasn't until after the traders and whalers came to the island that the national drink was invented. An escaped convict from an Australian penal colony is said to have taught the Hawaiians how to make a distilled liquor from the roots of the ti plant. To distill the ti root mash, the Hawaiians bought from the whalers the double iron pots used to boil down whale blubber. These were used in pairs and since they were flat on one side, when put together they resembled the rump of a plump matron. The Hawaiian word for rump is okole and the word for iron is hao, so they put the two words together and called their liquor okolehao.

I was pleased to learn, on my last visit to Honolulu, that some nice guy has started making genuine ti root okolehao. Properly aged in charred oak kegs, it is wonderful booze and the liquor originally used in the island Scorpion.

Someone told me that during the war, when liquor was rationed and non-existent most of the time, some of the islanders started making their own okolehao, and that many a Hawaiian had a keg of oke sloshing around in the back of his car, or suspended in the rafters with a rope hanging down. When he or members of his family went by they gave the rope a tug to turn the keg.

## KALUA PIG

The preparation for cooking the traditional Kalua pig underground hasn't changed much in modern times. About the only improvement is that the pig is either wrapped in chicken wire, lined with ti leaves, or lowered into the pit in a big wire basket, neither of which the natives of long ago possessed.

First the pit or imu is dug. It should be about 4 or 5 feet

long, 4 feet wide and about 4 feet deep, depending upon the size of the pig, or the number of pigs to be cooked. The Hawaiians like to cook big fat pigs, weighing 90 to 100 pounds. I prefer several pigs, each weighing about 25 pounds.

Next, stick a pole, several inches in diameter, right into the center of the pit. This is important because when you pull it out, the hole will be the means of lighting your fire. Lay kindling and wood on the bottom of the pit. Use lots of wood. On top of the wood arrange 60 to 75 imu stones. There are round smooth lava stones which can stand extreme heat without bursting and thus driving splinters of rock into the food. There should also be extra stones to put in the pig's *opu* (stomach).

When you are ready to light the wood, remove the center pole and light the fire through the hole left in the center. A lighter can be made by wrapping cloth around one end of a broom handle or bamboo pole and dipping it in kerosene. Let the fire burn until the wood is glowing embers and the stones are white hot.

Meanwhile the pig should be cleaned, scraped, slit down the stomach and drawn. Make slits in the skin, being careful not to cut through the skin into the meat of the pig. Rub coarse salt into the slits and rub several handfuls of the salt into the inside of the pig. Fill the stomach of the animal with heated imu stones and tie the legs together.

Lay several banana trunks across the width of the pit to form a sort of platform on which to set the pig, which is lowered into the pit in a wire basket, lined with ti and banana leaves and surrounded by yams, bananas, and fish, all tied up in ti leaf packages. Cover the food with a thick protective pad of banana and ti leaves. Over this lay a dozen or so burlap bags, and then shovel earth or sand over the whole thing. Let the food steam 4 to 5 hours.

## MODERN LUAU

Today's luau has undergone certain refinements. The ingredients may be the same but the process has changed a bit. On Oahu, the island where Honolulu is situated, the underground imu is used mostly by hotels or restaurants which make a specialty of the old-time presentation for the benefit of tourists. It is used on the outer islands principally by elegant resorts or on the big ranches.

While ti leaves still serve as the luau table covering, the feast is more apt to be served on tables than on the ground. Sometimes the tables are low and folks sit on cushions. Sometimes even knives and forks are provided. At each place is set a small dish or shell of Hawaiian (red) salt, a small container of red peppers, green onions and limed fish, No luau is ever complete without Lomi Salmon and Poi, both served in bowls, and the island dessert, haupia, made from coconuts and cornstarch. Of later years coconut layer cake has been added to typical luau menus.

The Kalua pig may be roasted in an oven or barbecued head down in a Chinese oven. For small celebrations or family luaus, the Kalua pig is often a pork roast done Hawaiian or Chinese style, or an oven-roasted suckling pig.

Laulaus are often steamed or cooked in pressure cookers. Yams or sweet potatoes may be oven-baked plain, or peeled and baked in a casserole with pineapple or bananas, or both.

The luau menu is often augmented by bowls of shrimp, Chicken Hawaiian, Hawaiian Curry, or Chicken Long Rice.

Luau food without the traditional Kalua pig is properly called a poi supper in the islands. Nowadays this can be a mixture of island foods, such as Poi Stew, mahimahi baked in ti leaves or sautéed and served with crushed macadamia nuts and slivers of pineapple. There are the usual baked or broiled bananas, Chicken Luau, island fruits, the everpresent Haupia, and coconut or banana cream cake.

# LUAU RECIPES—OLD TIME AND MODERN

*ROASTED KUKUI NUTS*

The kukui nut is an old-timer, served in small portions at luaus whenever available. They are roasted in the oven whole, shelled and then pounded into small pieces and mixed with a little Hawaiian red salt and a few of the hot red peppers which the Hawaiians love. It is one of those old island treats that never made it big. Macadamia nuts have more appeal and are now available everywhere.

*POI*

Made from the versatile taro root, poi is a product that requires the skill of an expert. Briefly, it is a grayish paste made by fermenting roasted taro roots. It is bought fresh or in cans, and is now available in powdered form. You can have instant poi by adding water. In addition to poi, the root is eaten like a vegetable—boiled, or sliced and fried. Or it can be boiled, mashed and formed into cakes which are fried in butter or baked. Serve hot with butter. It is even possible to make poi muffins.

From the tops of the taro plant come the tender leaves called luau, which are cooked like spinach or Swiss chard (only longer) and served with coconut cream or butter.

*TARO CAKES – I*
*You can see why they needed poi pounders*

Boil taro root until tender. Peel and while hot, pound smooth, adding as little water as possible. Mold into small cakes. Put in buttered pan. Place a dab of butter on each cake and bake until brown. Eat hot with butter.

*TARO CAKES – II*
*This is an old-time recipe and a little complicated*

Peel and cut one medium-sized taro root in half. Boil in plain water for 1½ hours, or until tender. Drain, mash fine while hot, adding 1 teaspoon salt. Keep left hand moist, with which to turn taro while beating with right until free from lumps. Put mass in stainless steel or porcelain bowl, cover and set away overnight, but not in the refrigerator. Next day, form into small flat cakes, half an inch thick. Put on baking sheet in cold oven. When thermometer registers 475° F., turn off heat. Cakes should rise three or four times their original height, and be crisp and dark brown color all over. Serve hot with butter.

*POI MUFFINS*

1⅓ cups flour
½ teaspoon salt
1 tablespoon sugar
4 teaspoons baking powder

⅔ cup poi
1 egg
3 tablespoons butter or margarine
½ cup milk

Sift dry ingredients together. Use poi as purchased. Do not mix with water. Blend poi with beaten egg, butter and milk; combine with dry ingredients and spoon into oiled muffin tin, ⅔ full. Bake at 400° F. for 30 minutes. If canned poi is used, reduce milk to ⅓ cup. Instant poi is now available. Follow directions for reconstituting. Makes 18 to 20 2-inch muffins.

We come now to opihis. Originally these were limpets, a gastropod, considered a delicacy by the Polynesians. Nowadays scallops may be substituted. In San Francisco we use tiny bay scallops, the meat of which is about the size of your thumbnail.

*OPIHIS*
*Fresh scallops cooked in lime juice*

1 pound scallops
2 teaspoons MSG
1 teaspoon salt
½ teaspoon white pepper

4 dashes Tabasco sauce
   (almost ½ teaspoon)
Juice of 6 limes

Use tiny scallops, if possible, which are closest to the tiny shellfish native to the Hawaiian Islands. If larger scallops are used, cut in quarters. Place ingredients in a stainless steel or ceramic mixing bowl and let stand for 6 hours in the refrigerator, stirring occasionally to let the lime juice thoroughly penetrate the fish. When ready to serve add the following:

2 tablespoons thick sour
   cream
3 tablespoons Coconut
   Milk

1 cup finely chopped
   green onions, including
   some of the tops

Serves 15 to 20.


Lomi Salmon, a somewhat late addition to the traditional luau, was made with salted salmon. It was first introduced to the Hawaiians by the early trading vessels stopping at Honolulu. It is still imported from the mainland.

*LOMI SALMON – I*
*The Hawaiian version with salted salmon*

1 pound salted salmon
4 large ripe, peeled
   tomatoes

1 bunch green onions
1 medium onion

Soak salmon in water several hours to remove some of the salt and soften. Meantime, chop the tomatoes. Clean and mince the green onions, including some of the tops. Peel and mince the dry onion. Drain the soaked salmon, remove skin and bones and break up with fingers. Rinse again if it is still too salty. Mix salmon with tomatoes and onions, and squeeze with hands until everything is broken up and well mixed. (This is where the *lomi* comes in. Lomi in Hawaiian means to press or massage.) Chill thoroughly. Serves 15 to 20.

*LOMI SALMON – II*
*Mainland style made with fresh salmon*

| | |
|---|---|
| 1 pound fresh salmon | 4 tablespoons chopped |
| 2 teaspoons MSG | onions |
| ½ teaspoon sugar | Juice of 6 limes |
| 2 teaspoons salt | 3 cups chopped, peeled |
| 4 dashes Tabasco sauce | tomatoes |

Remove skin and bones from salmon; dice and put in stainless steel or ceramic bowl. Add seasonings, onions and lime juice and let marinate for 6 hours in refrigerator, stirring from time to time. Meanwhile, chill the tomatoes. When ready to serve, knead the salmon with the lime juice and onions; add the tomatoes and mix well. Serve in small shells. Note: Finely chopped green onions or chives may be added for color. Serves 15 to 20.

The island laulau made with taro leaves can be cooked in a pressure cooker. A satisfactory substitute for taro is spinach, Swiss chard or Chinese bok choy. For mainlanders, here is a quick version, suitable for large groups. Swiss chard or bok choy is best.

*MAINLAND LAULAUS*

| | |
|---|---|
| 10 pounds green part of Swiss chard or bok choy | 1 tablespoon MSG |
| | 2 teaspoons sugar |
| 2 pounds cooked chicken meat | 2 teaspoons pepper |
| | ¼ cup lemon juice |
| 2 bunches green onions | 4 tablespoons cornstarch mixed with |
| 1 cup finely diced salt pork | ½ cup cold water |
| | 50 ti leaves |

Wash greens, remove any fibrous parts and the stems. Cut chicken into 1-inch pieces. Wash, trim and chop green onions, using the green stems also. Sauté salt pork in a heavy kettle; add green onions and sauté with pork for a few seconds, then add chicken and greens and sauté together for 5 minutes. Drain off most of the liquid; add seasonings and lemon juice and cook another minute. Mix cornstarch with cold water; stir into mixture, stirring constantly until remaining liquid is thick and clear. Place 1 kitchen spoonful of the thickened mixture on the end of a ti leaf, with rib removed, and roll up in the same manner as for the preceding recipe; then turn and roll up in another ti leaf and tie. Or the mixture can be bundled in the old-fashioned Hawaiian way, as illustrated. Put laulaus in pressure cooker for half an hour. Serves 25.

## LAULAUS
*Originally steamed in the imu with the Kalua pig*

| | |
|---|---|
| 4 pounds taro leaves | 3 pounds butterfish or |
| 5 pounds lean pork | mullet |
| 4 tablespoons Hawaiian | 48 ti leaves* |
| red salt | |

Wash leaves thoroughly. Remove the stem and fibrous part of the taro. Cut pork in about 20 pieces and mix thoroughly with the salt in a bowl. Cut fish in a suitable number of pieces. Arrange 5 or 6 taro leaves in the palm of your hand; place first a piece of pork in the center and then a piece of fish on top. Fold the taro leaves over to form a package. Next place the taro package (the laulau) on the end of 1 ti leaf (with rib removed**) and roll up; then turn and place it on the end of another ti leaf and roll up. Tie with string.

---

* Ti leaves are available at many florists. If not, your florist can order them from San Francisco.

** To remove the stiff rib of the ti leaf, cut off stem, then with a sharp knife, partially cut through the rib and peel off by rolling the ti leaf over your finger. If the leaves are young and tender you should have no trouble but if you have picked old, tough leaves, the rib is apt to split the leaf about midway.

The old-fashioned Hawaiian way was to cross 4 ti leaves in a circle, place the taro leaves, pork and fish in the center, and then pull the ends up and tie with fiber or string, to make little sacks.

Before we proceed further you should know how to go about getting Coconut Milk and Coconut Cream.

## HOW TO MILK A COCONUT

Let's assume that you have a coconut, or two, with the husk removed. By the time you buy a coconut on the mainland there usually isn't enough liquid left inside to bother with. There is simply sort of a jellied substance inside. If it *does* slosh around, open up the soft eyes at one end of the nut with a nail or an ice pick; drain out the liquid and save it to add to whatever you are cooking, as part of the liquid. Next, tap the coconut all around with a hammer and split it. Since you probably do not have a Hawaiian coconut grater handy (sort of a paddle-shaped gadget with a grater at one end) gouge the meat from the shell with a strong-bladed knife, or whatever will do the job. Since you are going to use the meat for making Coconut Milk, put it through a food grinder or chip it up and use your blender. One large coconut is supposed to yield 2 cups of grated coconut meat.

## COCONUT MILK

Pour 2 cups boiling water over 4 cups grated coconut meat. Let stand 20 minutes. Strain through double thickness of cheese-cloth, squeezing to remove all liquid. Store this liquid in the refrigerator. If it is to be heated, be sure to bring it just *to* the boiling point. Otherwise, it is apt to curdle. Makes 2 cups of Coconut Milk.

## COCONUT CREAM

To make 2 cups Coconut Cream you will need 6 cups of grated coconut meat to 2 cups boiling water. Proceed the same way as for Coconut Milk. Let the liquid chill for a few hours. The cream substance which rises to the top is skimmed off. This is called Coconut Cream. It may be served as a sauce or it may be whipped. Be careful about whipping, however, or you may end up with cocoa butter.

## CHICKEN LUAU – I

This is one of those old-time island dishes, a combination of chicken, tender taro leaves and Coconut Milk, which varies only with the inspiration of the cook. Some brown the disjointed chicken first and then simmer it. Others add boiling water and simmer the chicken without browning. The principle of the dish is to combine cooked chicken with cooked taro leaves (luau) and Coconut Milk.

| | |
|---|---|
| 3 pounds chicken | 2 cups boiling water |
| 1½ teaspoons salt | ½ teaspoon salt |
| ½ teaspoon white pepper | 2 cups Coconut Milk, |
| ½ teaspoon MSG | heated |
| 2 pounds luau | |
| (taro leaves) | |

Cut cleaned chicken in bite-sized pieces. Place in large kettle and barely cover with boiling water. Add seasonings after half

an hour cooking. Rinse luau, remove stems and fibrous parts. Cook in 2 cups boiling water until wilted. Drain and add fresh boiling water, ½ teaspoon salt and cook until tender. When chicken is done, drain off some of the liquid and place chicken in serving dish. Draw knife through drained luau and cut up coarsely. Add the luau to the heated Coconut Milk and pour over chicken. Serve hot. Serves 4 to 6.

*CHICKEN LUAU – II*
*Here is another version of this dish*

1 chicken, 4–5 pounds
3 cups chicken broth,
  heated
½ cup chopped celery
1 medium-sized onion,
  peeled and chopped
Salt, pepper and MSG to
  taste

¼ cup cornstarch mixed
  with
½ cup cold water
3 cups cooked luau
2 cups Coconut Milk,
  heated

Clean and cut up chicken; sauté to a golden brown, then add chicken broth (canned may be used). Simmer about 15 minutes and remove scum. Add vegetables and seasonings to chicken and simmer until chicken is tender, or about 2 hours. Remove chicken to serving dish to keep warm in oven. Reduce broth by simmering on stove until you have about 2 cups. Thicken slightly with cornstarch mixed with a little cold water. Meanwhile, drain the luau and chop coarsely. Pour the chicken broth over the chicken. Combine the luau and heated Coconut Milk and add this to the chicken and serve immediately. Serves 6.

## FISH BAKED IN COCONUT CREAM

This is a simple way of baking whole small fish, fish fillets or fish steaks. Prepare for the oven; season with salt and pepper and place in buttered baking dish. Pour Coconut Cream over fish and bake in medium oven for an hour or until done. In the islands, they prepare mullet, mahimahi and giant pampano in this manner. Here on the mainland, we can prepare most any of our delicately flavored fish with Coconut Cream.

## FISH BAKED IN TI LEAVES

The Hawaiians have been cooking fish in ti leaves for hundreds of years, and it is still a good way to do it.

Scale and clean a fish, weighing from 2½ to 3 pounds and rub with Hawaiian red salt. Dot with thin strips of salt pork and slices of lemon. Wrap fish in several ti leaves, after removing stems, and tie ends in place with ti leaf rib, raffia or string. Place in baking pan and bake in medium oven 1 to 1½ hours. Serves 4 to 6.

*STUFFED FISH BAKED IN TI LEAVES*

Rub the inside of a cleaned and scaled fish, weighing 3 to 5 pounds, with 1 teaspoon of salt. Stuff lightly with the following stuffing:

| | |
|---|---|
| 1 tablespoon minced onion | ½ teaspoon salt |
| 1 teaspoon minced parsley | ¼ teaspoon paprika |
| ¼ cup chopped celery | ¼ teaspoon pepper |
| 2 tablespoons butter or margarine | ½ teaspoon dill seed |
| | 1 cup small bread cubes |
| | ½ cup stock or chicken broth |

PLATE I. Suckling Pig Hawaiian, *page 34*

PLATE II. Hawaiian Curry Sauce with Chutney Aspic, *pages 52 and 53*

PLATE III. Tahitian Chicken and Bananas, *page 68*

Sauté onion, parsley and celery in butter or margarine; add seasoning, bread cubes and liquid. Mix well and stuff fish lightly; skewer or sew it together. Arrange 3 slices of bacon on top of fish, wrap in ti leaves, tie ends, and place in oiled baking pan. Bake at 325° F. for 20 minutes to the pound. Serves 6 to 8.

## POI STEW

*Just additional proof of the versatility of the taro root. Here it takes the place of potatoes in a stew.*

3 pounds taro root

3 pounds top round,
   sliced very thin

1 pound fresh mushrooms

3 tablespoons cooking oil

½ cup chopped green
   onions

3½ cups hot stock or
   chicken broth

½ cup soya sauce

3 teaspoons MSG

Salt to taste

¼ cup cornstarch
   mixed with

½ cup cold water

Boil taro root until tender. Cool, peel and cube. Pound steak, then slice into strips about the size of a ladyfinger. Wash mushrooms, leaving stems on but trim end; slice and then sauté in a few tablespoons of oil, stirring until they lose their whiteness—about half a minute. Add beef and sauté, turning and mixing. Add green onions. Mix well and continue cooking until onions are limp but haven't lost their green color. Add hot stock or chicken broth, soya sauce and seasonings, then add cooked taro root. Cover and steam for 5 minutes. Add salt if needed. Thicken with cornstarch and a little cold water. Serves 8.

## BARBECUED PIG CHINESE STYLE
*Sui Gee*

Select a small pig, 18 to 20 pounds. Remove most of the shoulder bones, and split the chine bone down the back from the inside, taking care not to cut the outer skin. The shoulder blade and pelvis are replaced by bamboo sticks so the pig doesn't lose its shape. Season pig inside and outside with salt, pepper and sage, rubbing them in well. Let stand for 2 hours. Meantime, prepare fruit and sweet potatoes for stuffing:

| | |
|---|---|
| 1 whole pineapple | 1 large cooking apple |
| 1 papaya | 2 sweet potatoes |
| 1 large banana | |

Wash and cut the pineapple, with skin and leaves left intact, into 10 pieces. Peel and seed the papaya and cut into 8 pieces. Wash and leave the banana whole, but trim stem end. Wash and quarter the apple. Peel the sweet potatoes and cut each into 8 pieces. Precook the fruit and sweet potatoes until about half done. Stuff the pig with the fruit and potatoes, and sew or skewer the stomach together. Hang the pig by wires in a preheated Chinese oven and let cook for half an hour. Remove and punch holes all over the skin with an ice pick to allow some of the fat to escape. Wash skin with hot water and honey— 4 tablespoons honey to a quart of hot water—and return pig to oven. Let cook about 4 hours over slow heat.

To serve, place pig on a large wooden serving board or tray, covered with ti leaves. Bank with leaves and flowers and pin a gardenia over Sui Gee's ear. Serves 15 to 18.

## SUCKLING PIG HAWAIIAN (PLATE I)

A festive dish at any time, served Hawaiian style, a suckling pig can be exciting and delicious. Order a whole pig, dressed weight from 10 to 12 pounds. Be sure to have your butcher clean the pig, remove eyes and prepare it for the oven. Season the pig inside with salt, pepper and sage. Brush the outside skin with marinade. Let stand 2 hours, brushing pig often with the marinade, then stuff with Hawaiian dressing.

### MARINADE

| | |
|---|---|
| 1 quart soya sauce | 1 teaspoon MSG |
| ½ cup sherry | 1 teaspoon salt |
| 4 tablespoons brown sugar | ½ teaspoon pepper |
| 4 tablespoons honey | 2 cloves garlic, crushed |

Mix ingredients thoroughly in jar; drop in the crushed garlic.

HAWAIIAN DRESSING

| | |
|---|---|
| ¾ cup butter | 1 papaya, seeds removed, |
| 1 cup chopped onions | peeled and diced |
| 1 clove garlic, minced | ½ teaspoon pepper |
| 1 cup chopped celery | 1½ teaspoons salt |
| 2 cups diced fresh | 7 cups diced, crustless |
| pineapple | bread |
| 1 cup peeled and diced | Aluminum foil |
| tart apple | |

Melt butter in a large skillet and sauté onion, garlic and celery. Add fruit and seasonings; let simmer until heated through. Add bread cubes and mix lightly. Taste and correct seasonings. Stuff pig loosely and sew or skewer stomach together. Skewer the hind legs into a hunched position; arrange forelegs forward and skewer in place so pig will sit well in a platter or serving board. Cover ears and tail with aluminum foil so they don't get too brown. Place pig in baking pan in preheated oven, 400° F. for 15 minutes. Reduce heat to 325° F. and continue roasting until tender, allowing 30 minutes to the pound. Baste every 15 or 20 minutes with juices from the pan, adding hot water as needed. Serves 8 to 10.

*KALUA ROAST PORK*

Even in Hawaii it is not always possible to cook a pig. A good substitute, especially for mainland luaus, is a pork roast flavored with liquid smoke, wrapped in ti leaves and foil and oven-roasted. Cook as many roasts as required, or 1 large one, depending upon the number of guests. Serve on a platter or tray covered with ti leaves, surrounded by baked sweet potatoes or baked orange cups filled with a mixture of sweet potatoes, pineapple and macadamia nuts.

If you are going to serve a loin of pork allow at least 1 chop per person. If you are going to serve a fresh ham or pork butt, allow half a pound per person. Here is a recipe for 4 pounds of meat.

| | |
|---|---|
| 4 pound pork roast | 1 banana leaf (if |
| 4 tablespoons Liquid | obtainable) |
| Smoke* | 5–6 ti leaves |
| 2 tablespoons salt | Aluminum foil |

Score meat on all sides with sharp knife and rub the smoked flavoring and salt into the meat on all sides. Wrap roast in whole banana leaf first, then in ti leaves. Tie firmly with string and then wrap in foil. Refrigerate overnight. Bake at 400° F., for 15 minutes, then reduce temperature to 350° F. and continue roasting 30 to 35 minutes per pound, or until tender.

### CHINESE-HAWAIIAN ROAST PORK

| | |
|---|---|
| 5 pounds loin of pork | 1 clove garlic, crushed |
| 1 pint soya sauce | 1 ounce okolehao or |
| 1 teaspoon MSG | bourbon |
| ½ teaspoon pepper | |

Have your butcher prepare the roast for easy slicing, removing the bony part with a meat saw. Trim away fat, leaving just a thin layer. Mix soya sauce with seasonings and liquor. Marinate roast for 2 hours, rubbing the sauce into the meat and turning it frequently. Use stainless steel, enamel or glass container for this. When ready to cook, preheat oven to 325° F. and roast meat 2½ to 3 hours, allowing 35 minutes to the pound. Baste during roasting period with additional sauce and pan drippings. Serves at least 8.

### BAKED SWEET POTATOES AND BANANAS

Those most congenial tubers, sweet potatoes, have never reached their potential on the mainland. They were brought to the Hawaiian Islands by the first Polynesian immigrants and the

---

* Liquid Smoke is a hickory smoke flavored liquid, the color of soya sauce. It can be found in the barbecue section of most markets. Colgin Hickory Liquid Smoke is manufactured in Dallas, Texas. Ingredients: Natural hickory smoke flavor, vinegar, flavoring, browned sugar and water sufficient to formulate.

islanders really know how to prepare them in dozens of ways. Here's one way.

6 medium-sized sweet
  potatoes
6 bananas
Butter
Salt and pepper

Brown sugar
Lemon juice
½ cup pineapple or
  orange juice

Boil the sweet potatoes in their jackets. Let cool, then peel, slice and arrange in alternate layers with sliced bananas in a well-buttered casserole. Start with the potatoes and end up with the bananas. Dot the layers of potato with butter and sprinkle with salt and pepper. Sprinkle the layers of bananas with brown sugar and a little lemon juice. Dot the top with more butter and add ½ cup pineapple or orange juice. Bake in a medium oven for 30 minutes. Serves 6 to 8.

*SWEET POTATOES MAUNA KEA*

3 tablespoons melted
  butter
2 cups sweet potatoes,
  mashed while hot
1 teaspoon grated orange
  rind
6 tablespoons orange
  juice

1 cup chopped pineapple
1 teaspoon salt
2 tablespoons brown sugar
Paprika
Grated coconut

Whip butter into mashed sweet potatoes, then add orange rind and juice, pineapple and salt. Pour mixture into baking dish, well buttered, swirling the top with a spatula or the back of a spoon. Sprinkle with brown sugar and paprika. Bake covered in hot oven for 30 minutes. Remove cover, sprinkle with coconut and brown under broiler. Serves 6.

As a variation to this recipe, alternate layers of sliced, firm bananas with layers of the sweet potato mixture and follow the same baking instructions.

*HAUPIA*

This is the traditional luau dessert. It has been poured into pans and cut into squares for generations. But why conform? I say mold it attractively and serve in shells or on dessert plates with galax leaves for doilies and top with chopped fresh or canned pineapple.

| | |
|---|---|
| 4 cups Coconut Milk | 4 tablespoons cornstarch |
| 1 cup sugar | mixed with |
| ¼ teaspoon salt | ½ cup cold water |

Heat Coconut Milk over low heat until it just reaches the boiling point. Add sugar, salt and cornstarch mixed and dissolved in a little cold water. Stir constantly until mixture thickens. Pour into oiled molds and chill. *Note:* It seems to me that a little vanilla wouldn't be amiss. Needless to say, the number of people this will serve depends on the size of the molds.

Since I am no great proponent of authenticity, let me say a word for the new packaged instant coconut puddings now on the market. Chilled and served with fresh or frozen grated coconut you have a delicious dessert. There are other ways to doll it up—whipped cream with a bit of well-drained, chopped pineapple, for instance—and it saves you hours in the kitchen. You can use whipped Coconut Cream, too. Top your coconut pudding with a tablespoon of this and a teaspoon of grated pineapple or chopped preserved kumquats.

For a luau buffet style, serve your coconut pudding in a large crystal bowl topped with clouds of whipped Coconut Cream or whipped cream spiked with a bit of Triple Sec. You might even fold in some fresh raspberries for color. Experiment a bit.

# THE HAOLE ENTERTAINS IN HAWAII

The luau takes care of celebrations and feting tourists, but what about everyday meals? What about the *haole* (Hawaiian for white or foreigner) who has a cook and likes to entertain? Her cook may be Japanese, Chinese or a mixture of Hawaiian and Japanese or Chinese. (The Hawaiian word for a Hawaiian whose parents were not pure Hawaiian is *hapa haole*.) What kind of food does she serve her guests?

It is probably a mixture of the recipes she brought to the islands and those of her cook, who has picked up a few ideas and recipes where she has worked in the past. The daily fare of the islands bears the stamp of many races of people, because everyone picks up an idea, a different seasoning or a little different way of preparing a dish from someone else.

So what's for dinner? With cocktails there may be Coco Shrimp, bite-sized Beef Teriyaki on picks, sliced Clam Roll and Rumaki or Cha Sui. Any or all of these may be served, depending upon the number of dinner guests.

Dinner may start with a cold Senegalese Cream Soup, served in chilled China clam shells and accompanied by a chilled California Gewürztraminer. The salad might be watercress and cherry tomatoes with finely chopped green onions and celery served with Mustard Dressing. For the main course, Pork Chops Hawaiian, Sweet Potatoes Mauna Kea and Chinese Peas and Water chestnuts could be accompanied by a chilled California rosé or Chardonnay. For dessert, a chilled compote of diced fresh pineapple, raspberries and mandarin orange sections, marinated in Triple Sec, would be a fitting finale. Or coconut ice cream served in a puddle of chocolate sauce and topped with grated fresh coconut.

So we start off with Coco Shrimp, a combination of Chinese and Japanese ingenuity, involving shrimp, rice, batter and deep-fat frying.

*COCO SHRIMP*

| | |
|---|---|
| 1 package long rice | 1 egg |
| All-purpose flour | Peanut oil for deep |
| Salt, pepper and MSG | frying (any vegetable |
| 1 pound large shrimp, raw | oil) |

Deep fry long rice in small batches until it puffs up; cool and crumble. Combine 3 parts crushed rice sticks with 1 part all-purpose flour, add salt, pepper and MSG and spread in a shallow pan or dish. Meantime, clean and devein the shrimp and cut in ¾-inch pieces. Dip the shrimp in well-beaten egg and then in rice stick and flour mixture, turning them so that they are well covered with the rice sticks. Fry in deep fat until rice sticks are a golden brown and the shrimp cooked through. Serve with mustard and chili sauce. To dry mustard add white wine to the proper dipping consistency. This is hot so watch it. To chili sauce, add a little grated horseradish. A nice touch is to put the mustard in one side of a porcelain butterfly dish and the chili sauce in the other wing. Serves 6 to 8 with cocktails.

*CLAM ROLL*

*This is a kissing cousin to the Chinese Egg Roll*

| | |
|---|---|
| 3 cans minced clams, drained | 2 tablespoons finely chopped green onions |
| ½ pound cream cheese | ½ teaspoon pepper |
| ¾ cup bread crumbs | 1 tablespoon MSG |
| ½ pound chopped black olives | Salt to taste |
| 2 teaspoons A-1 sauce | Thin Egg Skins |

Blend clams, cream cheese, bread crumbs, olives, A-1 sauce, onions and seasonings together until well mixed. Meanwhile make the Thin Egg Skins.

THIN EGG SKINS

| | |
|---|---|
| 6 eggs | ½ teaspoon salt |
| 1 tablespoon cornstarch | ¼ cup water |

Beat eggs well and mix with cornstarch, salt and water. Drop mixture into 8-inch frying pan by quarter cupfuls for each circle. When cooked, turn over for 2 seconds. These can be stacked on a plate until ready to use.

To make clam rolls, divide the clam mixture according to the number of skins you have. Roll out and then roll in egg skin, tucking the ends in and lapping the edges over well. Dip in a thin pancake batter and fry in deep fat until golden brown. Cut diagonally in slices to serve.

*CHA SUI*

This is that wonderful sliced roasted or barbecued pork which you dip into Chinese mustard, soya sauce and sesame seeds, and eat with cocktails. Use pork as lean as possible. For ordinary use, pork tenderloin is ideal, but expensive. If you are serving a raft of people, cut a boned leg of pork into strips. There are many ways of preparing this tidbit. Here's one.

| 3 pounds lean pork cut into strips | 1 teaspoon salt |
| 1 cup soya sauce | ⅛ teaspoon pepper |
| ½ cup sherry | ⅛ teaspoon MSG |
| ½ cup brown sugar | 2 cloves garlic, crushed |

Make sauce by combining all ingredients except pork. Marinate pork in sauce 2 to 4 hours, then roast or barbecue at high temperature for 5 to 10 minutes. Reduce temperature and continue cooking for an hour. Serves 12 to 16 with cocktails.

## RUMAKI

This is an island tidbit of Chinese origin with a Japanese name. Thoroughly integrated. There are many versions but essentially Rumaki is a combination of chicken livers, water chestnuts and bacon, marinated in spicy sauce and broiled or fried in deep fat. I like this recipe:

| 1 tablespoon sugar | 1 clove garlic, crushed |
| 1 large bay leaf | 2 cups soya sauce |
| 1 stick cinnamon | 1 pound chicken livers |
| 1 cup chicken stock | 1 can whole water chestnuts |
| 1 piece of fresh gingerroot | ½ pound thinly sliced bacon |
| 2 tablespoons star anise | |

Mix seasonings, stock and crushed garlic with soya sauce in saucepan and bring to a boil. Reduce heat and let simmer for 5 minutes. Add fresh chicken livers and bring to a boil again. Reduce heat and let simmer for 10 minutes, then remove chicken livers from sauce and let cool. (Save marinade for another day.) Meanwhile, cut water chestnuts in thirds. When chicken livers are cool enough to handle, slice and wrap a third of a strip of bacon around 1 piece of chicken liver and 1 piece of water chestnut. Secure with a toothpick. When the required number of rumakis have been assembled, fry in deep fat until bacon is crisp and serve immediately. Serves 8 to 10 with cocktails.

Besides the many races of people living in Hawaii which affect the island cuisine, many army and navy wives have brought with them recipes from far-off places, such as Senegalese Cream Soup, served chilled.

*SENEGALESE CREAM SOUP*

2 onions, peeled and minced

2 stalks celery, finely chopped

2 apples, peeled and chopped

3 tablespoons butter

2 tablespoons curry powder

4 tablespoons flour

4 cups rich chicken broth

Dash chili powder

Dash cayenne pepper

Salt

2 cups cream

¾ cup finely chopped cooked white chicken meat

Avocado slices for garnish

Sauté onions, celery and apples in butter until tender but not browned; add curry powder and stir for a few moments, being careful not to let it brown. Next stir in the flour to blend thoroughly with the ingredients; add the chicken broth, stirring constantly, a little at a time until it is well blended and slightly thickened. Add chili powder, cayenne pepper and salt. Cool slightly, then pour into a blender and blend for a few moments until the mixture is smooth, then chill. Before serving, stir in the chilled cream and add the chilled chicken meat. Correct seasonings. Serve in Chinese bowls or cream soup cups and garnish with slices of avocado. Serves 6 to 8.

*MUSTARD DRESSING*

1 cup mayonnaise

¾ cup oil and vinegar dressing

Juice of ½ lemon

1 tablespoon Dijon mustard

Salt and white pepper to taste

Dash of MSG

Combine mayonnaise with salad dressing, or a good French dressing, stir in lemon juice and mustard, and mix thoroughly. Season to taste. If you are out of Dijon mustard, a passable substitute is a blend of dry mustard with white wine spiked with a bit of lemon juice or wine vinegar.

*PORK CHOPS HAWAIIAN*

| | |
|---|---|
| Marinade | Salt, pepper and MSG |
| 6 thick loin pork chops | Oil for frying |
| 2 medium-sized onions | 6 slices canned pineapple |
| 1 large green pepper | 1 cup chicken broth |
| 3 stalks celery, finely chopped | |

Mix marinade and pour into shallow glass, enamel or stainless steel baking pan. (Soya sauce has an adverse effect on aluminum or other metals.)

| | |
|---|---|
| 1 cup soya sauce | ¼ teaspoon MSG |
| 1 teaspoon grated fresh ginger | ¼ teaspoon pepper |
| 1 clove garlic, crushed | ¼ cup Italian vermouth |

Remove excess fat from chops and marinate them for about an hour, turning them now and then. Meanwhile peel and slice onions so as to have 1 slice for each chop. Remove stem, seeds and inner ribs from green pepper and chop fine. Mix celery and green pepper and set to one side. When the chops have marinated long enough, brown in oil on both sides and place in bottom of large baking pan with lid, casserole or Dutch oven. Season with salt, freshly ground pepper and MSG. Place a slice of pineapple and a slice of onion on top of each chop. Mix celery and green pepper with some of the marinade and spoon over each chop. Mix the rest of the marinade with the chicken broth and pour into the bottom of the baking dish. Cover and bake in a moderate oven for about an hour. Add more broth if required. Serves 6. *Note:* Other wine may be used, such as port or sherry.

## CHINESE PEAS AND WATER CHESTNUTS

This delightful vegetable is also known as Chinese pea pods or snow peas. Wherever you have a Chinese population, you will find Chinese peas. They are pods containing immature peas, but they are a special variety and that is the way they grow— just pods, no peas. To prepare them you wash and snip off the ends and unstring them just the way you do string beans. Come to think about it, the strings seem to have been bred out of beans. You seldom find one.

Cook the snow peas—I like that name best—full length or cut in half or in 3 parts. This job is done quickly with a Chinese cleaver.

| | |
|---|---|
| ¼ cup chopped lean pork | 1½ cups hot chicken broth or stock |
| ¼ cup peanut oil | ¾ cup sliced water chestnuts |
| 1 teaspoon MSG | |
| 1 teaspoon salt | 1 tablespoon cornstarch mixed with |
| 1½ pounds Chinese snow peas | 3 tablespoons cold water |

Sauté pork in hot oil, add seasonings and stir in snow peas, which have been prepared for cooking. Keep stirring, then add broth. Cook until broth boils and peas are tender but still crisp and green. Stir in sliced water chestnuts and cook just long enough to heat through. Thicken broth with cornstarch and water. Add just enough of the cornstarch mixture to thicken the broth to clear, gravy-like consistency. Serves 6.

Mahimahi is one of the most delicious of fish from tropical waters. It is best, of course, when fresh, but it is now available everywhere frozen, and still great. Here are two ways to prepare mahimahi, which is the Hawaiian word for dolphin. You can experiment with these recipes using local fish of comparable texture.

## MAHIMAHI WITH MACADAMIA NUTS

Flour and sauté mahimahi fillets in butter. Prepare the following sauce:

### MACADAMIA NUT SAUCE

| | |
|---|---|
| 1 cup rich chicken broth | Juice of ½ lemon |
| 1½ teaspoons cornstarch mixed with | 2 tablespoons hollandaise sauce |
| 2 tablespoons cold water | ½ cup crushed macadamia nuts |
| 2 tablespoons butter | |
| Salt, pepper and MSG | Chopped parsley |

Thicken broth with cornstarch mixed with water. Stir constantly while it cooks. Add butter, seasonings and lemon juice. Fold in hollandaise sauce, add crushed nuts and spoon over sautéed fish. Top each serving with a little chopped parsley. Sauce for 6 to 8 servings.

Another way is to sauté chopped pineapple in butter and add crushed macadamia nuts. For 6 to 8 servings, sauté 1½ cups slivered, well-drained pineapple in 4 tablespoons butter until thoroughly heated and just tinged with a golden tan. Add crushed nuts and spoon over cooked fish.

Hawaii is the land of the soya marinade. Everyone has a pet recipe but after you have read a few it is difficult to see much difference. A friend gave me this one for barbecuing chicken.

## BASIC SOYA SAUCE MARINADE

| | |
|---|---|
| 1 tablespoon dry mustard | 1 medium-sized onion, peeled and grated |
| 1 teaspoon sugar | |
| 1 tablespoon grated fresh gingerroot | ¼ teaspoon MSG |
| | 1 cup soya sauce |

First, mix mustard with enough water to make a paste. Add mustard, sugar, ginger, grated onion and MSG to the soya sauce. Let stand overnight for best results. A glass jar with a screw top is a good container. If you are unable to obtain fresh ginger-root, try dried gingerroot but use less.

*BARBECUED CHICKEN*

Apply Basic Soya Sauce Marinade to halves of chicken and let stand about an hour at room temperature. Broil over charcoal or under preheated broiler 12 to 15 minutes, cut side up. Turn and continue cooking, brushing with remaining marinade as the chicken cooks. Cook another 12 to 15 minutes until the skin is browned and crisp, and the meat tender. Serve immediately.

Here is another way of cooking chicken in soya sauce, not just marinated, but in the sauce. The influence here is decidedly Chinese.

*SHOYU CHICKEN*

1 frying chicken, about
  3½ pounds
¾ cup soya sauce
1 tablespoon honey
½ cup brown sugar
1½ cups water
2 tablespoons grated
  fresh ginger
3 garlic cloves, crushed
1 star anise
¼ cup chopped green
  onions
2 tablespoons sherry
2 tablespoons cornstarch
  mixed with
4 tablespoons cold water
Chinese parsley for
  garnish

Clean chicken and wash carefully, saving the gizzard and liver. Combine soya sauce, honey, brown sugar, water and seasonings—everything but the cornstarch mixture. Let liquid simmer for 2 minutes, after bringing it to a boil, to dissolve honey and sugar, and develop the flavor. Add the whole chicken, including the gizzard and liver. Cover and simmer 40 minutes, or until tender. Remove chicken, cut into segments and arrange on platter. Add cornstarch and water mixture to sauce and bring to a boil. Simmer a few seconds, stirring constantly, until mixture is slightly thickened and clear. Pour over chicken and garnish with Chinese parsley. Serves 4.

Here is another island way of cooking chicken. The Chinese often cook chicken or duck whole and then cut it up for serving. They actually use a Chinese cleaver and chop the bird up into bite-sized pieces.

*FRIED SHOYU CHICKEN*

½ cup peanut oil
1 inch piece fresh ginger
2 cloves garlic, crushed
1 chicken, 3 pounds
  dressed
2 tablespoons port wine

½ cup brown sugar
1 cup soya sauce
1 cup water
Watercress or Chinese
  parsley

Heat frying pan and add peanut oil, ginger and garlic. Remove ginger and garlic and fry whole chicken, turning until it is browned all over, then add wine. Meanwhile in a deep saucepan melt sugar in soya sauce and water and bring to a boil. Place browned chicken in this soya sauce mixture. Cover and cook slowly until tender, turning from time to time. When done, cut into 1½ inch pieces and serve on platter with some of the sauce. Garnish with sprigs of watercress or Chinese parsley. Serves 4.

*CHICKEN LONG RICE – I*

1 chicken, 2–2¼ pounds
Flour
2–3 tablespoons peanut
  oil
2 tablespoons chopped
  onion
1½ cups chopped, peeled
  raw potatoes

1 cup chicken broth
Salt and pepper
MSG
2 cups cooked Chinese
  long rice (rice noodles)
  cut into 2 inch pieces
1 teaspoon chopped
  chives for garnish

Split chicken and cut each half in 2 pieces. Flour and sauté in oil until chicken is golden brown. Add chopped onion and the potatoes (which have been fried in deep fat for a few minutes) and continue to sauté with chicken. Add chicken broth, salt, pepper and MSG. Cover and let simmer a few minutes until chicken is tender. Add long rice and continue to simmer a few minutes more. To serve, arrange wing and leg portion of chicken on half of the rice noodles in an individual serving bowl or casserole. Garnish with ½ teaspoon chopped chives. Serves 2.

*CHICKEN LONG RICE – II*

1 large chicken, 3½ to
  4 pounds
Flour
¼ cup peanut oil
2 cups chicken broth
Salt, pepper and MSG
1 package long rice
2 tablespoons butter
1 medium-sized onion,
  minced

6 fresh mushrooms, sliced
¼ cup chopped green
  pepper
½ pound snow peas
1 canned pimiento,
  slivered
Chinese parsley for
  garnish

Disjoint chicken for frying. Flour and brown in oil. Add chicken broth, seasonings, cover and simmer until tender. Meanwhile soak rice in water while chicken cooks. Melt butter in a pot, add onion and cook until soft, then add sliced mushrooms and green pepper and cook about 5 minutes. When chicken is tender, add chicken broth to pot with the onion, green pepper. Drain the long rice and snip in 1 inch to 2 inch pieces with scissors, and add to broth. Let simmer a few minutes then add prepared snow peas. Cook about 10 minutes. Add the cooked chicken and pimiento and let simmer about 10 minutes longer. Serve on a platter and garnish with Chinese parsley. Serves 6.

While we are on the subject of chicken cooked Chinese style, here's a real Chinese fried chicken recipe, from San Francisco.

*FRIED CHICKEN BOBBY GEE*

| | |
|---|---|
| 1 chicken, 3 pounds dressed | 5 to 6 cloves garlic, crushed |
| 2 cups dark soya sauce | 2 ounces gin |
| 2 cups water | Peanut oil for frying |
| 2 chunks gingerroot, mashed | Chinese parsley |
| 2 teaspoons brown sugar | Green onions |

Split chicken and marinate in soya sauce, water, gingerroot, brown sugar, garlic and gin for an hour or so at room temperature, turning and loosening the skin so the sauce penetrates into the chicken. Fry the chicken in deep fat until tender. Test to be sure the chicken is cooked through. Remove from oil; cool slightly, then chop into pieces and arrange on serving dish. The Chinese often make a mixture of salt, browned in a skillet, and white pepper, which can be stored indefinitely. Sprinkle a little of this mixture on the chicken; garnish with Chinese parsley and slices of green onion. Serve immediately. Serves 4.

It seems that anything with pineapple in it immediately becomes Hawaiian. This is one version.

*CHICKEN HAWAIIAN*

| | |
|---|---|
| 1 chicken, 3½ to 4 pounds | Oil for frying |
| 1 cup soya sauce | 1 cup diced pineapple |
| 1 cup pineapple juice | Chicken broth |
| 2 cloves garlic, peeled and minced | Salt, pepper and MSG |
| 1 tablespoon grated fresh gingerroot | 2 tablespoons cornstarch mixed with |
| | ¼ cup cold water |

Disjoint chicken. Mix soya sauce, pineapple juice, garlic and gingerroot in a glass or stainless steel container and add chicken. Let marinate several hours, turning occasionally. When ready to cook, remove chicken and save the marinade for the sauce. Sauté chicken in hot oil until golden brown. Drain and place in baking dish or casserole. Add diced pineapple to marinade and bring to a boil. Pour over chicken, cover and bake in a moderate oven, 350° F., about an hour, turning and basting the chicken at intervals. Serve with steamed rice, piled in the center of a large chop plate or similar serving dish. Arrange chicken around the rice. Make a sauce of the drippings by adding chicken broth and seasonings to taste. Thicken with cornstarch and pass separately. Serves 5 to 6.

## BAKED SWEET POTATOES

Another way to serve baked sweet potatoes is to split them, mash the contents with butter, crushed pineapple, rum and seasonings, then refill the shells.

| | |
|---|---|
| 3 large uniformly shaped sweet potatoes | 2 tablespoons rum |
| 4 tablespoons butter | 2 tablespoons brown sugar |
| ½ cup well-drained, crushed pineapple | Salt and pepper to taste |
| 2 teaspoons grated orange peel | Nutmeg |

Wash potatoes and bake until tender. Test by squeezing. When done, cut in half lengthwise carefully. Scoop out the contents and mash thoroughly. Add butter, pineapple, orange peel, rum, brown sugar and season to taste with salt and pepper. Return to shells; swirl the tops and flick each with a dash of nutmeg. Return to oven to reheat and brown on top. Serves 6.

*HAWAIIAN CURRY SAUCE*   (PLATE II)

1 quart milk
2 cups grated coconut
2 tablespoons butter
1 large onion, peeled
  and minced
1 clove garlic, peeled
  and minced

1 teaspoon grated fresh
  gingerroot
1 tablespoon curry
  powder
½ teaspoon brown sugar
2 tablespoons flour
Salt to taste

Scald milk and add grated coconut meat. Let stand an hour, then strain through double thicknesses of cheesecloth and squeeze until the coconut meat is dry, then discard. Melt butter, add onion, garlic and ginger and sauté until pale gold and soft. Add curry powder and brown sugar. Mix thoroughly, stirring constantly, then stir in flour. Gradually add the milk squeezed from the coconut, stirring constantly until mixture thickens. When ready to serve, add salt to taste. If salt is added too soon to a sauce containing coconut milk it is apt to curdle. To this sauce you may add cooked shrimp, crab meat or diced chicken. Serve over steamed rice. Sauce for 6 to 8 servings.

Hawaiian Curry makes a good luncheon dish and Chutney Aspic is a superb accompaniment. For a buffet supper, the following recipe may be increased according to the size of the mold to be used. If you use a ring mold surround it with slices of pineapple on lettuce, and put the dressing in the center. This salad goes well with baked ham—in fact just about anything. One word of warning: this recipe is based on Trader Vic's Chutney, which is highly seasoned and dark in color. You will not have the same results with other brands, although the result may be quite acceptable.

*CHUTNEY ASPIC* (PLATE II)

2 packages lime-flavored
gelatin
½ cup boiling water
1½ cups unsweetened
pineapple juice
½ cup orange juice

2 cans (9 ounces)
crushed pineapple
1 cup Trader Vic's
Chutney, chopped fine
8 slices of pineapple

Dissolve gelatin in boiling water; add pineapple juice, orange juice, crushed pineapple and chutney. Let chill until it begins to congeal, then stir to keep the chutney from settling to the bottom. When thick, pour into oiled molds to set. Unmold on a slice of pineapple arranged on a bed of lettuce. Serve with a sour cream dressing. Serves 8.

*SOUR CREAM AND MAYONNAISE DRESSING*

2 cups mayonnaise
2 cups sour cream
2 tablespoons lemon juice

Salt, white pepper, MSG
to taste

Mix mayonnaise and sour cream until smooth, stir in lemon juice, and season to taste. A dash of Tabasco is good, too.

Another dandy luncheon dish for a Hawaiian theme is chicken salad served in pineapple shells. This one has water chestnuts, chopped nuts and a spiked dressing.

*KONA CHICKEN SALAD*

3 medium-sized ripe pineapples
2 small cans water chestnuts
6 cups diced cooked chicken
2 cups thinly sliced celery
2 tablespoons scraped or grated onion

1 cup chopped macadamia nuts or cashews
Chicken Salad Dressing
Salt, white pepper and MSG to taste
6 strawberries and 6 sprigs of mint

Cut pineapples in half, carefully, retaining the leaves. Scoop out the fruit, and dice, discarding the inedible core. Drain the water chestnuts and slice. Mix pineapple, water chestnuts, chicken, celery, onion and nuts with dressing. Add seasonings and mix. Pile into pineapple shells and garnish with strawberries and mint. Chill thoroughly before serving. Other fruits, such as orange sections, canned mandarin oranges, melon balls or canned, well-drained apricot halves may be used when strawberries are out of season. Watercress may be used instead of mint. Serves 6.

CHICKEN SALAD DRESSING

2 cups sour cream
1 cup mayonnaise
2 tablespoons lemon juice

3 tablespoons Triple Sec or Cointreau
Salt, white pepper and MSG to taste

This delightful luncheon salad has a curry accent. For a handsome effect serve in large China clam shells lined with endive or hearts of romaine. A China clam shell looks very much like a small tridacna shell, and is probably a member of the same family. When I say small, however, I mean large enough for a healthy portion of salad. To make shells sit evenly—some are inclined to tip over—fill coupe-shaped dinner plate with shaved ice and place shell in center. Another way is to take your shells to some handyman who can grind off the bottoms so they will sit flat.

*BENGAL SEAFOOD SALAD*

3 cups crab meat
3 cups small shrimp
½ cup minced onion
2 cups finely sliced celery
1 cup sliced water
   chestnuts
1 cup diced pineapple

½ cup pine nuts
¼ cup currants
¾ cup chutney, chopped
Juice of 3 lemons
Salt to taste
Hard-cooked eggs, ripe
   olives

Mix lightly all ingredients except eggs and olives and combine with the following dressing, reserving enough for a spoonful to top each salad. Garnish with hard-cooked egg sections and ripe olives. Serves 8 allowing 1½ cups of the mixture per person.

*BENGAL DRESSING*

3 cups mayonnaise
1 cup frozen Coconut
   Milk

1 cup sour cream
¼ cup curry powder

Mix mayonnaise, Coconut Milk and sour cream in a bowl, using whip or egg beater, gradually add curry, whipping until smooth.

# Tahiti

## TRIP TO TAHITI

I FIRST met Alfred Poroi and his wife, Susy, when they were in San Francisco. He is the former mayor of Papeete and the senator from French Polynesia. We renewed our acquaintance when I was the guest of Stanley Dollar on South Pacific Airline's inaugural flight from Honolulu to Tahiti. The visit was all too short but it put a bee in my bonnet which buzzed around until 1962. I wanted to get some Polynesian recipes and a fresh approach to Polynesian foods and customs, so in September of 1962 my bride and I took off for Tahiti where we spent a month getting to know and appreciate the lovely Tahitians. We had a ball.

Tahiti and the surrounding islands are a territory called French Polynesia. There are French citizens, a few Americans, British and other foreigners living there, and Chinese, which represent less than ten per cent of the total population. While the natives speak Tahitian amongst themselves, French is the island language and the cuisine of that area is predominately French.

The French may have influenced the Tahitian's cooking but they sure as hell haven't changed him. His life is uncomplicated. He lives in a simple house, fashioned from bamboo and woven palm leaves, with a thatched roof. He wears a length of bright pareu cloth wrapped around his loins and goes barefooted. There are fish in the sea, fruits and vegetables for the gathering. Bananas, breadfruit and coconuts grow in abundance. Nothing needs planting or cultivating. He works when he wants money to buy something and as soon as he has made the money he needs off he goes—to swim, dance or fish. He is great on fun so nothing gets done very fast unless it includes some pleasure.

The Tahitians are a wonderful, fine people in general, happy-go-lucky, with beautiful physiques and carriage. Some people predict that tourism will spoil Tahiti, but I don't think so. In the first place the native is not interested in changing his way of living to any great extent. Making a dollar doesn't interest him beyond what he can do with it *today*. Just as soon as you get out of the city and into the rural areas, you see how people have been living for hundreds of years—a simple life of friendliness and warmth. Nobody goes hungry. There are no orphanages. The Tahitians love children—anybody's children—and another baby is always welcome.

You hear a lot of cockeyed stories about les girls but they are not the tramps the stories make them out to be and a fellow will have just as much resistance on a boy-meets-girl basis as any place in the world. Well, almost. A lot depends on the fellow's manners and approach. One thing for sure, the Tahitian gal is 100 per cent woman. She has more charm in her little finger than most American women have in their entire bodies. It might be a good idea for more men to take their wives to Tahiti just to show them what real charm is.

For example, just a nice little thing happens in Tahiti when you pick up the telephone. You don't get a buzz in your ear nor does the operator grind out "nuuuuuummmmmmmmber puleeeeee-eeeze" in a tired monotone. The operator, instead, in a sweet little voice you can scarcely hear, with all the femininity at her disposal says, "J'écoute," which in English means "I am listen-ing." If the line is busy she just as sweetly says *"Occupé."* It sounds delightful.

Everyone should make at least one trip to Tahiti. Junk pre-conceived ideas about the place. Go with an open mind just to see how nice a guy, with a different slant on life, can be. He is interesting, friendly and kind. He has no worries and no problems. He has a helluva pretty country and once you visit the island you will understand why so many Americans would like to live in Tahiti.

The old French Tahitian is usually a sociable, nice guy; glad you are visiting him and anxious to see that you enjoy your stay. Most of the Parisian French are likable but there is a certain clique with that "I hate Americans" complex. As a French-speaking American, of French descent, I overheard some choice remarks about my compatriots.

A TRIP TO TOWN

Some people think Pepeete is just a dirty island town. Compared to Honolulu, it probably is, but it has charm and some fantastic shops. That island drives me crazy. And I don't mean just the sweet young things—I'd have to be a hundred years old not to notice them—but dammit, this island was made for the bon vivant. We stopped off at a little mom and pop grocery store for a couple of bottles of champagne. We came away with some pâté de fois gras, cut from a loaf in the refrigerator, some veal loaf that was excellent, some Kellogg's Corn Flakes, a can of Planter's Mixed Nuts, a can of Piff-O-Puff for cocktails and a Delic de Deux Cheese which I have difficulty finding even in the States.

While roaming through the store I made an incongruous discovery. Here we were, on an island inhabited by a native race, with a few French and a few Chinese, where the tourists certainly don't patronize grocery stores very often, and before my eyes were some Hostess Cup Cakes, some frozen Sarah Lee Cakes, and fresh nectarines, peaches and melons from California.

In the refrigerator there were three different brands of butter, sausages from France and Denmark, ham from Holland and dozens of different kinds of cheese, both aged and pasteurized. There was a complete array of ordinary fresh vegetables, plus some of the funny ones. The champagne was $2.50 a quart.

Wherever we went the selection was amazing. We found jams from England, Libby canned meats, an assortment of Del Monte canned foods, herring from Norway, canned squid and mandarin oranges from Japan, celery from Utah. There was all kinds of plunder in every store we visited. Not just the fancy food shops, but everywhere, and at a fair price, considering that it was all imported.

Out in the countryside, every grocery store had a can opener on the wall. Whenever a native bought a can of food—and the Tahitians adore canned asparagus—the storekeeper just automatically took the top off. The natives don't have can openers.

Most of the stores are run by Chinese and a few by Frenchmen. The French, however, cater to the French. The Chinese is interested in selling his merchandise and he doesn't give a damn if you are German, French, American or Tahitian. He's a nice guy who tries to take care of you and he gives you a good price.

## PAPEETE HAS STYLE

The women in Tahiti are very style conscious, smartly dressed and ultra feminine. The beat look is never going to make it there. In the first place, women in Tahiti want to look like women, alluring and chic. In the second place, there are many Chinese dressmakers, with Paris couture training, who will put together any fashion or style from beautiful French cottons or other imported fabrics, all custom made and fitted, and the cost is anywhere from 25 dollars to 150 dollars, depending upon the fabric and the amount of detail you want. You can buy ready-made dresses, too, in smart styles and good quality of fabrics, quite inexpensively. You may have to go to several shops for a particular piece of cloth or a pair of shoes but they are there, right in the middle of nowhere. To me, it is fantastic.

Nothing will ever take the place of the pareu in Tahiti, however. It is the work or play garb of the native. Pareu cloth comes in a variety of colors and patterns. These are cut and hemmed while you wait. The gals wind the lengths of cloth around themselves, under their armpits, and tuck in the end. The fellows wrap a length around their hips like a skirt and tuck in the end. Or they will pull one end up between their legs and stick it in at the waist. They wear their pareus this way when they are fishing or climbing trees. I look terrific in a pareu, with my big belly and wooden leg. That's a combination that is hard to beat, but what the hell, it was comfortable.

## WHAT TO DO IN TAHITI

Prices of food, hotels and living in general are not cheap. There are restaurants, dozens of them, with perhaps only twenty-five or thirty people in them when we were there. Whatever was offered was good.

Entertainment depends upon what you like, and there is something for everyone. During the day you can tour the island, climb mountains, visit the other islands, go boating, fishing or

swimming. Tahiti and its surrounding waters provide a sportsman's paradise. The fishing is fantastic, best between December and July. For many years, Tahiti held the record for the largest marlin ever caught. It weighed over a thousand pounds.

Besides marlin there are various species of tuna, barracuda, giant groupers, sailfish, wahoo, and giant dolphin. The Polynesian name for this fish is mahimahi, found throughout South Pacific waters, and one of the most delicious of fish.

At night, there is shrimp fishing in the rivers with spear and lamplight. Sometimes the natives paddle out to the reef in canoes and fish for the giant sea centipede called varo. It tastes something like lobster meat and is delicious roasted. The Chinese cook them with Chinese black bean sauce and egg, like Lobster Cantonese, and they are out of this world.

There was a small 9 hole golf course when I was there last. I understand that this was taken over for a new hotel site, but that there are plans in the future for golfers. There is a miniature golf course for those who want to practice their putting. Tennis is popular, played on the courts at Fautaua Sports Stadium. About 3 miles out of Papeete you can hire horses by the hour or day.

Wherever you go in Tahiti you are overwhelmed by color. The sky, the trees and the ocean are so vivid and colorful that they seem unreal, a fantasy. There is the splash of pink and yellow hibiscus everywhere, growing wild.

As far as anything cultural—aside from a few art galleries—there is the Museum of Tahiti, called the Musée, located on the Rue Brea, a block and a half from the waterfront. There you will find some interesting artifacts and books on old Polynesia. Several years ago a group decided to create a memorial to Gauguin, to be called the Gauguin Museum. Since the islanders let all of the Gauguin originals get away from them, only reproductions will be displayed along with art of the South Seas.

Night life is furnished by the hotels and nightclubs. Entertainment at Hotel Tahiti is sophisticated and great fun. This is one of the better spots, featuring a South Sea atmosphere in its bar, and Tahitian dancers and musicians. Tahitian women are swivel-hipped and more men get into the action, with agile knee action and hip movement. Tahitian dancing is fast, suggestive and sexy.

On the other side of the coin are Quinn's and Lafayette. They are both buckets of blood but hilarious. You must have heard of Quinn's. Anything you have heard is an understatement. It is a night spot of international fame, the meeting place for Tahitians, sailors, soldiers and tourists. The Tahitian band, which has made a number of successful records, plays hot, fast music, which somehow takes your mind off the smoke and heat.

Four of us decided to take it in one night. While we were

ordering drinks, two Tahitian teen-agers sat down nearby and ordered a couple of beers. They couldn't have been more than fourteen. Two sailors came along and before long there was a sympatico going. I was sitting with my wife, who is not an unattractive woman, and a soldier came over and asked her to dance. We explained the situation and he understood. He was just lonesome.

Quinn's is just a typical, tropical nightclub, right on the waterfront, with co-educational toilet facilities, but everybody goes there. The music is terrific. You see all kinds of dancing from Tahitian to the latest U.S.A. dance fad. If you bear this in mind you will enjoy the place.

When Quinn's closes, which is before midnight, you can go on to Lafayette, a few miles out of Papeete. It is very much like Quinn's, but the tempo is stepped up. The music is hotter, the dancing more abandoned, and the drinking wilder.

Then there is Vaima. That is the place to go during the daytime. It is right on the waterfront, up from Quinn's. You sit there and drink beer and everybody in Papeete who is looking for anyone will look there. You can pick up a girl, meet your friends, watch the boats, or eat breakfast, lunch or dinner. It is where traffic flows in Papeete.

## LE MARCHE

If you are in a grocery store, a meat market, gift shop or a drugstore and you ask for something they don't have in stock, the clerk always says "le marche," so off to le marche we went one morning about five o'clock. What a madhouse. It was so crowded you could hardly see the stalls. Everyone who has anything to sell brings it to market.

Unlike Mexican or Caribbean markets, it is clean, washed down every night and the merchandise is neatly arranged in piles—big yams, small yams, ufi (sweet potatoes) of various sizes, taro roots as big as your head, taro leaves for pota, big fish, little fish, bonita and tuna on long racks, head down and tied up by their tails. There was little fish that looked as though they belonged in an aquarium, flat ones with yellow and black stripes, pretty little red ones, lobsters, crayfish and fresh water shrimp. You have to buy it quickly and get it home pronto because the fish was caught during the night. The coolness of the morning quickly passes and there is no ice.

If you want fresh fish you must go to le marche or do without, so your cook gets up at dawn and off she goes on her little motorbike. Everyone in Tahiti has a motorbike—just a motor attached to a conventional bicycle. You see them all over the island, and they go for miles on a quart of gasoline. How anyone ever finds his own is a mystery to me but no one ever seems to take the wrong putt-putt. There is nothing more appealing than the sight of a Tahitian girl, a hibiscus over one ear, sitting with her knees together, her long hair flying out behind her, putt-putting down the road.

Besides fresh fish, you can buy a live chicken or a duck at le marche. And what vegetables! String beans, cabbages with small heads, lettuce with no heads, leeks, onions, breadfruit. Breadfruit is something everyone should taste. If you ever get a chance, try it cut up and French fried.

A Tahitian woman sat in a corner making flower crowns from Tiare Tahiti (the Tahitian jasmine). Next to her a man sold eggs—little brown eggs, fatter white eggs, and still bigger brown eggs.

There was the woman who sold fruit. They have a grapefruit, called pamplemousse, almost as big as your head. The perfume and flavor are delightful. You can buy them for 10 or 15 cents apiece. There were star apples, pretty purple plums as big as baseballs, papaya and a fruit I know as cherimoya. There were vanilla beans, big fat yellow bananas, small, fat, orange-colored bananas, small black figs, oranges and limes. One Tahitian must have had a tamarind tree for she sold only tamarind pods in little

PLATE IV. Tahitian Mahimahi Dali Dali, *page 73*

PLATE V. Mainland Luau, table setting, *page 87*

piles. Did you ever eat the fruit? You peel off the heavy brown skin and there is a sticky fruit like a lichee with a big seed. You pop the seed into your mouth and work off the fruity pulp which is tart and unique in flavor. In India the tamarind is used in some curries. The Italians make a syrup out of them and so do the Mexicans. The Tahitians just eat them.

Tahitian packaging is decidedly far out. Peanuts are sold in pop bottles with corks in them, which isn't as silly as it sounds. This keeps both the bugs and the rats from getting to them. We think we have done something great, dry roasting peanuts, but the Tahitians have been doing this since no one remembers when. You buy milk in a bottle that is only half full. I never did find out the reason for that. Loaves of bread are a yard long and you just carry them under your arm. The natives and working class drink cheap red wine imported in 50 gallon steel drums. French vintage wines are available but only the rich can afford them.

## WE DINE IN PAPEETE

Our first evening in Papeete was spent with the Porois. Susy, remembering my interest in native Tahitian dishes, included a number of them in her menu, including Poisson Cru, which is French for raw fish.

The meal started off with mahimahi prepared in lime juice. The fish is diced and well salted. Let it stand a bit, then wash thoroughly. Add fresh lime juice to mix completely with the fish and let it stand several hours, mixing from time to time. Add pepper and finely chopped onion—just a suspicion. Don't overpower the fish because mahimahi has a very delicate flavor. Just before serving, Coconut Cream is poured over the fish. If you don't have Coconut Cream use chopped tomatoes with a little salad oil and some finely chopped sweet pepper. Scallops and lobsters can be prepared this same way. Cut the scallops in half inch cubes and slice the lobster very thin.

Included in the menu that first night were baked bananas, taro cut into chunks and steamed, a white sweet potato called ufi, baked breadfruit and pota. The pota was delightful, served very much like the Hawaiian laulau—a mixture of chicken, salt pork, taro leaves, seasonings, thickened with cornstarch and steamed in ti leaves. In this country, where it is often impossible to secure fresh taro leaves, Swiss chard makes a satisfactory substitute. The leaves of the Chinese bok choy are even more flavorful.

*POTA U.S.A. STYLE*

| | |
|---|---|
| 4 tablespoons diced salt pork | ½ cup chicken stock |
| ½ cup chopped cooked chicken | Salt, pepper and MSG to taste |
| 5 cups coarsely chopped Swiss chard leaves or green part of bok choy | Juice of ½ lemon |
| | 4 tablespoons Coconut Milk |
| 4 tablespoons chopped green onions | 2 teaspoons cornstarch mixed with |
| | ¼ cup water |

Sauté salt pork until browned; add chicken, chard and green onion. Stir in chicken stock, seasonings and lemon juice. Simmer until chard is tender. Add Coconut Milk and bring just barely to a boil. Thicken with cornstarch, stirring constantly, adding just enough to thicken the mixture. If Coconut Milk is not available, substitute heavy cream. Serves 6.

With this we were served chicken cooked with ginger and Coconut Cream which was delicious. The way Tahitian food is eaten was interesting to me. You pour the Coconut Cream, which the Tahitians call miti ha'ari, into a soup plate in front of you. You put the food on top of the Coconut Cream and sort of mix it around with your fingers as you eat.

The Tahitians make their miti ha'ari the same way the

Hawaiians make their Coconut Milk or Cream except that they use seawater instead of plain water in the process. Miti means sea or ocean in Tahiti and ha'ari is the Tahitian word for coconut. Wherever you eat there is always miti ha'ari on the table, usually in a catsup bottle with holes punched in the cap.

## CHICKEN WITH GINGER

Cut up 2 young chickens, weighing about 2½ pounds apiece. Shake pieces in a paper bag with flour seasoned with salt, pepper and MSG. Sauté chicken in butter (I'd mix safflower oil with the butter) until the chicken is tender and nice and crisp. Then take a piece of fresh gingerroot about the size of your thumb and chop it very, very fine. Use red ginger if it is available. Put the chopped ginger in a piece of muslin or double thickness of cheesecloth and squeeze the juice into some Coconut Cream. Pour this over the fried chicken and slip it into the oven for a few minutes. Don't leave it in there too long or the Coconut Cream will break down. This treatment is also good with fish. Serves 6.

Another delightful dish was fillets of mahimahi sautéed in butter mixed with peanut oil, seasoned with salt and pepper. The fillets were placed in a baking dish, the following sauce poured over them and baked in a medium oven for a few minutes.

## SAUCE FOR MAHIMAHI SUSY POROI

| | |
|---|---|
| Juice of 2 limes | 2 tablespoons arrowroot |
| 2 tablespoons sugar | mixed with cold water |
| 1 tablespoon vinegar | to a thin paste |
| ¼ cup water | Salt and pepper to taste |

Mix the lime juice, sugar and vinegar in a saucepan with the water. Add arrowroot mixture and stir over fire until sauce is clear and thick, adding more water if necessary. When sauce is smooth season to taste and pour over fish.

The Tahitians serve bananas with everything but cooked with chicken the result is outstanding.

*CHICKEN AND BANANAS* (PLATE III)

3 fryers, split
½ cup oil
Salt and pepper
Nutmeg
3 cups chicken stock

12 ti leaves
12 bananas, peeled and
   halved
¾ cup butter

Cut chicken halves in 2 pieces per serving; sauté in oil until golden brown. Add seasonings and chicken stock; let simmer a few minutes. Place 2 pieces of chicken (breast and thigh) in individual baking dishes lined with 2 ti leaves, leaving enough extending on each side to fold over. Sauté bananas in butter; place 4 strips of banana on top of chicken. Fold ti leaves over the chicken and bananas, and then cover entire dish with aluminum foil. Bake in medium oven half an hour. Serves 6.

One of the outstanding soups I tasted in Tahiti is easily made wherever fresh fish is available. Those of you who do not care for the flavor of saffron or turmeric may omit them, but you should try it at least once.

*TAHITIAN FISH SOUP*

4 pounds assorted fresh
   fish
1 gallon water
2 cups white wine
1 bay leaf
3 large onions, peeled
   and sliced
1 cup sliced celery
1 cup chopped raw
   carrots
2 large raw potatoes,
   peeled and chopped

½ teaspoon imported
   saffron *OR*
1 tablespoon grated
   turmeric
1 clove garlic
2 teaspoons salt
¼ teaspoon pepper
¼ teaspoon thyme
2 teaspoons MSG

Clean and cut up fish—rock cod, bass or whatever is available. Put fish, heads and tails in large soup kettle and cover with water, about a gallon. Bring to a boil, add white wine and bay leaf. Let simmer until fish falls apart, about 1½ hours. Dispose of bones, fins, heads, etc. Sauté onions and celery in butter until they are golden brown. Pour sautéed vegetables into stock, rinsing the pan with some of the stock and add it to the pot for extra flavor and color. Add carrots, potatoes and seasonings. Simmer for another hour, or until vegetables are mushy. Remove soup from fire and force everything through a food mill, or blend the entire soup with the vegetables and fish in a blender, a little at a time. Return to kettle and bring to a boil. Correct seasonings. The soup should have the consistency of a cream soup. Serves 8 to 10.

*POISSON AU GRATIN*

Clean a 3 pound fish—salmon, bass or whatever edible fish is available. Bone but leave the skin intact, after scaling. Stuff with the following bread dressing, saving enough to cover the top of the fish. Allow about half a cup of dressing for each pound of fish and put the rest on top.

| | |
|---|---|
| 2 tablespoons chopped onion | ½ teaspoon salt |
| 2 tablespoons melted butter | ⅛ teaspoon pepper |
| ½ cup chopped celery | ½ teaspoon dried dillweed |
| 2 tablespoons chopped parsley | 1½ cups fresh bread crumbs |
| ¼ cup diced tomato | 1 egg, beaten |
| | Milk to moisten |

Sauté onions in butter, add celery, parsley and tomato in pan. Add seasonings and mix well. Combine with bread crumbs and stir in beaten egg. Add enough milk to make a loose dressing. Mix well. Stuff fish, saving about 1 cup of dressing for the top, and place fish in oiled baking pan. Spread dressing on top of fish. Prepare a Sauce Vin Blanc and pour over the stuffed fish before baking. Bake in 325° F. oven 40 to 45 minutes, or until done. Serves 6.

*SAUCE VIN BLANC*

½ cup white wine
1 bay leaf
2 cloves
3 black peppercorns
1 small piece fresh
  gingerroot

1 teaspoon chopped
  shallots
Quick Light Cream Sauce
2 tablespoons whipped
  cream

Mix first six ingredients and reduce by half over medium heat. Strain and add to 1 cup of the following sauce, and fold in whipped cream.

QUICK LIGHT CREAM SAUCE

Blend 2 tablespoons melted butter with 2 tablespoons flour and add 1 teaspoon salt. Add roux to 1 cup milk in a small pan. Set pan over heat and beat with rotary egg beater until sauce thickens.

Good beef, in Tahiti, comes from New Zealand and we enjoyed a wonderful steak in Arue, a few miles out of Papeete. I was fortunate enough to secure this recipe and several others from Puooro-Plage.

*STEAK AU POIVRE A LA HONGROISE*

Turn a fillet or minute steak in oil and then in crushed black or white peppercorns. Crush the peppercorns on a cloth or several thicknesses of waxed paper with a rolling pin. Cook steak in butter with chopped shallots to taste. In an extra pan—the kind you use for Crepes Suzettes—the sliced marrow of a beef marrowbone, add the cooked steak and flame with cognac. Remove the steak to a warm pan or platter and to the same pan in which the steak was flamed, add a small glass of Madeira wine. Let it reduce over flame and add a teaspoon of Dijon mustard and 2 tablespoons of fresh cream (half and half) and ½ teaspoon paprika. When this is thoroughly mixed, return the steak to the pan and cook 2 minutes. Salt to taste and serve with the sauce. Serves 1.

### POULET AU GINGEMBRE

Cut a fricasse chicken in serving pieces and cook in seasoned broth. On the side, cut up some fresh ginger very fine and mix it with Coconut Milk. When the chicken is about done, heat the Coconut Milk and thicken it slightly with a little cornstarch mixed with cold water. Add some chopped pimiento. Drain the chicken and add to the coconut sauce. Let simmer gently for a few minutes and serve with rice.

From this recipe we experimented with younger chickens and a little difference in the preparation and we think the result is outstanding.

### CHICKEN REA

Quarter 3 broilers and simmer in seasoned chicken broth or consommé to cover, with 1 onion, peeled and sliced, and a suspicion of garlic. When the chicken is about half cooked, add 1 teaspoon salt. When chicken is tender—be sure it is not over-cooked—remove to serving platter to keep warm, arranging one breast and one thigh together for each serving. Sort of tuck them together. Serve with following sauce.

SAUCE

1 cup white wine
1½ cups chicken broth
3 tablespoons minced red
   ginger
1 teaspoon turmeric
   powder

2 cups fresh frozen
   Coconut Milk
Salt, white pepper and
   MSG to taste
Watercress or parsley

Heat wine and chicken broth with ginger and turmeric. Let

simmer to blend thoroughly. Add Coconut Milk gradually, stirring carefully. Do not overheat as the Coconut milk is apt to break down. Point up with salt, white pepper and MSG to taste. Pour sauce over chicken. Garnish with watercress or parsley. Serve immediately. Serves 6.

Chicken Rea is wonderful with Rice Papeete, a sort of Tahitian rice pilaf which Susy Poroi served us one evening.


*RICE PAPEETE*

| | |
|---|---|
| 8 cups cooked rice | ½ teaspoon Lingham's |
| ¼ cup butter | Chilly Sauce |
| 8 ounces seedless raisins | Salt, pepper and MSG |
| 8 ounces chopped dried | to taste |
| bananas | |

Sauté rice with butter in frying pan. Add raisins, bananas and Chilly Sauce and mix thoroughly. Stir until heated through. Season to taste and serve on a platter, or chop plate, surrounded by sautéed bananas, or you can arrange the Chicken Rea and sauce around the mound of rice. Serves 6.

This next recipe involves an old Chinese secret, preparing chicken for Chicken Velvet. The theory is to coat the chicken with the cornstarch and egg white to seal it, then poach it in oil. If done properly, it really is as smooth as velvet. The sauce is delightfully mild and the ingredients should not be cut up too fine or overcooked so as to provide a contrast in texture to the smoothness of the chicken.


*CHICKEN CURRY AMUI*

| | |
|---|---|
| 1 3 pound chicken | 2 egg whites |
| ½ teaspoon salt | 2 tablespoons oil |
| ½ teaspoon MSG | 2 cups oil |
| ½ ounce sherry | Curry Sauce |
| 2 tablespoons cornstarch | |

Remove meat from bones and cut into ½ inch slices. Season with salt, MSG and sherry, mixing well, then add cornstarch and mix thoroughly. Add unbeaten egg whites and 2 tablespoons oil. Mix thoroughly and let stand 10 to 15 minutes. Meanwhile, heat about 2 cups of oil in a wok or pan. The exact amount of oil will depend on the size of the pan used. There must be enough oil to cover the chicken. Bring temperature to 250° F.; add chicken and keep stirring so pieces will not stick together. Poach for about two minutes to seal coating. Chicken should be cooked but not the least bit colored. Test for doneness. When done lift from oil immediately with perforated spoon and drain in a colander or strainer. Add to Curry Sauce which follows and reheat. Serve immediately over steamed rice. Serves 6.

CURRY SAUCE

| | |
|---|---|
| 1 tablespoon curry powder | ½ cup chicken broth |
| 1 tablespoon butter | 1 quart half and half |
| 1 onion, chopped | 4 tablespoons cornstarch mixed with |
| 2 stalks celery, chopped | ½ cup cold water |
| ½ cup sliced mushrooms | Salt and MSG to taste |
| 1 cup diced, peeled apple | |

Sauté curry powder in butter, being careful not to let it scorch; add vegetables and apple and mix thoroughly. Add stock and let it simmer for a few moments, until ingredients are tender but not overcooked. Add half and half and bring just to a boil. Thicken with cornstarch mixed with water, stirring constantly until mixture thickens. Season to taste and add cooked chicken. *Note:* Cooked shrimp or crab may be used in place of the chicken.

*MAHIMAHI DALI DALI* (PLATE IV)

Mahimahi is the Polynesian name for the dolphin. It is usually frozen and shipped in cases of 5 pound fillets, and not usually found in retail outlets. Restaurants are the best source. As it becomes more popular it will probably be packed frozen for the retail trade.

Should you obtain mahimahi from your favorite restaurant, let the fillet thaw, skin it and cut into 4 inch pieces. Trim the black center portion, then cut the fillet into quarter inch thicknesses, crosswise. Season with salt, pepper and MSG, dust lightly with flour and sauté in butter. Allow 3 pieces per person.

In a separate pan, sauté thin slices of peeled papaya, cut lengthwise. Don't use a papaya that is too ripe, and allow at least 3 slices per serving. Peel 1 banana per serving. Cut in half lengthwise, or cut in half crosswise and sauté in butter.

## A WEDDING IN TAHITI

One of the highlights of our stay in Tahiti was a wedding—a French Tahitian wedding. When we were invited I pictured a native feast, something like a luau, with Tahitian dancing. But what a pleasant surprise. It turned out to be just about the nicest wedding party I have ever attended.

First of all, and what I especially liked, we weren't expected to attend the wedding ceremony. A civil ceremony was held first and a church service took place in the early afternoon. Then everyone went about their business until about seven-thirty or eight o'clock that evening, when the real celebration took place.

The party was held at the home of the bride's parents, but there was no dull receiving line to endure. The bride and groom held court in the living room and as the guests arrived, singly or in groups, they paid their respects, chatted for a moment and then strolled out into the garden where the feast was to be held.

The array of food was fantastic. A whole calf was turning on a spit, alongside of a whole lamb, both of which had been brushed with a most delicious marinade and let stand several hours before barbecuing. You can use this sauce for most any meat or fowl, but it is particularly good with lamb.

*MARINADE FOR LAMB OR VEAL*

| | |
|---|---|
| 1 cup salad oil | 1 tablespoon pepper |
| ½ cup red wine vinegar | 3 teaspoons dried |
| 1 jar Dijon mustard | marjoram |
| 2 tablespoons | 5 cloves of garlic, peeled |
| Worcestershire sauce | and crushed |
| 2 teaspoons salt | 1 large onion, peeled and |
| 2 teaspoons MSG | grated |
| 2 tablespoons curry | 2 stalks celery, minced |
| powder | |

Blend sauce and let stand several days or at least overnight, prior to using. Apply liberally to meat with a brush three or four hours before meat is to be barbecued.

Quarts of beer and champagne were chilling in tubs of ice. There was a big keg of rum punch that was simply great, and 5 gallon jugs of good French wine in reed jackets. Before I describe the rest of the spread, here is the recipe for the punch:

*TAHITIAN WEDDING PUNCH*

| | |
|---|---|
| 2½ cups crushed | 1 fifth gold rum |
| pineapple—※2 can | 2 fifths white wine |
| 1 cup sugar | Slices of fruit and berries |
| 1 cup lemon juice | or gardenias |
| Rind 2 lemons | |

Mix ingredients in large crock or keg and stir thoroughly. Let stand 6 hours in a cool place. Strain into punch bowl with cake of ice and let chill 2 hours before serving time. Garnish with slices of fruit and berries or gardenias. Increase according to the number of people to be served.

Here is a dandy punch for a wedding or any kind of a

reception where punch is the star of the show, but you'll need a whopper of a punch bowl. Serves 25.

*CHAMPAGNE PUNCH*

| | |
|---|---|
| 1 whole large ripe pineapple | 1 fifth cognac |
| 1 pound bar sugar | 1 fifth Jamaica rum |
| 1 fifth curaçao | 12 quarts champagne |
| | Gardenias, berries or fruit |

Slice pineapple, core and cut in pieces; place in large crock and add sugar, curaçao, brandy and rum. Let stand overnight. Be sure sugar is dissolved. Next day, pour over a cake of ice and let stand 2 to 3 hours before using. Meantime have champagne chilling. When ready to serve, add champagne. Garnish with gardenias, berries or sliced fruit.

Places were set at long tables laden with all kinds of goodies— olives, several kinds of sausages on bamboo sticks, varieties of cheese, bowls of salad, and little finger sandwiches of baked ham. The bread was spread with butter lightly touched with garlic which gave the ham a wonderful flavor. And there were cakes of infinite variety.

About a hundred and fifty people were all talking and having a gossipy good time. When the bride and groom showed up at their long table, everyone sat down, the orchestra began playing and the party began to shape up. The meat was sliced and Tahitian girls in pareus, flower crowns and leis rushed plates of food to everyone. Other vahines kept guests supplied with rum punch or beer and there were carafes of wine on the tables which were replenished as soon as they were emptied.

When most of the guests had finished eating, the musicians played a lovely Tahitian song, like a waltz or a two-step. The bride and groom went to the center of a sort of dance floor which apparently had been installed for the occasion, and there they stopped. The groom started to fidget with his wife's long white dress and it looked as though he was taking her dress off. And by golly, he was doing just that. It fell from her shoulders, she stepped out of it and there she stood in a white satin sheath, knee high. No shoes. Just as cute as a mouse's ear. And then the two of them began a lovely dance together out under the stars. As the dance ended, the floor filled with the guests who danced to the same lovely Tahitian song.

When the music stopped, an elderly woman stepped to the center of the floor. Suddenly everyone was quiet and she began to speak in Tahitian. It was almost like a chant and she pointed first to the newlyweds and then to the guests. Susy Poroi whispered that she was giving the couple their new Tahitian name.

As she finished, a Tahitian man, tall and straight, with a fine physique, walked to the center of the floor. He stood as I have never seen anyone stand, leaning slightly forward, with one foot just a little ahead of the other. He, too, spoke in Tahitian and he too gave them a name, and he named their first and second born. Then came his ia ora na (farewell), and he retired from the floor. Susy said it was then up to the bride and groom to pick the name they liked best, to use from that day on.

The ceremony over, the orchestra broke into the hottest music I've ever heard and the party was on. It was still going strong when Helen and I left, and it continued on, I was told later, until about four in the morning. The remaining guests took time out to clean up a bit, and then carried on all the next day, with some differences.

There were no professional musicians but just guests who brought guitars, ukuleles or a drum. Others brought ham, cheese, sausages. Others brought rum, beer or wine. And the dancing continued. This became a real Tahitian party.

Here is a dish the Tahitians recommend for the day after.

*PAGOA*

2½ pounds fresh salmon
or tuna
10 lemons
2 medium-sized tomatoes,
peeled and diced
2 onions, chopped
2 cloves garlic, peeled
and finely minced
2 canned pimientos,
drained and chopped

1 large firm cucumber,
peeled and diced
2 tablespoons chopped
sweet pickles
½ cup chopped parsley
Sauce Vinaigrette
3 hard-cooked eggs

Bone and cut the fish into small cubes; put in a large stainless steel or china bowl and barely cover with a strong solution of salt water. Add the juice of 10 lemons. Let marinate, stirring from time to time, in the refrigerator, for about 2 hours. Meanwhile, put tomatoes, onions, garlic, pimientos and cucumber in a bowl; cover and chill. When fish is "cooked" by the lemon juice, strain off the liquid, add the chilled vegetable mixture, chopped pickles and parsley. Stir well and mix with Sauce Vinaigrette. Serve in soup plates, garnished with wedges of hard-cooked eggs, accompanied by French bread and butter and wash down with cold beer. Serves 6 to 8 hung-over people.

*SAUCE VINAIGRETTE*

½ cup olive oil
3 tablespoons wine
vinegar
½ teaspoon dry mustard

½ teaspoon salt
½ teaspoon freshly
ground pepper

Mix two tablespoons of the oil, the vinegar, mustard, and seasonings, stirring until smooth. Beat in the rest of the oil with a wire whisk, a little at a time. Chill. Mix again before using. You can increase the quantities and store it in a screw-cap jar in the refrigerator for use as needed.

# A TAHITIAN TAMAARAA

The Tahitian Tamaaraa is the equivalent to the Hawaiian luau, but more exciting. The music and dancing have a faster beat. The Tahitians dance with more abandon, the men get into the act and everyone drinks more. Rum punch is usually reserved for parties but everyone drinks beer or wine every day. There is a difference, too in the way the traditional pig is cooked.

Before we left Tahiti we gave a Tamaaraa for the friends who had entertained us during our stay. It was prepared at the home of the Porois, so I was able to watch the preparations and get my oar in too.

About a hundred people were invited. There was a keg of rum punch which was started two days in advance of the party. I have since served it at private parties in San Francisco with sensational results. It can make a stone tiki dance.

*TAHITIAN RUM PUNCH*

| | |
|---|---|
| 12 bottles light rum | 6 large grapefruit |
| 12 bottles Jamaica rum | 8 ripe bananas |
| 2 pounds raw sugar | 2 ripe pineapples |
| 4 or 5 whole vanilla | 6 bottles dry white wine, |
| beans | chilled |
| 6 dozen oranges | 15 gallon keg or crock |
| 6 dozen lemons | Sliced fruit and gardenias |
| 6 limes | |

Pour rum into your container. If you use metal, be sure it is stainless steel. *Never* use a galvanized container. The action of the fruit juices and alcohol on the metal can make you and your guests deathly ill. Add the sugar and vanilla beans. If you can't get Demarara sugar (or Kleen Raw) use coarse brown sugar. Stir until the sugar is dissolved. Halve the citrus fruits, squeeze the juice into the rum and drop in the shells. Peel and slice the bananas; peel, core and slice the pineapples and drop both bananas and pineapples into the rum mixture. Let stand in a cool place for 2 days, stirring every 2 or 3 hours during the day.

On the day of the party, remove pulp and rinds. Pour the rum mixture over ice in a large punch bowl. Let the mixture chill thoroughly for several hours and just before serving add the chilled wine. If you haven't a punch bowl, just add ice to the container and let it chill for several hours, then add chilled wine. Decorate with sliced fruit—oranges, lemons, limes and float a few gardenias. Serves 125 to 150.

Because Tahitian coconuts are too large for punch cups, some of the Tahitian boys cut bamboo in the mountains and made punch cups from the sections just for the party. There was plenty

of good French wine for those who didn't care for punch and flower crowns for all. A troupe of Tahitians dancers, about to take off for the U.S.A. on a promotion of the islands, enlivened the party.

Meantime, preparations were underway for the underground cooking of the feast. Two pigs were cooked, along with fruits and vegetables. The Tahitians don't like to cook a great big pig. They claim the big ones take too long to cook and everything else is overcooked. So we had two pigs, each weighing about

25 or 30 pounds. A pit, about 2½ feet deep, 6 feet long and 4 feet wide, was dug. The Tahitians call their underground oven an ahimaa. Wood of a non-resinous nature was laid in the bottom in sufficient quantities to heat the special stones which were piled on top of the wood. These stones are porous, taken from lava beds, which can stand great heat without exploding.

It took about an hour for the fire to burn down, so there has to be plenty of wood underneath the stones to get them to a white heat. When the fire had burned down, palm boughs, stripped of their leaves, were placed on top of the stones. The

pigs, which had been opened up by splitting the chime bone, were seasoned with soya sauce, salt, pepper and garlic. They were placed, skin side up on top of the boughs, and around them were tucked little packages of peeled bananas, taro root cut in 2 inch cubes, peeled sweet potatoes and pota, tied up in banana leaves which had first been passed slowly over flames. This wilts the leaves and keeps them from tearing so foods can be wrapped more easily.

Chicken in bamboo containers were added to the ahimaa, as well as pota of two different kinds; fish wrapped in ti leaves; and breadfruit, peeled, cut into pieces and wrapped in banana leaves. When everything was in place, green bamboo poles about

2 inches thick were placed on top with spaces between which allowed a breathing space for steam and heat to cook everything completely.

The Tahitian underground cooking differs from the Hawaiian in two respects. First, the pigs are laid out flat—they don't put hot stones in the stomach cavity—and second, the arrangements of the bamboo poles, which is the reason the pigs come out crisp in Tahiti instead of mushy.

Finally, on top of the green bamboo poles, plenty of banana leaves were spread, then ti leaves and woven mats of several thicknesses. Last, about four inches of earth was spread on top. The food cooked two and a half to three hours, no longer.

While the food cooked, everyone dipped into the punch, drank wine or beer, cooling in tubs of ice. Soon there was music and the dancers got into high gear. Meantime, other preparations were being completed.

Young vahines, wearing cotton print dresses or pareus and flower crowns, dashed about setting the tables, while the matrons chopped and stirred.

One of the operations underway was the Poisson Cru, made in an enamel dishpan. The Tahitians use mahimahi instead of the Hawaiian salt salmon, but the process is the same as for Lomi Salmon II. Just substitute mahimahi for the salmon.

I was fascinated with the chicken cooked in the bamboo. Cut up chicken meat was mixed with minced onion, a bit of garlic and seasoned with herbs, salt and pepper. The mixture was poked into a section of green bamboo, closed at one end by the joint, and the open end was stuffed with ti leaves. These were put in the pit with the rest of the food to steam. The Tahitians cook eel the same way.

When I returned to San Francisco we experimented with the idea of Chicken Bamboo for our Truly Polynesian menu and developed the following recipe.

*CHICKEN BAMBOO TAHITIAN*

For 6 people, split 3 chickens weighing between 2¼ and 2½ pounds each. Poach them in chicken broth (canned will do) with a bouquet garni tied in muslin, salt, white pepper and MSG. Poach gently until the chicken is tender and the bones are loose. When cool enough to handle, skin and remove the breasts carefully. Put in a container with some of the broth, cover and put in an oven at low heat to keep warm. Bone the rest of the chicken and cut into bite-sized chunks. Make the following sauce from the remaining broth:

| | |
|---|---|
| 3 tablespoons minced shallots | 2 cups cream sauce (béchamel) |
| 3 cups sliced fresh mushrooms | 1 teaspoon Worcestershire sauce |
| 2 tablespoons butter | Salt, pepper and MSG to taste |
| 1 tablespoon curry powder | 2 tablespoons Coconut Milk |
| 2 teaspoons garlic powder | Chopped parsley for garnish |
| 1 cup white wine | |
| 4 cups chicken broth | |

Sauté shallots and mushrooms in butter until limp and slightly golden in color, then stir in curry powder and let cook a few seconds; keep stirring. Add the garlic powder and blend into mixture, then stir in wine and let simmer for a few seconds. Add chicken broth. If you find that you have more than 4 cups of broth from the poached chicken reduce it over heat to 4 cups. Stir in cream sauce, Worcestershire sauce and seasonings. Heat and stir, then stir in Coconut Milk. In 6 individual serving dishes, such as shallow ceramic or shirred egg dishes, arrange portions of bite-sized pieces of chicken, add some sauce, then top with breast of chicken and more sauce. Garnish each with chopped parsley. Serves 6.

Getting back to our farewell Tamaaraa, when it was time, the earth was carefully removed, then the mats and banana leaves and finally the boughs. The most delicious aroma arose with the steam. There was much commotion as the food was lifted out and served on steaming platters and bowls, on long tables. The dining area was open but roofed with thatch which kept it cool. There were pitchers of wine on the table, containers of milk along with the bamboo cups of punch and bottles of miti ha'ari, the Tahitian Coconut Milk.

For dessert a baked pudding was served made of fruits and pia, which is Tahitian for arrowroot.

*TAHITIAN PO-É*

| | |
|---|---|
| 3 ripe papayas | 2 cups raw sugar |
| 6 ripe bananas | (Kleen Raw) |
| 1 can Clemente Jacques | 2 pieces vanilla bean, |
| sliced mangoes | crushed |
| 3 cups crushed pineapple | 1 cup arrowroot |
| 3 cups pineapple juice | Coconut Cream |

Peel papaya, cut in half and remove seeds. Peel bananas and place in bowl with papayas and mash. Drain mangoes, saving liquid, and add to bananas and papayas. When reduced to a fine pulp, mix in crushed pineapple and pineapple juice. Add the raw sugar and continue to mix. Add crushed vanilla beans. Mix arrowroot with mango syrup and stir until smooth, then mix with pulp. Pour mixture into buttered baking pan so that it is about an inch deep. Bake on middle rack of oven for one hour at 400° F. If top is not browned, slip under broiler for a few seconds. Cut into 3 inch squares and let cool in pan. Serve in shells with Coconut Cream, whipped cream or a mixture of whipped cream and whipped sour cream. Serves 20 to 25, depending upon size of servings or number of squares per serving.

Someone once asked me to compare Hawaii with Tahiti. You really can't because they are two entirely different cultures. Hawaii is the melting pot of many races. In Tahiti, the native Tahitians predominate. There is a strong French influence with a Chinese accent, and you are somewhat startled at first to find Chinese speaking fluent French.

One thing that does stand out is the difference between the Hawaiian luau and the Tahitian Tamaaraa. The Hawaiians decorate their tables more festively, are lavish with fruit, flowers and ti leaves. The Tahitians, more practical, use just plain tables —often just boards on sawhorses. The Tahitians use more Coconut Cream and Coconut Milk than the Hawaiians. They pour wine in pitchers or carafes and drink it from jelly glasses. About the only imaginative, primitive touch is the bamboo container for punch and a food dish that is fashioned from large bamboo sections, split in half. The rounded bottom is sliced off so that it sits firmly on the table.

The Tahitians tend to wear flower crowns more than the Hawaiians but their flower garlands or leis are simpler. Another difference is in the music and dancing. While they still sing the old chants and songs, the Tahitians have taken current tunes, changed the tempo and given them their own words. Their dancing is usually at a faster tempo, while the Hawaiian hula is more languid.

The Tahitians are so nutty about music and dancing that they form teams all over Tahiti and the outer islands to compete for prizes. These competitions take place whenever there is a fête, held in Papeete in a sort of park, with tables and benches. The big celebration of the year is Bastille Day, held on the fourteenth of July, which to the French is comparable to our Fourth of July.

There are fêtes held at other times. Although I can't remember what the celebration was all about, there was one while we were in Tahiti. We paid 10 dollars to go to it, which entitled us to seats and all the champagne we could drink. As soon as we sat down a vahine came along and plunked down a bottle of good champagne and two jelly glasses. While we sat there drinking and watching the dancing, kids went by with bottles of pop, just like kids at home. Only the adults drank the bubbly.

There were dancing teams from all over—Mooréa, Bora Bora, Riatea and even Rapa. The dancers were mostly Tahitian but a few French girls were on the teams, and the dancing was native style, exclusively. Team after team put on their exhibitions, and they were magnificent. Some teams consisted of both men and women; others were all women or all men.

Finally, the best team was selected by a group of judges, the prizes awarded, and then everyone started to dance—conventional or Tahitian, depending upon the music. There was sort of a raised pavilion, surrounded by palms, for the dance floor, but it was pretty rough. If you didn't have on heavy shoes you were apt to get a sliver in your toe.

# Mainland Luau

HERE on the Pacific Coast the luau may seem overdone, but it is still novel to many inland people who have never been to Hawaii—even to some who have. Held indoors, on your patio, in your back yard or the city park, in a rented hall or the country club, the mainland luau is one of the most pleasant, exciting, informal ways to give a party for a lot of people. It is a wonderful way to give fund raisings, church suppers, a graduation party or a lodge picnic. It's fun just for no reason at all, except to get a bunch of people together who like to sing, dance, drink, eat and talk.

If you are past the age of sitting cross-legged on the floor, skip it. If you are up to cushions, put a door on blocks of wood or cement blocks. Use your outdoor picnic tables or put plywood slabs on wooden horses.

For a real bash, set up a long buffet table, cover it with ti leaves, use flowers and fruit for decorations and let guests help themselves. Your florist can secure ti leaves for you at a moderate price and if you find anthurium, strelitzia (bird-of-paradise), torch ginger and other tropical exotics out of your price range, forget them. Use any showy, bright blooms available. Camellias, begonias, gladiolas, chrysanthemums, lilies, zinnias, calendulas —whatever is available. And large leaves, such as caladium, callas, magnolia, ferns, hydrangea, to name a few, can augment the ti leaves. If ti leaves are unavailable, sword ferns make good table coverings. Use assorted fruits—a pineapple for the top center, with hands of bananas, oranges, avocados, limes, lemons or whatever fruits are immediately available, even apples. I have seen beautiful arrangements include wedges of cut watermelon which are used for dessert.

For evening parties, indoors or out, aloha lights are festive and glamorous. If you can't find these locally, you can use colored hurricane chimneys or colored glass vases with warming candles in the bottom and set them amid the fruit and flower decorations. Shells for the tidbits and side dishes can be bought from a nearby import outlet. You find these all over the country nowadays, where you can probably obtain coconut or bamboo cups, as well. Sometimes hardware stores carry baking shells in various sizes.

Not everyone can cook underground, but you can always get somebody with a big oven to cook the pig. The local baker or most any restaurant will cook one for you. When you get it, wrap it in foil and plenty of towels. It will keep hot for a long time. Use whichever of the recipes in the Hawaiian or the Tahitian Tamaaraa chapters seem most practical. Check available ingredients and then decide. You can use a combination of both.

Perhaps you don't want to do a pig. In the photograph of our Mainland Luau (PLATE V) we have used Pork Chops Hawaiian and baked chicken legs. Nowadays you can buy chicken parts, and chicken legs are good finger food for luaus. The Opihis, which are scallops in lime juice, and Lomi Salmon or Poisson Cru (French for raw fish) are easily done. The third shell contains small California bay shrimp. You can use marinated canned Louisiana shrimp instead.

While the Hawaiians use more imagination in their table decorations, the Tahitians always seem to have more fun, so I suggest Hawaiian decorations and Tahitian music. Use the best features of each for your party. Tahitian music is faster with more beat. The Tahitians wear flower crowns and both the women and the men dance. You can buy Tahitian records. RCA Victor has put out an album called "Tahiti—Yesterday and Today" by Quinn's Combo. There may be others. You'll want some Hawaiian records too, but mix them up. Use the Hawaiian music for singing and for background while everyone is eating.

Everybody likes to get out of character now and then, to relax and unleash the shackles of propriety. The gals like to play the siren, dance a little naughty and shake their fannies around. Guys like to get into the act and clown around. The best way to do this is to dress the part. A South Pacific party should be a costume affair. The gals in pareus, muumuus or other island garb, sandaled or barefooted, with flowers in their hair and leis around their necks; the guys in aloha shirts and shorts or pareus and flower crowns. You just provide the atmosphere and the excuse to "go native" and your party is bound to click.

One outstanding party, I recall, was a costume party where all the guests were asked to come dressed as characters from the South Pacific. Some came as beachcombers. One couple came as the minister and Sadie Thompson in *Rain*. Others came as characters from Michener's *Hawaii*. There was a Bloody Mary and a Nellie Forbush in a sailor suit and others more glamorous but not so easily identified. It was some party.

To set the scene, remove as much furniture as possible. Strew the floor with colorful cushions. Borrow some if need be. If the rooms lend themselves to such decorations, hang swags of fish net around, studded with starfish and shells and laced with strings of flowers. You can thread flower heads on linen thread or any heavy thread using a big needle, for effective decorations. You can make leis this way too. Use flowers and plants in profusion. Plants can even be rented for the occasion.

The firewater for your party should be a good strong rum punch. Get two big bowls or kegs and put one on the front doorstep or in the entrance so that from the beginning folks will have the feeling that "this is going to be great!" Wherever the party is being held—the living room, garden, terrace or basement, there should be a welcome drink for each guest. If it is a big party, have several punch bowls scattered around in convenient spots.

The punch container is important but it needn't be fancy. A keg or a half barrel, a 5 gallon tin or a steel drum will do. It doesn't make much difference what you use as long as it holds enough. You can tie some matting around it, branches of leaves and flowers, or build a fence around it. Here is where some imagination will come in handy.

For the punch itself, I prefer Tahitian Rum Punch. That's the best, and use the recipe as given in the Tahitian chapter. Don't make it any weaker. Weak punch is the greatest party-pooper that ever happened to a defenseless guest. If your friends know that you have a strong brew, they'll watch it. On the other hand, don't make it so strong that your guests gag on it.

The drinking containers should be original and fun. Coconut cups or bamboo cups would be ideal. Nice shiny tin cans, with the edges turned are practical. Get them from a store that sells home canning supplies.

Don't overlook the wine idea. On one trip to Tahiti I attended a ball in Papeete's park given by the governor. There were hundreds of people there, the women in smart cottons and the men in aloha shirts. There was dancing on a palm-decorated dance floor to both French and American music. As guests arrived they were assigned to tables and immediately several bottles of champagne appeared. Everyone drank champagne and had a ball. Try it some time. If champagne is out of the range of your entertaining budget, get a cask of wine and have the head knocked out, then just ladle it into glasses.

Just remember—and I can't emphasize it enough—once your party starts to boil, don't let it die. Keep it in the groove at all times. Don't let anyone make a speech or sing a solo with the orchestra, or whatever music you are having. Keep the dancing going and the liquor flowing. Serve food before everyone gets too loaded, but keep the punch cups filled during dinner. And enjoy your own party. It takes a lot of planning and lots of work ahead of time so you can join the party and have a good time, too, but if you are having fun you know that your guests are too.

Ever since *Trader Vic's Book of Food and Drink* was published, in 1946, we have been bombarded by requests for more parties and more recipes. Hardly a day goes by that we don't receive a letter asking for help with a tropical dance or a luau. We have been asked to cater parties in Oregon, Texas and as far east as Pennsylvania. And we have catered quite a few.

One of the most fabulous luaus we ever catered was held poolside at a country club nearby. There were about 150 guests. Instead of cooking pigs underground we had Chinese barbecue ovens made from oil drums and hung the pigs inside to cook at the scene of the party. A colorful awning was spread over the adjoining area and braziers burning charcoal were set around the edge to keep out the chill night air. The pool was decorated with glass floats, anchored to the bottom with cords and weights so they wouldn't bump against the side of the pool. An outrigger canoe was afloat, filled with tropical flowers. The water was studded with little floating candles that twinkled like stars. Man-made palm trees were placed about at strategic spots. The pavilion was hung with lanterns and surrounded with kerosene-burning luau torches.

Low tables were covered with ti leaves and down the center there were lavish arrangements of tropical flowers, flown in from Honolulu. Every few feet we placed candles in colored glass bubbles which added warmth and color to the party. Colorful cushions were provided for seats and the food was served on wooden plates and in shells of assorted sizes and shapes.

For entertainment we had several Tahitian and Hawaiian dancers, a Samoan sword dancer and a group of French-Tahitian musicians sang and played. I don't know how the invitations were worded but the women wore chic prints and the men wore aloha shirts and slacks.

The rum punch was served in a long wooden canoe-shaped bowl. Giant tuberous begonias floated amid the chunks of ice. It was a beautiful party. The flickering torches were reflected in the water, the sky was cloudless and star-studded, and there was a moon.

Polynesian foods and decorations needn't be confined to luaus and dinners. You can give a brunch, luncheon or cocktail party with a tropical theme, using the same ideas for table decorations—ti leaves, fruit and flowers—and foods served in wooden bowls and shells. Giant clam shells can be filled with shrimp or filled with shaved ice embedded with containers of caviar. Abalone or small clam shells can be used for various dips.

# Japan

SEVERAL years ago we took a trip to the Orient. Japan was our first stop, then Hong Kong and Thailand. In no land, anywhere, have we ever been treated with such consideration and courtesy as we were in Japan. Never was there the least indication, by word or action, that these people had ever been our enemies.

Wherever you go in Japan, the people are interested in you as an individual, not as a tourist. They don't try to sell you anything, they do not expect to be tipped and they have a great pride in whatever they are doing. If you display any interest, and if they can speak English, they will explain at length about their work or occupation.

We flew first to Tokyo, the world's largest city. There are ten and a half million people at last count and I think they missed a few. It is a city that is constantly in the process of rebuilding. The activity is tremendous. All day long there is that rush of people and cars that you find in our major cities at five o'clock when the white-collar workers pour out of the skyscrapers.

It is a fantastic city of contrasts—ugly, garish and noisy in the downtown areas—but in the back streets and in the poorest part of town you will find a bit of beauty. A neatly swept doorway, a small tree or plant to one side of the entrance, some stones artfully arranged, are a part of the poorest home.

There are children everywhere, happy children at play. On holidays you see whole families sight-seeing. The Japanese take their children everywhere, and they are all well behaved. No whining, no tantrums. You seldom see a Japanese child crying.

During the week, the older children are not in sight during

the day but around five o'clock you see children all over Japan on their way home from school, all in school uniforms, both girls and boys. In Japan children go to school all day. In the rural districts, on Sundays, you see the playgrounds full of activity, with parents sitting in the bleachers watching games or calisthenics.

Once you find your way out of the major cities in Japan the scenery is delightful. There are no ugly signs, no billboards to hide the beauty of the countryside. Of course, even in the cities, I find nothing objectionable about most Japanese signs, unless they are neon lighted, because the calligraphy is so interesting.

One thing that particularly interested me was the way the embankments were treated in road building. All over Japan you see stones, rough cut but square, neatly set into the soil. Throughout the country you see this type of stonework used for retaining walls or sorts of moats and there didn't seem to be any mortar in evidence.

The Japanese are temple happy, seemingly. Actually there are more shrines than temples. Buddhist places of worship are temples and Shinto places are shrines. You can tell them apart by the red gateways, or torii, in front of all shrines. No matter where you are, you may go down a little road and there amidst a forest of tall trees, will be the torii leading to a shrine. Often there will be slabs of stone, about 4 feet wide, 2 inches thick and 10 to 15 feet high, carved with Japanese characters, telling a story. Wherever you travel throughout the country you find beauty in simple form. This is the way the Japanese dress, the way they furnish their homes and the way they eat.

The Japanese cuisine is so exquisitely simple and pure in flavor that most Caucasians don't enjoy it. It has lots of eye appeal and ceremony but lacks sufficient flavor and satisfaction for the average Westerner. We are used to more distinct flavors, heavier textures, sauces and extremes in temperature. We either want our food very hot or very cold. The Japanese don't seem to care much one way or the other. They will pour hot broth over chilled vegetables in a lacquer bowl, put the cover on it and place it before you with much ceremony, and graciousness. Whatever the Japanese do, they do with grace and beauty.

Tradition has dictated the proper way to behave, walk, talk, cook and eat. There are certain foods for every season, holiday or occasion. Every movement of a dance, every garnish of a dish, the position of every picture and flower arrangement, the way to wear a kimono has been taught and handed down from generation to generation. You name it and there is a rule for it in Japan. Perhaps this is their strength and salvation. The ability to fall back on certain precepts, when plagued with typhoons, earthquakes, epidemics and war, must give them the strength to rebuild time after time, to pick up the pieces of their lives and go on.

The average Westerner is familiar with those dishes which are most popular with patrons of Japanese restaurants in cosmopolitan cities in the United States. Most travelers to Japan have experienced the banquet or party food which best goes with the sake, served at all important dinners and banquets. Many have been privileged to attend at least one tea ceremony. A capsule description of Japanese foods breaks down to five categories:

1. *Court dishes*, created in the Imperial Court during the Nara Period, but not practiced now except on very special occasions.

2. *Party dishes*, meant for entertaining. Arrangement, contrast and purity of form is important. Every dish is designed to highlight the sake.

3. *Ceremonial dishes*, for celebrations and mourning.

4. *Tea Ceremony dishes.* Every dish and vessel used must conform strictly to the teachings and taste of the tea ceremony master or Chajin.

5. *Household dishes.* These are side dishes eaten with the traditional boiled rice of the Japanese. They are usually highly seasoned and differ in contents from home to home.

It is this last category which we are concerned with here, the everyday foods and side dishes of Japan. Here are a few I have enjoyed, presented with minor adjustments for Western tastes.

The main seasonings used in Japanese cooking are soy sauce, salt, sugar, vinegar, miso (soy bean, salt and rice malt mixture), oil and sake. A clear soup is made of konbu seaweed (tangle), dried bonito shavings and water, called Dashi. This is used as a stock very much the way we use a clear broth to make sauces or a court boullion for fish dishes. It is easy to make. The difficulty lies in securing the ingredients. For our purpose, canned chicken broth makes a satisfactory substitute.

*DASHI*

| | |
|---|---|
| 1 teaspoon tangle | Pinch Ajinomoto |
| 5 cups water | (Japanese MSG) |
| ½ cup dried bonito shavings | |

Put tangle in water in a saucepan and bring to a boil. Remove tangle and add bonito shavings. When the water boils again, remove pan from heat and let stand. When the shavings sink to the bottom of the pan, drain and use clear liquid as stock. Makes 5 cups.

*BEEF TERIYAKI*

| | |
|---|---|
| 2½ pounds sirloin steak cut into 4 portions | 4 tablespoons sugar |
| 1 cup soy sauce | 1 large piece fresh gingerroot |
| 1 cup water | 1 clove garlic, crushed |
| ¼ cup sake | |

PLATE VI. Cocktails and dinner for four, Japanese style, *page 108*

PLATE VII. Hong Kong Empress Chicken, *page 138*

PLATE VIII. Hong Kong Cho Gu Chicken, *page 141*

Grill steak and cut each serving into ½ inch squares. Combine remaining ingredients and bring to a boil. Ladle sauce over each portion of cut grilled steak. Serve with steamed rice. Serves 4.

JAPANESE BROILED LAMB CHOPS

4 lamb chops, 1½ inches thick
½ cup soy sauce and ½ cup water

1 clove garlic, minced
1 tablespoon chopped fresh gingerroot

Put lamb chops in a glass bowl or casserole. Mix soy sauce, water, garlic and ginger; pour over chops and let marinate in refrigerator overnight. Bring chops to room temperature before cooking. Place chops on broiler and brush with sauce. Broil about 6 minutes, then turn and brush with additional marinade. Broil for 4 minutes or until browned and done. Bring balance of marinade to a boil and strain. Serve with chops with hot rice. Serves 4.

CHICKEN YAKITORI

1 cup sake or sherry
1 cup soy sauce
3 tablespoons sugar
2 teaspoons pepper

1½ pounds raw chicken meat, cut in large cubes

Mix sake, soy sauce, sugar and pepper and bring to a boil. Marinate chicken 15 minutes, then skewer and broil. Brush several times during cooking, turning to brown on all sides. Serves 2 to 3.

One of the most acceptable of all Japanese cooking is tempura. There are tempura bars in Tokyo which specialize in dipping shrimp, vegetables, scallops, fish fillets or small fish in batter and frying them in deep fat. The Japanese plan tempura as a dish of assorted fish and vegetables according to the season. There are several kinds of fish, such as shrimp, mussels, sea-eels, sillagoes (they look like sardines), squid, greens, chrysanthemums—flowers and leaves—scallops, and eggplant, for example.

The batter, of course, is the all important ingredient for a good tempura and it is mostly a matter of experimenting until you find the one you like best. Shrimp is probably the most popular subject. Of all of the vegetables, zucchini is probably the best suited for this form of cooking, but eggplant lends itself well to batter cooking and so does sliced cauliflower. String beans and asparagus can be given the tempura treatment if they are partially cooked.

## TEMPURA BATTER – I

| | |
|---|---|
| 1¼ cups cake flour | 1⅓ cups water |
| 4 tablespoons rice flour | 1 egg yolk, beaten |
| 4 tablespoons cornstarch | 1 egg white, beaten stiffly |

Sift flour, rice flour and cornstarch together. Add half of the water to beaten egg yolk and add flour mixture, mixing from outside to center of the bowl. Stir in rest of the water, then fold in stiffly beaten egg white. Dip seafood or vegetables, carefully dried, in batter and fry in sesame seed oil or half sesame seed oil and peanut oil or salad oil.

## TEMPURA BATTER – II

| | |
|---|---|
| 1⅓ cups all-purpose flour | 2 egg yolks, beaten |
| 1 teaspoon salt | ¾ cup flat beer |
| 1 tablespoon melted butter | 2 egg whites, beaten |

Mix flour, salt and butter with beaten egg yolks and gradually stir in the beer. Cover and allow batter to rest in refrigerator from 2 to 12 hours. Just before using, fold in 2 beaten egg whites. Be sure food to be fried is thoroughly dry.

## TEMPURA BATTER – III

½ cup flour
½ cup cornstarch
½ teaspoon salt

¼ teaspoon MSG
1 egg, separated
½ cup water

Sift dry ingredients. Beat egg yolk and add water, then add dry ingredients, stirring lightly. Beat egg white until stiff but not dry and fold into batter.

## SHRIMP TEMPURA

This is different from ordinary batter-fried shrimp in the way the shrimp are cut and the way the batter is mixed. Start with 1 pound raw, unpeeled, or green, shrimp with an 18 to 20 count. That is, 18 to 20 to the pound. Wash and shell, leaving the tails on. Pinch tails to remove water and dry thoroughly in paper towels so the batter will adhere. Devein, then slice down the length of the shrimp but not clear through. Spread and flatten, then turn over and score slightly so the shrimp will not curl when fried. Dip shrimp, holding by the tail, into one of the tempura batters just listed—I, II or III—and fry in hot oil at 375° F. until golden brown. Serve with Tempura Sauce.

## TEMPURA SAUCE

½ cup light soy sauce
2 tablespoons sake
½ cup water
¼ teaspoon grated fresh
  gingerroot

1 teaspoon sugar
Green onions, sliced

Mix soy sauce with sake and water, add gingerroot and sugar. Bring to a boil, then cool. With the sauce serve sliced green onions in separate bowl. Grated white radish may also be served in a separate bowl.

If you are going to fry vegetables, here are a few tips for preparation. Zucchini should be washed and dried. Cut away the end stems and cut lengthwise in quarters. Asparagus may be split if large. If young and tender, no precooking is necessary. String beans will do better if parboiled about 5 minutes. Cut in half or in 4 inch lengths. An electric fryer or skillet is good for tempura frying. For vegetables set control at 375° F. Shrimp and other fish may go a little higher. The main idea is to have the oil hot enough to give the food a crusty, golden coating. Don't put more than a few pieces of food in the fat at a time or you will reduce the temperature and cause the fried pieces to become soggy and fat-soaked.

This is probably the most famous and the best liked of all Japanese dishes in this country. It lends itself to informal entertaining, particularly among the young and limber who dote on sitting on sabutans at cocktail level tables.

*BEEF SUKIYAKI*

2 pounds top sirloin  
½ pound carrots  
2 medium-sized cooking onions  
¼ pound fresh mushrooms  
2 bunches green onions  
4 stalks celery  
½ pound fresh spinach  
2 packages silver noodles  

1 cup soy sauce  
¼ cup sugar  
½ cup chicken stock  
2 squares broiled tofu (bean curd)  
1 can bamboo shoots, 12 ounces  
Steamed rice  
1 egg per person  
2 ounces beef suet

*Preparation:* Have your butcher slice the meat bacon-thin for you. Wash carrots, trim ends and julienne so they will cook quickly. Peel and slice the two onions very thin. Wash and slice the mushrooms lengthwise, trimming the stem end first. Wash, clean and cut the green onions diagonally in 1 inch lengths, including the tops. Slice the celery diagonally. Wash the spinach and drain. Soak the silver noodles in warm water to soften, then cut in 3 inch lengths. Mix soy sauce, sugar and chicken stock in small bowl. Cut the broiled soy bean curd (tofu) into 12 squares. Slice the bamboo shoots crosswise very thin.

*Arrangement:* Arrange the sukiyaki ingredients separately on a large chop plate or platter, grouping them attractively. Place cooking unit on table. This may be an electric frying pan or a skillet on a hibachi. There should be pitchers of soy sauce and jugs of sake on the table. For each diner there should be a pair of chopsticks, a bowl for rice, a bowl for the sukiyaki, a small sauce dish and a bowl with an egg in it. Each diner breaks his own egg into the bowl and beats it with the chopsticks.

*Method:* Preheat cooking unit. When the skillet is hot, put a piece of suet into the skillet to melt, rubbing it around the bottom of the pan with a pair of chopsticks. When fat is hot, start putting in pieces of vegetables, starting with the carrots. Put a little of everything in, including pieces of meat, until about half of the vegetables and meat are in the pan. The vegetables should be pushed to one side of the pan and the meat cooked until the blood shows, then turned. At this point add a part of the soy sauce mixture, mixing it with everything, and let cook about 5 minutes. Add silver noodles and tofu and continue to cook until everything is done. Start dishing the food, a little of everything, into the sukiyaki bowls, with a spoon. Then melt some more suet, and cook the last half of the ingredients. Serves 5 to 6.

*DIPPING SAUCE FOR SUKIYAKI*

¾ cup light soy sauce     ¾ cup chicken broth

3 tablespoons sake or dry     6 tablespoons sugar
sherry

Mix the soy sauce, sherry, broth and sugar. Let stand before using. It may be served in a small pot or soy sauce container and passed so that each guest may pour his own or you can pour it into the sauce dishes ahead of time when you place them on the table.

One of Japan's country dishes which has become quite well known is Chicken Mizutaki. Like all such dishes it varies from one part of the country to another and probably has undergone a few changes on the trip over here. Basically it is a poached chicken, started in the kitchen and finished at the table over a charcoal burner or electric unit. Vegetables and seasoning ingredients are added at the table and the chicken and vegetables are spooned into serving bowls.

Which brings me to one of the most intriguing and picturesque cooking utensils to emanate from the Orient. It is sometimes called a Mongolian stove, and sometimes called a Chinese hot pot. What is it? Well, it is a metal bowl set on a charcoal brazier, with a chimney in the center through which the heat rises. There is a lid with a hole in the center to fit around the chimney. The bowl, much like a moat, is half filled

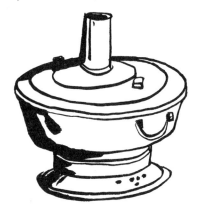

with chicken or meat broth which is heated by burning coals in the bottom of the burner, and in a grate in the chimney, at the level of the bottom of the bowl. It is surprising how quickly the broth boils.

The idea started, so legend has it, in Mongolia when tribesmen gathered around their campfires at night for supper. They speared chunks of mutton and dipped them in boiling cauldrons of water to which they had added dried vegetables, herbs and whatever they happened to have in their saddlebags or could forage from the mountainsides.

Peking, the mecca of gourmet dining in bygone days, adapted the idea to restaurant dining and fashioned elaborate pots of brass and pewter which were used for formal banquets. Over the years their use spread to all parts of Asia and now, to this country. While Mongolian stoves are not widely distributed or standard items in a hardware store, they can be found in Chinatown and sometimes in import outlets. Several years ago one of our leading magazines devoted to high-style homemaking and interior design showed a picture of a beauty called a hoko-nabe, 13 inches across, charcoal-burning and costing in the neighborhood of $32.50, which would indicate that Japan is exporting them to the United States. I hope so because for parties and informal entertaining they are great. They are decorative, too, with all the charm of a samovar.

In Hong Kong there are restaurants which feature the Mongolian-style dinner, the way it was done in Peking. A group of people are seated at a round table. There are bowls of cooking wine, vinegar, sesame jam, shrimp sauce, soy sauce and hot pepper sauce from which each diner takes spoonfuls to make his own sauce in his dipping bowl. Before each diner are small plates of paper-thin sliced lamb. The stove is placed in the center of the table and contains well-seasoned soup. When the soup boils, the diners pick up lamb slices with chopsticks and hold them in the boiling soup for ten to fifteen seconds. As soon as the lamb changes color, it is withdrawn and cooled in the dipping sauce and then eaten. Later silver noodles are added to the boiling soup and after everyone has had enough lamb, the soup is ladled into soup bowls for the last course. Hot damp towels are provided for face and hands and diners are charged for the number of empty meat saucers before them.

Of course, you don't have to have a Mongolian stove to have a Hot Pot Party. You can use a hibachi and set an interesting pot on it for the soup. An electric unit could be used, too. To give your party a festive air, select bowls and sauce dishes, porcelain spoons for the soup course, and plates for the meat. You can put a circle of wood on a stand that is coffee table height and let everyone sit on cushions. While you can't have a centerpiece, you can use interesting fat candles on Chinese candlesticks with spikes. You will want ashtrays and cups for tea or wine. When the meal is over, before you serve dessert or after dinner drinks, pass little finger towels, dipped in hot water, faintly perfumed and folded on small plates, one for each guest. Instead of letting guests make their own dipping sauce I suggest that you provide one:

HOT POT DIPPING SAUCE

½ cup soy sauce
½ cup lemon juice
½ cup dry sherry
½ cup chili sauce

½ cup peanut butter
½ cup chopped green
onions

Blend and adjust flavor to taste. You may want to add more soy sauce or more sherry. If you are not sure about the chili sauce, start out with ¼ cup and increase cautiously.

LAMB HOT POT

6 large mushrooms
sliced
1 large onion, thinly
sliced
2 cloves garlic, minced
1 tablespoon oil
8 cups chicken broth
1 cup celery, thinly
sliced diagonally

1 cup carrots, thinly
sliced
1 teaspoon salt
1 teaspoon MSG
¼ teaspoon white pepper
¼ cup chopped green
onions
3 pounds lamb, sliced
paper-thin

Sauté mushrooms, onion and garlic in oil until mushrooms lose their white look. Add chicken broth and bring to a boil. Add celery and carrots, salt, MSG and pepper and let simmer until vegetables are about half done, then add chopped green onions. Meantime arrange meat on small plates for each guest. Pour broth and vegetables into unit to be used at table. Guests dip lamb in boiling broth to cook, then dip into sauce before eating. Soup is ladled into bowls after meat course has ended. Serves 6.

*BEEF HOT POT*

4 cups consommé
2 cups chicken broth
2 cloves garlic, crushed
1 teaspoon minced fresh
  ginger
¼ teaspoon pepper
1 teaspoon salt
1 teaspoon MSG
1 cup celery, thinly sliced

½ cup chopped green
  onions
2 cups bok choy, sliced
  diagonally
1 cup carrots, thinly
  sliced
3 pounds sirloin, sliced
  paper-thin

Heat consommé and broth in a large saucepan, add seasonings and bring to a boil. Add vegetables. When they are about half cooked, pour into unit to be used at the table. Meantime, arrange the slices of beef attractively on plates for each guest. Each diner should have, in addition to a plate of beef, a bowl for rice, a soup bowl and a dish of sauce. Serves 6.

DIPPING SAUCE

2 cups soy sauce
½ cup dry sherry
1 teaspoon sugar

¼ teaspoon pepper
¼ cup lemon juice
1 teaspoon MSG

But let's get back to Chicken Mizutaki. Whether you finish your Mizutaki in a Mongolian stove or in a pot on an electric unit, here is a recipe with suggestions for variations.

*CHICKEN MIZUTAKI*

1 chicken, 4 pounds
4 cups chicken broth
1 large onion, thinly
  sliced
1 teaspoon MSG
1 teaspoon salt
¼ pound fresh
  mushrooms, sliced

6 green onions
1 bunch watercress
1 can bamboo shoots–12
  ounces
2 carrots

Have your butcher clean and split the chicken, then chop it into 2 inch pieces with a cleaver. Wash chicken, skin and bones too, and place in a heavy saucepan and cover with chicken broth. Canned broth is satisfactory. Add sliced onion and bring to the boiling point, then simmer gently for an hour. Skim from time to time. When chicken has been cooking for half an hour, add the MSG, the salt and the sliced mushrooms. Meantime, clean and slice the green onions diagonally in 1 inch lengths; wash and trim the watercress, removing coarse stems. Slice bamboo shoots crosswise as thin as possible. Clean, trim and slice the carrots diagonally, very thin. Arrange attractively in separate groups on a chop plate or tray. When chicken is tender bring it and the broth to the table in a suitable container. Place on whatever cooking unit you are using and regulate heat so it barely boils. Bring platter of vegetables to the table also. When guests are seated, commence adding vegetables to the simmering broth, a few at a time. To serve, spoon portions of the meat and cooked vegetables into serving bowls. Serve with cooked rice. Using chopsticks, guests dip bite-sized pieces of chicken and vegetables into the following seasoning sauce. Serves 6.

*MIZUTAKI DIPPING SAUCE*

½ cup lemon juice
1 cup soy sauce
½ cup dry sherry
½ teaspoon sugar
1 teaspoon grated fresh
  ginger

¼ cup chopped green
  onions
¼ teaspoon white pepper
½ teaspoon MSG

Combine ingredients and let stand an hour or so before using. You can substitute beef for the chicken. In fact, take the ingredients for the Beef Sukiyaki, including the bean curd and cook it in a mixture of chicken broth and consommé, as for the Beef Hot Pot. The possibilities of this sort of cooking are endless.


One of Japan's best and least known condiments is wasabi radish powder, possessing the fiery elements of both mustard and horseradish but a flavor of its own. It is usually associated with sashimi, the Japanese name for finely sliced raw sea bream or tuna, and sushi, which is seasoned cold rice patted around various kinds of fish, egg and pickled ginger, eel, shrimp, seaweed and other delicacies which the Japanese enjoy. Wasabi is the flavor highlight of many of these goodies. I think it has possibilities as a seasoning in this country. It comes in a 2 ounce can and is mixed with water which produces a delicate though artificial green color.

Japan has much to offer in the way of inexpensive decorations, nice serving ideas and table appointments which are particularly adapted to young people just starting out on their own. Whether the sofa is a day bed piled with cushions or custom-made cushions on a door provided with legs, Japanese decor blends. We have tried to convey this idea in our photograph (PLATE VI) of shrimp in the black lacquer box, the usabata with the Irish bells and the white porcelain cups with lemon twists floating in what should be martinis. Not shown is the white porcelain teapot of martinis chilling in another black lacquer box filled with crushed ice.

## WASABI COCKTAIL DIP

| | |
|---|---|
| ½ cup whipped sour cream | 1½ tablespoons wasabi powder* |
| ½ cup mayonnaise | Dash of salt |

Combine whipped sour cream and mayonnaise in a porcelain bowl. Mix wasabi powder with a little cold water until it is smooth and runny, then stir into sour cream mix. I like 2 tablespoons but it is better to start light and work up to it. Season to taste with salt. We fudged a bit on the color, too.

Next time you serve artichokes, mix a little wasabi powder in the mayonnaise.

* Please refer to Index for a list of sources of various foreign or odd ingredients mentioned in all recipes.

# Hong Kong

NO MATTER where you have been or what you have seen, you are never prepared for Hong Kong. It is an overcrowded city of contrasts, of great wealth and abject poverty, beautiful mansions and squalid slums, breathtaking beauty and filth. It is a hodgepodge of Hong Kong Chinese, refugees from Red China, Europeans and tourists from all over the world.

The British administer it but the Chinese furnish the manpower and do all the business. You can buy anything if you know where to look. Beautiful fabrics are available—woolens from England, silks from Thailand and Japan, as well as Hong Kong's own satins and brocades.

I remember Mrs. Bergeron being busy for several days, selecting materials and ordering clothes. She ordered a suit one day, had a fitting the next and picked it up on the third day. Meanwhile she matched shoes with swatches of selected materials. Fifty to seventy-five dollars bought her a Christian Dior designed suit of wonderful material and workmanship.

Food, both Chinese and European cuisine, was in great variety and the preparation was excellent. The Chinese have always revered a good cook. They have considered cooking an art for thousands of years. Two thousand years before the birth of Christ, they knew how to hunt game, fish, cultivate their land and cook food. In the Chou Dynasty (1122–249 B.C.), considered the great classical age of China, the preparation of food was deemed an art. It still is, except in Red China where the great leap forward has nothing to do with gourmet dining.

Many of our finest restaurants, not necessarily Chinese, employ Chinese cooks, most of them Cantonese. They have an instinctive feeling about food and quickly learn Continental cuisine. The more delicate flavors and delightful combinations of meat, vegetables and sauces have made Cantonese-style cooking the most popular in this country.

The southern part of China, where Canton is located, has a greater variety of vegetables, more rice and plenty of fresh seafood. In the northern part of China, where more wheat and less rice is grown, more noodles are eaten. In some of the more elegant Chinese restaurants in this country, mainly in New York and San Francisco, you will find some dishes from Shantung, Shanghai and Peking, referred to as northern China cooking. These are richer and more highly seasoned.

The Western world has adopted many of the principles of food and preparation from the Chinese without realizing it. We have adopted soy sauce and learned the value of the soy bean. We know that it is better to cook vegetables in very little liquid to save the vitamins, and have been advised by home economists for years to save the liquid for soups and gravies.

The Chinese, however, thicken the broth in which vegetables are cooked and serve it as a sauce, a practice we would do well to copy. Monosodium glutamate, which enhances the flavors of food, was a Chinese invention. They call it vetsin.

Chinese food is long on preparation and short on cooking. Because it consists mainly of vegetables—sliced, diced or minced —cooked quickly with meat sliced paper-thin in such a manner as to retain all of the food value, it is the most healthful cuisine in the world. All of the vegetables are prepared ahead of time and arranged in bowls, the meat is prepared, and the seasonings, oil and cornstarch for thickening are all ready, because the actual cooking takes just a few minutes and there is no time to stop and peel or chop anything. Once you start all systems are GO.

The most important part of cooking Chinese or any other oriental style is to cook the food enough to sterilize it but not enough to destroy the vitamins. Vegetables must retain their color and a certain crispness. To do this you must have the proper equipment and sufficient fuel or heat. Hot, fast cooking is one of the secrets.

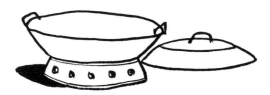

The Chinese use a wok, which has a round bottom and sits in a metal collar, over high heat. In this country this equipment is usually used over gas. But our American Chinese are progressive and you can now buy a specially contrived wok for use on electric stoves. Browsing through a super-hardware store on Grant Avenue in San Francisco, I found a fantastic array of modern Chinese cooking utensils, stainless steel woks, cleavers, chopping blocks and tools of all kinds—Chinese, but updated. They even had an electric Mongolian hot pot.

Most of these recipes can be cooked in a frying pan with a lid that fits, but if you really want to learn to cook Chinese style, go all out and buy a wok, a lid, a ring and the necessary implements. These consist of a long-handled pancake turner, a long-handled ladle and, if you contemplate using your wok for deep-fat frying, a Chinese strainer is most useful. The long handles keep you from being spattered with hot oil. Chopsticks are handy, too, when you know how to use them. Especially when you want to fry pieces of chicken in a wok. Chopsticks are better than a fork for lifting food into a wok and taking it out.

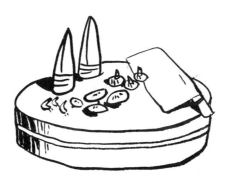

Perhaps the most useful pieces of Chinese equipment are a cleaver and a chopping board. Once you have used a Chinese cleaver you will never be without one. It can be used for slicing, chopping, mincing, flattening out a piece of veal, chicken or pork, giving a clove of garlic a good bang to make it easier to peel, and lifting what you have sliced or chopped into the wok.

The preparation of the food is most important. Straight slicing is used for tender meats and vegetables which require very little cooking, such as onions, mushrooms, summer squash or zucchini. Coarse-grained meats or the cheaper cuts, and such vegetables as carrots, celery, bok choy and turnips, are sliced diagonally in order to expose the greatest surface to heat and seasonings. It is the combination of various vegetables, sliced or chopped in a variety of ways, with thinly sliced meats, seasonings and broths which provide the texture and color as well as the flavor of Chinese dishes. A hint here. To slice meats paper-thin, partially freeze the meat to be sliced. You really don't freeze it. You just over-chill it.

The Chinese believe that there should be several textures to a well-prepared dish. The sauce, or gravy, should be rich in flavor, clear and smooth. This smoothness is generally accomplished by the use of cornstarch for thickening. There must be no lumpiness, greasiness or muddiness in the sauce. Only tender, young vegetables are used, which must retain their color and crispness in cooking. Meats and poultry must be fresh. If fresh fish is used it must be really fresh, preferably alive when selected. Dried seafoods, vegetables and herbs are used for flavoring soups and broths.

*Procedure:* Every ingredient for a dish should be prepared and placed in separate containers before starting to cook. In order to retain the flavor and texture of the food be sure to add the various ingredients in the order given.

*Seasonings:* There are certain ingredients which develop the original flavors of food, such as salt, vinegar, soy sauce, sugar and MSG (vetsin). Others remove undesirable tastes and flavors in such foods as fish, kidneys, liver, etc. These are sherry, green onions, garlic and ginger.

At this point it might be well to clear up some confusion about soy sauce, soya sauce, shoyu, thick soya, pure soya, etc. Soy and soya are Chinese and shoyu is Japanese and all are the products of fermented soy beans. For some dishes the Chinese prefer a lighter soy or soya sauce, often referred to as pure soya. They also use a thick soya for certain dishes. The Japanese shoyu is more delicate in flavor. The difference in spelling is about as important as the spelling of our national condiment —catsup, ketchup or catchup.

OTHER SEASONINGS

*Fermented Black Beans (Dow See):* These are black salted beans. A little water is added to clean and soften them, then they are crushed with a pestle or the back of a spoon and added, along with garlic, to dishes with strong-smelling ingredients, such as Lobster Cantonese.

*Chinese Parsley:* This is the same as the Mexican cilantro or our coriander.

*Fresh Gingerroot:* This fresh, knobby tuber, when used with discretion, imparts a delicate flavor to food. It is better to omit ginger entirely than to use the dried, ground product.

The Chinese often use a combination of spices known as "Spices of Five Fragrances," which may be purchased mixed in powdered form. Purchased separately, whole, they are:

1. *Chinese Star Anise:* In addition to being one of the favorite spices of the Chinese, it is good for digestion, and is a carminative.

2. *Fennel:* This is a narrow oval seed, resembling a caraway seed in appearance, only it is about twice as large. It has a slight licorice aroma and flavor.

3. *Cloves:* This is a spice we all know. It is used by the Chinese both as a seasoning and a tonic.

4. *Chinese Cinnamon:* This, like our cinnamon, comes from the bark of a tree, but it is less delicate than the true cinnamon. When used in medicine it is considered one of the best restorative spices and is also an excellent carminative.

5. *Chinese Pepper:* This is a single dark, blackish red seed, pungent and aromatic, from a shrub grown in both China and Japan (Xanthoxylum piperitum).

Sesame seed oil is used as a flavoring in much the same way that Westerners use butter. It is often added to other oils just for the flavor. Peanut oil is the cooking fat of the Chinese but any vegetable or unsaturated oil may be used. Most dishes start in a little oil.

There are seven principal methods of Chinese cooking:

1. *Stir-frying:* This is cooking vegetables, or a combination of meat and vegetables, in a little oil over a hot fire, stirring constantly. A small amount of stock or broth is added, the pan is

covered and the foods steam for a few moments. The liquid is then thickened with cornstarch mixed with cold water.

2. *Pan-frying:* Frying in a small amount of oil.

3. *Deep-fat frying:* Frying in a large amount of oil.

4. *Fricasseeing:* Meats or fowl are fried or braised and then simmered until done in stock, sauce or gravy.

5. *Steaming:* There are special steamers for food but you can achieve something adequate by cutting the bottom as well as the top from small cans, such as those used for tuna or minced clams. Set three of these in the bottom of a large kettle. Set the smaller container of food on the cans, add boiling water to the bottom of the kettle, cover and let cook. For small amounts of food, a double boiler accomplishes the purpose.

6. *Roasting, barbecuing or grilling:* These processes need no explanation.

7. *Stewing:* The ingredients are fried or braised and then stewed slowly in a sauce. If the sauce consists largely of soy sauce, it is called Red Cooking. White Cooking is stewing without soy sauce.

Aside from the Chinese use of seasonings and soya sauce, and the stir-frying process, other processes aren't too different from ours, but the end products differ greatly.

One of the greatest differences between Chinese and Western foods is that the Chinese use no dairy products. Hundreds of years ago, the Chinese used no beef. They had water buffalo but because this was a valuable work animal it was not used for food. The pig was the favorite for food because it produced litters and was not useful for field work. Chickens and ducks, too, were used for food. While they produced eggs and food for the table, they were not useful otherwise. Lamb was introduced to the Chinese in the far north by the Mohammedans who followed Jewish dietary laws which prohibited the eating of pork. You seldom find lamb dishes in a Chinese restaurant. I am tempted to say never, at least not in this country, but there are always exceptions. Lamb is used, along with beef, chicken or fish, and assorted vegetables for the Mongolian Hot Pot dinner.

One of the demands of present-day cookbooks is that the ingredients be listed in the order in which they are used, which is helpful, and that each recipe specify the number of servings. This too is helpful, but is somewhat difficult with Chinese recipes because most dishes, particularly the stir-fried dishes, are too much for one person and often, but not always, just right for two. It depends on the dish.

The Chinese like variety in their meals and at a Chinese dinner several dishes are served at a time and everyone takes a little of each dish, not with a serving spoon, but with chopsticks. The food is transferred to a bowl in front of the diner. No one dish is intended for one person.

You have probably noticed, when dining in Chinese restaurants, that dinners quite often are listed at so much per person. This is for the guidance of people not familiar with the Chinese way of serving. Appetizers will be listed and a soup, then for two persons three dishes will be listed; for three persons one more dish will be added to the list and for four persons, a fifth main dish will be added.

Restaurants, serving both Chinese and Continental dishes, have Westernized the serving of Chinese dishes to please Caucasians who want their food served on a plate. In Trader Vic restaurants the food is brought to the table on service wagons, in small chafing dishes to keep it hot en route from the kitchen, and the captains dish up a little of each dish ordered on each diner's plate.

Some Chinese dishes can be increased without difficulty. Others cannot. In the first place, if you put too much food in a wok you are apt to stir it all over the stove or the floor. In the second place, it is impossible to cook individual ingredients properly when too many are piled into the wok or cooking vessel. The essential high heat simply doesn't penetrate properly and the result is apt to be an unpalatable, soggy mess. I would never recommend more than doubling a recipe, until you are thoroughly familiar with your equipment, the ingredients and what you expect of the end product.

There are many Chinese dishes which can be incorporated into an American meal. This is particularly true of vegetables cooked Chinese style. For the American woman learning to cook Chinese dishes, one dish at a time is enough. It takes practice and a thorough familiarity with timing and procedure to turn out an entire Chinese meal. This is one of the reasons why so many Chinese people dine out and why they generally entertain in restaurants. Aside from restaurants, only the very wealthy have the cooks and equipment required to prepare a formal Chinese dinner or a banquet.

If you want to serve Chinese food, I suggest that you plan the menu so as to have just one stir-fried dish with perhaps a stewed or fricasseed dish, a soup, rice or noodles, and Westernize your service somewhat. And on your first try, don't invite too many guests.

Start out with some of the simpler appetizers or hors d'oeuvres which can be prepared ahead of time. Decorate your table in an oriental manner, using colorful place mats and napkins, and Chinese accessories.

The soup could be brought to the table in covered dishes to keep hot and Chinese porcelain spoons are far better than metal spoons for enjoying soup. The rest of the food could be served from a serving table or wagon, on heated plates and passed. In this way everyone sees the serving dishes and the finished, decorated product, and there is no confusion trying to pass dishes. The host or hostess takes on the duties of a captain or waiter.

A word about ingredients before we go on to recipes. Important ingredients in Chinese cooking are mushrooms, bamboo shoots, fresh gingerroot and soy sauce. The Chinese prefer dried black mushrooms for stewing and cooking with soy sauce, and they are used in some stir-fried dishes. Wash them well, then cover with warm water and let stand 15 or 20 minutes until they soften and are spongy. Squeeze out the liquid, remove the stems and proceed as directed in the recipe.

When a recipe calls for ginger, it means fresh gingerroot.

You can use dried gingerroot sparingly but it isn't the same. And it is better to omit ginger entirely from a recipe than to use the powdered variety. I am told that you can plant a root in a flowerpot and then dig up a small piece as needed. But whether you dig it up or buy it at a Chinese grocery store, wash it, scrape or peel it before using and freshly grate just the amount called for in the recipe—or less, if you aren't enchanted with the flavor. It is potent and a flavor some people have to learn to like.

Before you start to cook a Chinese dish be sure all preparations are completed and that every ingredient you are going to need is right at hand. Once you have started to stir-fry a dish there is no time to start looking for soy sauce or chop some green onions. Check all of your ingredients before you start. If you are going to use stock or chicken broth, have it heating on the stove. Have the cornstarch and water close by but don't mix until you are ready to use it because the cornstarch settles to the bottom and will lump.

Chinese-style cooking is heaven-sent to the person who lives alone. No other style of cooking so lends itself to dining solo. All you have to do is decide on the recipes you would like to try and buy small quantities of the foods which won't keep long. For example, you can cook zucchini Chinese style. Three small zucchini, sliced very thin, makes about a cupful. Heat a small saucepan or frying pan which has a lid, and add a teaspoon of oil. Stir-fry the squash until it is completely coated with fat and the color is bright green. Add 2 tablespoons hot water or hot chicken broth, cover and cook for about one minute. The squash should be bright in color, hold its shape, and be just tender but still a little crunchy. Add a teaspoon of seasoned chicken stock base (Spice Island) in lieu of salt. Stir until smooth. There is something in the base which, when mixed with the chicken broth or water, forms sort of a glaze, very much like the glaze of the broth thickened with cornstarch.

Brussels sprouts are the most mistreated vegetables in the world. They take to the Chinese treatment like a duck takes to water, and the variations are limitless. This recipe isn't truly Chinese but the theory is the same, and it can be applied to other vegetables with delightful and surprising results.

*PAKE BRUSSELS SPROUTS*

| | |
|---|---|
| 1 pound Brussels sprouts | ½ cup boiling water |
| 2 tablespoons oil | 1 teaspoon butter |
| ½ teaspoon salt | Grated Parmesan cheese |
| ¼ teaspoon white pepper | |
| ¼ teaspoon dried dill weed | |

Clean sprouts, remove any wilted or spotted leaves and trim stem end. Soak in salted water about 10 minutes. Slice sprouts lengthwise, starting at the top or side. If tiny, split in 2. Otherwise, make 3 or 4 slices out of each sprout. Heat pan and add oil, then add sliced sprouts and stir-fry until well coated with oil and bright green in color. Add seasonings, stir and add water. Cover and cook for 2 minutes or until tender but still crunchy and bright green. Serve immediately, adding butter for flavor, and sprinkle with grated cheese after placing in serving dish or on dinner plate. Serves 6.

## PAKE HORS D'OEUVRES

The hors d'oeuvre was originally intended to whet the appetite, and usually preceded dinner at the table. Its present-day use was an invention of American hostesses to keep guests from starving or getting stoned during the cocktail hour which sometimes is prolonged. The variations are many and sometimes elaborate but everyone seeks the unusual.

Certain Chinese tidbits seem to have an affinity for cocktails. Pake is the Hawaiian word for Chinese, which is a good name for these hors d'oeuvres. The fact that they were never intended for this role is of no importance. The following are great with drinks and pleasantly bridge the gap from the cocktail hour to dinner.

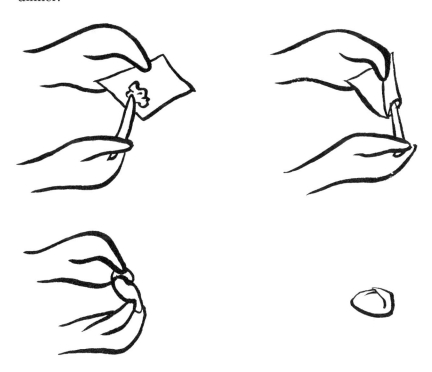

*WON TON*

| | |
|---|---|
| ½ pound pork | ½ teaspoon salt |
| ¼ cup chopped mushrooms | ¼ teaspoon pepper |
| | 1 egg yolk |
| 1 tablespoon minced green onions | Won ton squares |
| | Peanut oil |

Mince pork, mushrooms and onions very fine, then mix thoroughly with seasonings and egg yolk. Place ½ teaspoonful of the pork mixture in the center of a won ton square (these may be purchased in Chinatown), and twist as illustrated. Fry in hot peanut oil as needed. Drain and serve with catsup mixed with a little horseradish or Chinese mustard. Makes filling for 125 to 130 won ton.

Here is another filling for the same won ton squares. We call this hors d'oeuvre

*CRAB RANGOON*

| | |
|---|---|
| ½ pound crab meat | Won ton noodle squares |
| ½ pound cream cheese | 1 egg yolk, beaten |
| ½ teaspoon A-1 sauce | |
| ¼ teaspoon garlic powder | |

Chop crab meat and blend with cheese and seasonings. Put ½ teaspoon of mixture in center of noodle square, fold square over cornerwise. Moisten edges slightly with beaten egg and twist together. Fry in deep fat until delicately browned. Serve hot. Makes filling for 190 to 195 squares.

*PAKE MEATBALLS – I*

| | |
|---|---|
| 1 pound ground pork | ½ teaspoon salt |
| ¼ cup minced mushrooms | ½ teaspoon sugar |
| 1 small can water | ½ teaspoon MSG |
| chestnuts, (5–6 ounces) | ¼ teaspoon garlic powder |
| drained and minced | 1 egg, beaten |
| 2 tablespoons soya sauce | 2 tablespoons cornstarch |
| 1 tablespoon sherry | Oil for frying |

Mix pork with mushrooms and water chestnuts; add soya sauce, sherry, salt, sugar, MSG and garlic powder, then beaten egg, and mix thoroughly. Sprinkle meat mixture with cornstarch and shape into balls about an inch in diameter. Fry in deep fat until golden brown. Drain. Serve on toothpicks and serve very hot, with Chinese mustard and catsup. Makes 30 to 35 meatballs.

*PAKE MEATBALLS – II*

| | |
|---|---|
| 2 cups soft bread crumbs | ½ teaspoon Worcestershire |
| ½ cup beef or chicken | sauce |
| stock | ½ teaspoon salt |
| 1 pound ground beef | 1 small can (5–6 ounces) |
| 1 tablespoon scraped | water chestnuts, |
| onion | drained and minced |
| 2 tablespoons soya sauce | 1 egg, beaten |
| ¼ teaspoon Tabasco sauce | Oil for frying |

Soak bread crumbs in stock, add to ground beef. Add onion, soya sauce, Tabasco, Worcestershire, salt, water chestnuts and beaten egg. Mix throughly and shape into balls about an inch in diameter. Can be prepared ahead of time. Fry in hot oil, as needed. Drain and serve hot with toothpicks. Makes about 50 meatballs. Serve with Chinese mustard and catsup.

*CHINESE HOT MUSTARD*

Mix a very hot dry mustard with water, a little at a time until smooth and thin enough for a dip. Turmeric may be added for color.

*CHINESE CATSUP*

If you can't find Trader Vic's Chinese Catsup at your nearby market, try adding some horseradish to ordinary catsup or chili sauce. Experiment a little. *Note:* If you are interested in knowing where to buy Trader Vic's seasonings and sauces, write to Trader Vic's Food Products Co., P.O. Box 8603, Emeryville, California 94608.

Here is another version of Chinese Barbecued Pork, one of the best accompaniments with cocktails. This, too, may be served with Chinese mustard and catsup, with the addition of toasted sesame seeds. You dip the slice of pork first in one or both sauces, then in the sesame seeds.

*CHA SUI (Barbecued Pork)*

| | |
|---|---|
| 2 pounds pork tenderloin | 1½ teaspoons salt |
| 3 ounces Bourbon or | 3 tablespoons sugar |
| dark rum | 3 tablespoons soy sauce |

Cut pork tenderloin into two long strips. Mix rest of ingredients into a paste and rub into the meat. Let stand for an hour or two so the flavor penetrates the meat, then barbecue or broil slowly for one hour. When cool, cut into thin diagonal slices and serve with Chinese mustard and catsup. Serves 8 to 10 with cocktails.

*STUFFED SHRIMP*

This is the verbatim translation of the Chinese name for this appetizer. Actually it consists of a sort of shrimp forcemeat, made into small balls, poached, cooled, wrapped in a thin piece of bacon, secured with a toothpick, dipped in a thin batter and fried in deep fat to a golden brown. It is a delicious hors d'oeuvre.

1 pound shrimp or
  prawns, shelled and
  deveined
1 bunch parsley
¼ cup toasted almonds
½ cup bread crumbs

2 teaspoons salt
1 teaspoon pepper
½ teaspoon MSG
Bacon strips
Dipping Batter II (Thin)

Put shrimp, parsley, almonds, crumbs and seasonings through a meat grinder until very fine and well mixed. Put in pastry bag and form into small balls. Poach balls in boiling water for 15 minutes, then lift out carefully with a slotted spoon or Chinese skimmer and let cool. When cool enough to handle, wrap in half pieces of very thinly sliced bacon and secure with toothpicks. Chill until ready to use. At serving time, dip in a thin batter (No. II) and fry in deep fat until golden brown.

*DIPPING BATTER I*

1 egg
1 tablespoon cornstarch
1 cup flour
1½ teaspoons baking
  powder

2 teaspoons salt
1 tablespoon sugar
½ teaspoon MSG
1 cup milk
1 cup water

Beat egg slightly; add dry ingredients sifted together, then stir in milk and water slowly. Beat until smooth.

*DIPPING BATTER II (Thin)*

To Dipping Batter I add ¾ cup more water and ¼ cup more milk.

*CHICKEN LIVERS*

Cut up chicken livers in bite-sized pieces and dip in Batter I. Fry in deep fat until brown. They should be crisp but not over-cooked.

This tidbit is an all time favorite but not too good for stand-up cocktail parties. Egg Rolls are better at smaller groups where there are tables handy for glasses, cigarettes and hors d'oeuvre trays or plates.

*EGG ROLLS*

4 cups bean sprouts, washed and dried

1 cup shredded bamboo shoots

2 cups shredded water chestnuts

3½ cups slivered cooked chicken

¾ cup slivered cooked ham

¾ cup slivered barbecued pork

1 cup finely chopped parsley

1 cup chopped mushrooms

½ cup finely chopped green onions

Salt and pepper to taste

3 tablespoons oil

Be sure all ingredients are cut in very fine slivers—almost shredded. Mix together and cook in a little oil for 10 minutes, stirring occasionally to prevent sticking. Let mixture cool, then

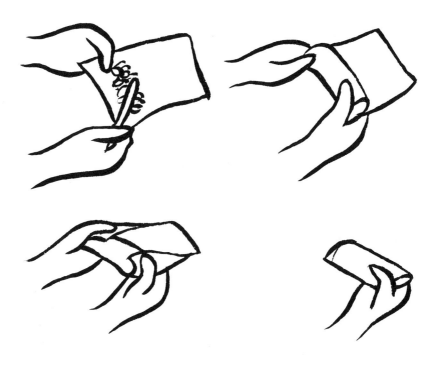

spoon onto Egg Skins (recipe for which follows), using about half a cup for each skin. Fold the ends in and completely seal, like an envelope. Dip in thin batter, Dipping Batter II, and fry in hot oil for 5 minutes, turning carefully to brown on both sides. Be careful, when lowering rolls into the hot oil that they do not become unrolled and their contents spilled.

When done, remove and slice diagonally in 1 inch or 1¼ inch slices and serve hot. A nice touch is to serve these on compotes lined with galax or grape leaves and garnish with chopped chives or slivers of green onion. This makes enough filling for about 28 to 29 rolls.

EGG SKINS

| 12 eggs | 2 teaspoons salt |
| 2 tablespoons cornstarch | 1½ cups water |

Beat eggs, add cornstarch, salt and beat in water. Heat oil in bottom of wok or 8 inch frying pan and pour quarter cupfuls of the batter into the pan. Fry lightly, then turn and fry on other side. Makes 16 egg skins.

*CHO CHO*

Alternate inch pieces of the white part of green onion (split in two if large) with pieces of chicken ½ inch by 1 inch, allowing 3 pieces of onion to 2 pieces of chicken, on a 5 inch bamboo skewer. Cover ends of sticks with foil to prevent burning. Line up in a shallow pan and broil until tender and browned, turning once. Allow at least four skewers per person. Serve on compotes or platters lined with galax leaves, or ti leaves cut to fit.

## SOUPS

Noodles are an interesting facet of Chinese cooking and custom. While rice is the mainstay of the southern Chinese, noodles made from wheat are the daily fare in the north. Noodles, however, are a symbol of longevity and are always served at birthday celebrations. They can be made from rice, corn and peas, as well as wheat. The translucent noodles are called silver noodles, cellophane noodles and long rice. Recently I bought a package of translucent noodles labeled NICE—Bean Threads, manufactured by the Ching Sham Food Products Fty in Hong Kong. There is more to this than meets the eye.

Here are two recipes illustrating the use of the translucent noodle, call it what you will. Real Sharks Fin Soup requires the services of an expert, and it is expensive, so many are the attempts to imitate the real thing.

*MOCK SHARKS FIN SOUP*

6 cups rich chicken consommé

6 tablespoons chopped, cooked chicken meat

6 tablespoons cooked silver noodles

1 tablespoon finely chopped parsley

1 tablespoon sieved hard-cooked egg yolk

Heat consommé to boiling point, add chicken and silver noodles and heat just long enough to heat chicken and noodles. Ladle into Chinese soup bowls and top each with a half teaspoon parsley and half teaspoon sieved egg yolk. Makes 6 portions.

PLATE IX. Kwan Yin and trio of Chinese dishes: Abalone Macao, *page 145;* Zucchini with Mushrooms Chinese Style, *page 151;* Singapore Noodles, *page 161*

PLATE X. Lobster Cantonese, *page 146*

PLATE XI. Curried Lamb Cheeks, *page 169*

*MOCK BIRD'S NEST SOUP*

1 bundle long rice
6 cups rich chicken broth
4 large mushrooms
½ teaspoon MSG
1½ teaspoons salt
1 cup finely minced
   fresh pork
1 cup finely chopped
   cured ham

½ cup chopped water
   chestnuts
2 egg whites, lightly
   beaten
2–2½ teaspoons chopped
   Chinese parsley

Cut long rice, with scissors, in quarter inch lengths and soak in hot water 30 minutes. Heat chicken broth. Meanwhile, wash mushrooms, trim stem ends and chop. Bring broth to a boil, add mushrooms, seasonings, pork and ham. Let simmer half an hour. Drain long rice and add to broth with water chestnuts. Simmer 5 minutes more. Stir beaten egg whites into hot broth and serve immediately. Garnish each bowl of soup with ¼ teaspoon chopped Chinese parsley. If not available, substitute regular parsley and use a little more—about ½ teaspoon per bowl. Serves 8 to 10.

*BLACK MUSHROOM SOUP*

¼ cup dried black
   mushrooms
1 clove garlic
1 tablespoon sesame oil
2 quarts rich chicken
   broth
1 piece gingerroot, size
   of hazelnut
3 tablespoons soy sauce

½ cup finely diced
   cooked chicken
½ cup diced bamboo
   shoots
½ cup finely diced
   cooked ham
½ cup finely chopped
   green onions

Soak mushrooms in warm water for 15 minutes, or until soft and spongy. Squeeze out liquid and chop very fine. Crush the garlic and sauté in oil for a second or two, then remove and save. Sauté the mushrooms about 5 minutes in the same pan. Bring chicken stock to a boil in a soup kettle; add garlic, mushrooms, ginger and soy sauce. Simmer several hours. Before serving, strain and add chicken, bamboo shoots, ham and green onions. Let simmer a few minutes to heat added ingredients thoroughly. Serve in Chinese soup bowls. Serves 8 to 10.

*MANDARIN SOUP*

1 cup raw, lean pork
1 tablespoon peanut oil
1 cup finely sliced
   mushrooms
½ cup diced carrots
1 cup sliced celery
½ cup diced water
   chestnuts
6 cups chicken or beef
   stock

½ cup finely chopped
   spinach
1 teaspoon MSG
1 teaspoon salt
1 egg, slightly beaten
2 tablespoons cornstarch
   mixed with
⅓ cup cold water

Cut pork in very fine strips; sauté in oil, then add mushrooms, carrots, celery and water chestnuts and continue to sauté, stirring constantly for a few seconds. Add hot stock, cover and let simmer until vegetables are tender but not overcooked. Add spinach and seasonings, and stir in egg quickly. Add cornstarch and water, a little at a time, stirring constantly, until desired consistency is obtained. Serve immediately in Chinese soup bowls. Serves 8 to 10.

*CHINESE WATERCRESS SOUP*

1 pound watercress
4 ounces lean pork,
   chopped fine
1 teaspoon cornstarch
1 teaspoon salt
½ teaspoon pepper
¼ teaspoon sugar

½ teaspoon grated
   gingerroot
1 tablespoon soy sauce
1 tablespoon peanut oil
3 cans hot chicken broth
   (about 5 cups)

Wash and discard thick stalks of watercress; chop. Mix pork with cornstarch, seasonings, sugar, gingerroot and soy sauce. Heat oil in pot and sauté pork mixture a few seconds, until pork is cooked but not browned. Add boiling chicken broth, bring to a boil again and let simmer, with cover on, about 10 minutes. Add watercress, cover and simmer another five minutes. Serve immediately in Chinese soup bowls. Serves 4 to 6.

*CHINESE CLAM SOUP*

2 ounces finely chopped lean pork
1 teaspoon cornstarch
1 tablespoon soy sauce
½ teaspoon salt
½ teaspoon pepper
½ teaspoon grated fresh gingerroot
1 tablespoon peanut oil
4 large mushrooms, finely sliced

4 stalks celery, finely sliced
2 cans minced clams, No. ½ Flat
2 bottles (8 ounces) clam juice
2 ounces smoked ham, slivered

Mix pork with cornstarch, soy sauce, salt, pepper and ginger. Sauté in oil until pork is cooked but not browned. Add mushrooms and celery and stir-fry for a few seconds. Meanwhile drain off the juice from the clams and add it to the pan with the 2 bottles of clam juice. Simmer about 10 minutes. Taste and correct seasonings. Add slivered ham and minced clams and simmer just long enough to heat through but not long enough to toughen the clams. Serve immediately. Serves 4 to 6.

## MEAT DISHES

Many of the recipes to follow will indicate 2 to 4 persons. This means that if you are serving American style, using the dish as your main event at dinner, it will serve only two persons. If, however, you are serving Chinese style, with several comparable dishes, you can serve four persons. You can divide or multiply accordingly.

If you have but one steak in the refrigerator and have the urge to invite a friend for dinner, you can slice the steak very thin, cook it with vegetables, Chinese style, using onions, celery, green pepper, and whatever you happen to have in the crisping bin of your refrigerator. Use canned chicken or beef broth for the liquid and thicken it with cornstarch mixed with cold water or cold broth. The following recipes will give you some idea of the many possible combinations.

As you read through these recipes you will notice that vegetables are cut the same way as the meat. For instance, if the meat is to be shredded or sliced julienne style, the vegetables will be prepared the same way. If the meat or chicken is diced, the vegetables will also be diced. This does not apply to the vegetables used for seasoning, such as onion. Where flank steak is unavailable, other cuts of beef may be used.

*GREEN PEPPER BEEF*

½ pound flank steak
½ teaspoon salt
¼ teaspoon pepper
¼ teaspoon MSG
2 tablespoons cornstarch
1 tablespoon soy sauce
1 tablespoon brandy
2 tablespoons peanut oil
½ cup julienne green
   peppers

½ cup julienne green
   onions
¼ cup soup stock or
   chicken broth
1 tablespoon oyster sauce
1 tablespoon cornstarch
   mixed with
3 tablespoons cold water

Julienne flank steak, making strips 1 to 1¼ inch long and about ⅛ inch thick. Season with salt, pepper and MSG. Dust meat with cornstarch and mix with soy sauce and brandy; let marinate 15 minutes. Heat oil and fry meat until slightly browned. Remove meat from pan and reserve. Add peppers and green onions and stir a few seconds, then return meat, add broth and oyster sauce and bring to a boil. Thicken with cornstarch mixture and stir a few seconds. There should be just enough gravy to hold the meat together. Serve 2 to 4.

Oyster sauce is used to season many Chinese dishes. It may be bought in bottles in Chinese grocery stores. It is also sold in fancy food stores, called Grieg's Oyster Sauce.

*OYSTER BEEF*

½ pound sirloin of beef
1 cup sliced button
   mushrooms
2 teaspoons peanut oil
2 teaspoons chopped
   green onions
1 tablespoon oyster sauce
2 teaspoons Sang Chow
   Soya Sauce*

¾ cup chicken broth
½ teaspoon MSG
2 tablespoons cornstarch
   mixed with
¼ cup cold water
Salt to taste

Slice meat in ⅛ inch slices. Saute mushrooms in oil, 10 to 15 seconds, then add beef and green onions and stir-fry about half a minute. Add oyster sauce and Sang Chow Soya Sauce and stir a few times. Add chicken stock, cover and steam for about 20 seconds. Remove cover, add MSG and salt if it is needed, but the salt content of the oyster sauce and soya sauce

---

* The Chinese use more than one kind of soy or soya sauce. The best sauce for everyday use is imported. If you use domestic soy sauce, it is necessary to cut it with water, as it is heavy and concentrated. Japanese shoyu soy sauce is also good. Pure soya, Sang Chow, comes from Formosa. It is the classical soy sauce of the Chinese, pale, clear and delicate in flavor. They also use a thick soy sauce, like a paste. This is used in small quantities for flavor, when not much liquid is wanted. The term soy and soya is optional.

is very high. Mix in cornstarch mixture and stir until thickened. Serves 2 to 4.

*TOMATO BEEF*

½ pound flank steak
2 tablespoons cornstarch
1 tablespoon soy sauce
1 tablespoon brandy
2 tablespoons peanut oil
¼ cup chopped onion
⅓ cup sliced celery
¾ cup green pepper cut in about 1 inch squares
2 whole tomatoes, each cut in 8 segments
¼ cup sliced water chestnuts
1 cup chicken broth or soup stock, heated
2 teaspoons catsup
½ teaspoon salt
1 teaspoon sugar
1 tablespoon cornstarch mixed with
3 tablespoons cold water

Slice flank steak about ⅛ inch thick. Mix with cornstarch, soy sauce and brandy. Let stand about 15 minutes while you prepare the rest of the ingredients. Heat pan and add oil; add steak and stir-fry until golden brown. Remove from pan and reserve. Add onion and celery and sauté 10 to 15 seconds, then add rest of vegetables and stir a few times. Add heated broth, cover and let steam about 1 minute. Remove cover, add beef and mix well. Cover again and let steam for another 15 to 20 seconds. Add seasonings and stir a few times. Thicken slightly with cornstarch mixture. The sauce should not be too thick. Serves 2 to 4.

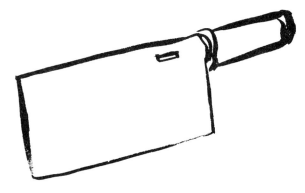

## BEEF WITH CAULIFLOWER AND SNOW PEAS

½ pound tender beef
½ teaspoon salt
¼ teaspoon pepper
2 tablespoons cornstarch
1 tablespoon soy sauce
1 tablespoon brandy
1 clove garlic, crushed
2 tablespoons peanut oil

¼ cup chopped onions
¼ pound snow peas
1 small cauliflower
1 cup chicken broth or
  soup stock, heated
2 tablespoons cornstarch
  mixed with
¼ cup cold water

Slice beef in narrow strips, season with salt and pepper and roll in cornstarch, then add to soy sauce and brandy in a mixing bowl and mix well. Let stand for 15 minutes. Sauté garlic in oil. Remove and discard. Add meat and stir-fry until slightly brown, then remove and reserve. Stir-fry the chopped onions a few times until limp, then add snow peas and cauliflower, broken into flowerlets and sliced. Stir a few times and add heated broth or stock. Cover and let steam for a minute or so, then add meat, cover and let steam for an additional 15 to 20 seconds. Vegetables should be tender but still crunchy. Thicken with cornstarch mixture and stir until thickened. Correct seasonings and serve with steamed rice. Serves 2 to 4.

## PAKE HAMBURGERS

1 pound ground beef
1 egg, beaten
½ cup finely chopped
  water chestnuts
3 tablespoons minced
  mushrooms
2 tablespoons minced
  onions

1 tablespoon oyster
  sauce
½ teaspoon MSG
⅛ teaspoon pepper
Salt

Mix ground meat with egg, vegetables, oyster sauce and seasonings. Shape into two patties about ¾ inch thick. Place on broiler pan about 4 inches from the unit and broil 6 minutes. Turn, sprinkle with salt lightly and broil other side 4 minutes. Serves 2.

*SWEET AND SOUR PORK*

1 pound pork tenderloin
2 tablespoons sherry
½ teaspoon chopped
 fresh ginger
Egg Batter
Cornstarch
Oil for deep frying
3 tablespoons peanut oil
1 cup pineapple cubes
1 green pepper, sliced
½ cup sliced celery
½ cup sliced Chinese
 snow peas

½ cup white vinegar
1 cup pineapple juice
¼ cup brown sugar
½ teaspoon salt
1 tablespoon catsup
½ teaspoon Worcestershire
 sauce
1 large tomato, cut in 8
 pieces
2 tablespoons cornstarch
 mixed with
¼ cup cold water

Cut pork in half lengthwise, then slice in ⅛ inch thick slices. Marinate in sherry and ginger for 10 minutes, dip in Egg Batter (given below) and roll in cornstarch. Deep-fry in oil until golden brown. Drain and keep warm. Preheat pan and add peanut oil. Add pineapple and all vegetables, except tomato, and stir-fry for a few seconds. Add vinegar, pineapple juice and seasonings; bring to the boiling point and let simmer for half a minute. Add tomato—first cut in half and then each half quartered—and let cook a second or so, then add cornstarch mixture. Stir until thickened and add pork last. Mix quickly two or three times and serve immediately with steamed rice. Serves 4 to 6.

EGG BATTER

1 egg
½ cup flour

½ teaspoon salt
¼ cup water

Beat egg slightly, add flour and salt, and stir in water slowly; beat until smooth.

Here is what Chinese restaurants do with leftover barbecued spareribs. In fact, they see to it that they have leftover ribs. If you have any left from a cookout you can do the same. Cut first in 4-rib sections then chop the sections in 4 pieces. Last, cut between the ribs, making bite-sized pieces.

| | |
|---|---|
| 2 tablespoons peanut oil | ¼ cup brown sugar |
| 1 side small meaty barbecued spareribs | 1 cup pineapple juice |
| | 2 teaspoons catsup |
| 3 slices pineapple, diced | ½ teaspoon salt |
| 1 green pepper, cut the same size as the pineapple | ½ teaspoon MSG |
| | 2 tablespoons cornstarch mixed with |
| ½ cup white vinegar | ¼ cup cold water |

Heat pan, add oil, then add spareribs, pineapple and green pepper, and stir-fry a few seconds. Add vinegar, sugar and pineapple juice, cover and steam for about 2 minutes. Add seasonings, thicken with cornstarch mixture, and mix thoroughly. Stir until thickened. Serve with steamed rice. Serves 4.


*CHINESE BRAISED LAMB*

| | |
|---|---|
| 1 pound choice lamb | ¼ cup sherry |
| 2 tablespoons peanut oil | 1 teaspoon brown sugar |
| 3 cups stock or chicken broth | ½ teaspoon salt |
| | ⅓ cup finely sliced green onions |
| 1 large turnip, peeled and halved | |
| 1 clove of garlic, smashed | 2 tablespoons cornstarch mixed with |
| ½ cup soya sauce | ½ cup water |

Cut lamb in 1½ inch squares. Preheat stew pot, add oil and braise lamb. Add stock or broth, turnip and garlic; cover and simmer for an hour, skimming if necessary. Remove turnip and garlic and discard. Add soya sauce, sherry, sugar and salt; cover and simmer another hour, or until meat is tender. Remove lid, add onions and simmer uncovered until liquid is reduced, to about 2 cups for richer flavor, then thicken slightly with cornstarch mixed with cold water. Serves 2 to 4.

CHICKEN WITH ALMONDS

½ pound white meat of chicken
2 tablespoons peanut oil
1½ cups diced celery
1 cup diced bamboo shoots
1½ cups diced bok choy
½ cup water chestnuts, sliced lengthwise
1 cup button mushrooms

1 teaspoon salt
4 cups chicken stock, heated
½ teaspoon MSG
2 teaspoons thick soya
2 tablespoons cornstarch mixed with
¼ cup cold water
½ cup whole toasted almonds

Cut chicken meat in strips ¼ inch thick, ½ inch wide and 1¼ to 1½ inches long. Sauté lightly in peanut oil, add vegetables and salt, and stir-fry a few seconds. Add chicken stock and bring to a boil. Cover and let steam 1 to 1½ minutes. Add MSG, thick soya and cornstarch mixture, and mix a few times quickly. Add toasted almonds, stir a couple of times and serve immediately. *Note:* Don't add too much thick soya, but just enough to give the dish an amber color. The sauce should not be thick, but should drip readily and freely. Serves 4.

EMPRESS CHICKEN   (PLATE VII)

8 chicken legs
8 chicken thighs
12 ounces prosciutto ham
¼ cup sherry
¼ cup pure soya (Sang Chow)

1 teaspoon salt
¼ teaspoon pepper
½ teaspoon MSG
2 tablespoons oil
Cornstarch

Wash chicken legs and second joints and bone them carefully, leaving the skin intact. Chop prosciutto ham very fine, and fill the cavity of each leg and thigh. Mix sherry, pure soya, seasonings and oil in a bowl and marinate chicken 10 to 15 minutes. Roll pieces in cornstarch, rubbing it in to make a good coating, and fry in deep fat until golden brown. Keep warm in oven while you make the following sauce:

SAUCE FOR EMPRESS CHICKEN

| | |
|---|---|
| 12 Chinese dried black mushrooms | ½ teaspoon salt |
| 2 tablespoons oil | 1 ounce sherry |
| ¼ cup chopped onions | 1 ounce pure soya (Sang Chow) |
| 1 tablespoon minced gingerroot | 3 tablespoons cornstarch mixed with |
| 3 cups chicken stock | ½ cup cold water |

Wash and soak mushrooms in warm water for 15 to 20 minutes. When spongy, squeeze out water and cut into strips ¼ inch wide. Heat pan and add oil; sauté onions and chopped ginger together. Add mushrooms and stir-fry a few seconds, then add chicken stock, salt, sherry and soya and bring to a boil. Thicken with cornstarch mixture, then add fried chicken pieces and let heat through. Serve with steamed rice. Serves 6 to 8.

SESAME CHICKEN

| | |
|---|---|
| 1 chicken, 2–2½ pounds | ½ cup sesame seeds |
| Salt, pepper and flour, mixed | ½ teaspoon salt |
| 2 eggs, beaten | ¼ teaspoon pepper |
| 2 tablespoons milk | Peanut or safflower oil for frying |
| 1 cup flour | Light Cream Sauce |

Wash and dry, then disjoint chicken. Dust with seasoned flour, then dip pieces of chicken into batter of beaten eggs mixed with milk, then roll in flour mixed with sesame seeds and seasonings. Deep fry in peanut or safflower oil at 350° F., until light brown and tender. Serve with Light Cream Sauce made with chicken broth and cream. Serves 2 to 4.

LIGHT CREAM SAUCE FOR SESAME CHICKEN

| | |
|---|---|
| 4 tablespoons butter | 1 cup rich chicken stock |
| 4 tablespoons flour | ½ cup whipping cream |
| ½ cup half and half | ½ teaspoon onion salt |

Melt butter over low heat, add flour and blend over low heat several minutes, stirring constantly. Mix half and half, chicken stock and whipping cream and gradually add to butter and flour mixture, stirring constantly. When smooth, stir in onion salt. Add plain salt if necessary. Let cook over hot water in double boiler 15 to 20 minutes, stirring occasionally.

## CHICKEN CANTONESE

| | |
|---|---|
| ½ pound white meat of chicken | ½ cup sliced water chestnuts |
| ½ pound Chinese snow peas | 1 teaspoon MSG |
| ¼ cup peanut oil | 1 teaspoon salt |
| ½ cup bamboo shoots | 4 cups chicken stock |
| 1 cup sliced bok choy | 2 tablespoons cornstarch mixed with |
| 1 cup sliced celery | ½ cup cold water |
| 1 cup sliced button mushrooms | |

Slice chicken in strips, about ½ inch wide, 1½ inches long and ¼ inch thick. Wash and string Chinese peas and cut cross-wise in half. Stir-fry chicken in peanut oil for about 10 seconds. Add vegetables and seasonings and stir-fry for another 10 seconds. Add chicken stock, bring to a boil, cover and steam for about a minute. Stir in cornstarch mixture, mix throughly and quickly. Sauce should not be too thick, but should drip or run freely and readily. Serve 2 to 4.

*CHICKEN WITH PINEAPPLE*

½ pound white meat of chicken

3 tablespoons peanut oil

2 slices pineapple

¾ cup sliced water chestnuts

1 green pepper

1 cup bamboo shoots

1 cup sliced bok choy

1 cup sliced celery

1 teaspoon salt

1 cup white vinegar

¾ cup white sugar

1 cup pineapple juice

½ teaspoon MSG

3 tablespoons catsup

2 tablespoons cornstarch mixed with

¼ cup cold water

*Preparation:* Cut chicken meat in slices ¼ inch thick, ½ inch wide and 1¼ to 1½ inches long. Slice pineapple into half inch wedges. Wash pepper, remove stem end, ribs and seeds, and cut into pieces about 1 inch square. The rest of the ingredients, the bamboo shoots, bok choy and the celery, should all be sliced approximately the same size: 1 inch by 1¼ inches by ⅛ inch thick.

*Method:* Preheat pan, add oil and stir-fry chicken lightly. Add vegetables, pineapple and salt, and stir-fry about 10 seconds. Mix vinegar, sugar and pineapple juice together and add to pan. Stir and bring to a boil; cover and let steam for 1½ minutes. Add MSG, catsup and thickening, and stir a few times quickly until sauce is clear. Serves 4 to 6.

*CHO GU CHICKEN*   (PLATE VIII)

3 tablespoons peanut oil

½ pound sliced white meat of chicken

1 can straw mushrooms (13 ounces)

¾ cup sliced bamboo shoots

½ pound Chinese snow peas

¾ cup sliced water chestnuts

½ teaspoon salt

2 cups chicken stock

1 teaspoon thick soya

½ teaspoon MSG

2 tablespoons cornstarch mixed with

¼ cup cold water

*Preparation*: Cut chicken meat in slices ½ inch wide, 1¼ to 1½ inches long and ½ inch thick. Drain and use mushrooms whole, preferably, but if too large, cut in half. Cut bamboo shoots in slices 1 inch by 1¼ inches by ⅛ inch thick. Wash and string Chinese snow peas, and cut in half across. Slice water chestnuts crosswise in about ⅛ inch thickness.

*Method*: Preheat pan, add oil and stir-fry chicken lightly. Add vegetables and salt and stir-fry a few seconds, then add chicken stock. Bring to a boil, cover and steam half a minute. Add thick soya, MSG and cornstarch mixture and stir a few times until sauce is clear. The thick soya should just give the sauce an amber color, so don't use too much. Serves 4 to 6.

*PRECIOUS CHICKEN*

¼ cup peanut oil
1 cup diced celery
1 cup sliced button
  mushrooms
½ cup shredded Chinese
  snow peas
½ cup diced bamboo
  shoots
½ cup sliced water
  chestnuts

4 cups chicken stock
2 teaspoons salt
2 teaspoons MSG
3 tablespoons cornstarch
  mixed with
¼ cup cold water
1 pound white meat of
  chicken
Dipping Batter I
Peanut oil for frying

*Vegetable procedure:* Preheat pan and add oil. Add vegetables (diced in about ¼ inch cubes) and stir-fry for 10 to 15 seconds. Add chicken stock, bring to a boil, cover and steam for 1 to 1½ minutes. Add 1 teaspoon salt, 1 teaspoon MSG and cornstarch mixture and stir thoroughly until thickened. This is the bed for the chicken, which should be cooked while the vegetables steam.

*Chicken procedure:* Slice chicken in strips about ½ inch wide, 1¼ inches long and ⅛ inch thick. Season with salt and MSG, remaining teaspoon of each. Dip in Dipping Batter I used for Chicken Livers and deep fry in peanut oil until golden brown.

When done, pour over bed of vegetables. Do not fry the chicken in advance, but fry while vegetables are cooking. Serves 4 to 6.

CHINESE ROAST CHICKEN

3 green onions, chopped
2 pieces fresh gingerroot
½ cup sherry
1 cup soy sauce
1 teaspoon sugar
1 teaspoon salt
4 cups water
1 chicken, about 3
    pounds
Green onions or Chinese
    parsley

Mix chopped onions, gingerroot, sherry, soy sauce, sugar and salt with water in stew pot. Bring to a boil. Meanwhile, wash and draw chicken. Put whole chicken in boiling liquid, cover and let simmer for half an hour. Remove and put on rack in roasting pan in hot oven. Roast half an hour to 45 minutes, until chicken is browned and tender. Served Chinese style, the chicken is split in two with a cleaver, then each half is chopped into five or six pieces and arranged, skin side up on a serving dish. Garnish with slivers of green onions or sprigs of Chinese parsley. The hot broth is served separately as a dipping sauce. Serves 4 persons.

A variation for American kitchens would be to disjoint the

cleaned chicken, simmer the pieces in the soy sauce mixture, then roast in a hot oven. Serve in a ring of steamed rice, garnish with green onions, slivered, and/or Chinese parsley. Thicken the soy sauce mixture and pass as a sauce.

## PINEAPPLE DUCK

2 tablespoons oil
1 Long Island or white
   domestic duck,
   weighing about 4
   pounds
1 teaspoon salt
¼ teaspoon pepper
4 slices canned pineapple

1 large green pepper
2 cups broth
½ teaspoon MSG
1 tablespoon soy sauce
1 tablespoon cornstarch
   mixed with
2 tablespoons cold water

*Preparation:* Clean and quarter duckling. Cover with boiling water and simmer gently until tender. Remove from broth (save it) and let duck drain. Cut up the pineapple. Wash and clean the pepper, removing stem, inside ribs and seeds, and cut into inch-sized squares.

*Method:* Preheat heavy skillet and add oil. Add pieces of duck, salt and pepper and brown gently, turning frequently. When browned, add the pineapple and green pepper and stir-fry a few seconds. Add the broth (in which the duck was simmered), MSG and the soy sauce. Cover and simmer about 10 minutes. Thicken slightly with cornstarch mixture. Serve hot with steamed rice. Serves 2 to 3.

## DRESSED DUCK WITH SWEET AND SOUR PLUM SAUCE

1 Long Island or
   domestic duck,
   weighing about 4
   pounds
1 tablespoon Spices of
   Five Fragrances
1 teaspoon salt

1 cup water chestnut
   flour
Sweet and Sour Plum
   Sauce
Almonds or macadamia
   nuts

Clean and draw duck. Simmer in kettle with boiling water, spice and salt until tender. Cool and remove meat from bones, discarding skin. Lay meat on a platter which has been covered with the water chestnut flour, then rub and pat this in to make a nice thick cake about ½ to ¾ inch thick, or the depth of the platter. Steam the duck right in the platter, in a steamer, about ½ hour until the water chestnut flour has gelatinized and turned into a thick, heavy, jellied crust. Let cool, then cover with foil and refrigerate until ready to use. To prepare, cut in serving pieces. Fry in deep fat and serve with Sweet and Sour Plum Sauce. Top with crushed toasted almonds or macadamia nuts. Serves 4.

SWEET AND SOUR PLUM SAUCE

| | |
|---|---|
| ½ cup water | 2 tablespoons catsup |
| 1 cup plum jelly | 2 tablespoons vinegar |

Bring ingredients to a boil. If not thick enough, thicken slightly with a teaspoon of cornstarch mixed with cold water. Serve hot on pressed duck.

*ABALONE MACAO*   (PLATE IX)

| | |
|---|---|
| ½ pound abalone steak | 2½ cups chicken stock, hot |
| ½ cup sliced bamboo shoots | 1 teaspoon sugar |
| ½ pound Chinese snow peas | ½ teaspoon MSG |
| 3 tablespoons peanut oil | 2 tablespoons cornstarch mixed with |
| 3 tablespoons oyster sauce | ¼ cup cold water |

Cut abalone in 2 inch long strips, about ⅛ inch thick. The bamboo shoots should be about the same size. Wash and string snow peas and cut each in three pieces. Heat oil in preheated pan and fry abalone quickly, then stir in bamboo shoots and snow peas quickly. Don't overcook or the abalone will lose its tenderness. Add oyster sauce, hot chicken stock and seasonings. Bring to a boil and cover. Steam about 10 seconds. Thicken with cornstarch mixture and serve immediately. Serves 4 to 6.

*CHINESE POACHED FISH*

1 whole fish, 3–5 pounds (striped bass, black cod, pike or perch)
½ cup soy sauce
2 slices gingerroot
1 large onion, thinly sliced

1 cup chopped Virginia ham
¼ cup chopped green onions

Clean and scale fish but do not skin. Leave head and tail intact. Lay fish gently on greased poaching tray, if you have a fish poacher. Add enough cold water to immerse fish. Add soy sauce, ginger, sliced onion and chopped Virginia ham and bring to a boil. Reduce heat, cover and let fish simmer for 5 to 8 minutes per pound. If you don't have a poacher, use roasting pan with a cover. Tie fish in muslin or cheesecloth so it may be easily lifted from the pan and lay it on a rack— a cake rack or something similar that fits—will serve the purpose. Proceed the same as for a fish poacher. When fish is cooked, remove to platter. Pour some heated soy sauce over the fish and sprinkle it with the chopped green onions. Allow ½ pound per person.

*LOBSTER CANTONESE*   (PLATE X)

1 pound Icelandic lobster meat
1 tablespoon fermented black beans
3 tablespoons peanut oil
1 clove garlic, minced
¼ cup chopped onions
¼ cup chopped fresh mushrooms
¼ cup chopped celery

3 whole canned tomatoes
⅓ cup sherry wine
1½ cups chicken stock, hot
3 eggs
2 tablespoons cornstarch mixed with
¼ cup cold water
1 teaspoon MSG
1 teaspoon salt

Cut thawed lobster meat into inch-sized chunks. Lobster tails may also be used, fresh or frozen. Wash and soak black beans in 2 tablespoons warm water to soften them, then mash with a mortar and pestle, or with the back of a spoon. Preheat pan and add peanut oil. Stir-fry garlic, black bean paste, onions, mushrooms and celery in oil for about 10 seconds. Add lobster meat and tomatoes, which have been chopped into four or five pieces each; stir-fry another minute. Add sherry and stir a few times, then add chicken stock. Bring to a boil, cover and let steam 1 to 1½ minutes. Meantime, beat eggs in a bowl; mix the cornstarch with water. Remove lid, stir in MSG and salt, then stir in beaten eggs and mix quickly until the eggs flake. Stir in the cornstarch mixture, a little at a time, and mix thoroughly until sauce thickens. Should you find the sauce too thick, immediately add a little more hot chicken broth. Serves 2 to 4.

*CURRIED CRAB LEGS CANTONESE*

| | |
|---|---|
| 1 pound crab legs | 2 teaspoons MSG |
| 1 tablespoon imported India curry powder | 1 teaspoon salt |
| | ¼ teaspoon pepper |
| 2 tablespoons peanut oil | 3 eggs, beaten |
| 3 cups chicken stock | 1 tablespoon cornstarch mixed with |
| 2 medium-sized tomatoes, peeled and chopped | 3 tablespoons cold water |

Sauté crab legs and curry powder in peanut oil about 10 seconds, stirring gently to keep powder from browning and the crab legs from breaking up. Add chicken stock and steam for half a minute. Remove crab legs to serving dish and put in oven to keep warm. To remaining liquid, add tomatoes, MSG, salt and pepper and let cook with lid on for 10 seconds. Remove lid, add beaten eggs and stir quickly until they flake. Add cornstarch and water mixture slowly, stirring constantly until the mixture thickens. Taste and correct seasonings. Pour over crab legs and serve with steamed rice and sambals, such as pine nuts, or chopped cashew nuts, currants, chopped bananas, grated frozen or fresh coconut, diced cucumber, etc. Serves 2 to 4. *Note:* One pound shrimp or prawns may be substituted for the crab legs.

*PAKE CRAB*

| | |
|---|---|
| 1 cooked crab | ½ teaspoon salt |
| 1½ cubes butter | ¼ teaspoon pepper |
| 2 cloves garlic, chopped very fine | ½ teaspoon MSG |
| | 4 ounces French vermouth |
| 3 tablespoons A-1 sauce | |

Remove the butter from the cooked crab and save. Clean crab and crack it. Melt butter in wok or large heavy skillet with a lid, add garlic and seasonings, vermouth and crab butter and heat through. Add the crab, cover and allow to steam about 5 minutes. Serves 1 or 2 persons, depending upon the size of the crab and the rest of the menu.

This makes a good party dish, especially in honor of the beginning of crab season which, in San Francisco, occurs November 15. Serve plenty of crabs in big abalone shells with the holes plugged. Supply diners with bibs for uninhibited crab-picking. A hearty green salad, plenty of fresh, hot sour dough French bread with garlic butter, wine and a simple dessert—such as fruit and cheese or an ice—make a simple menu, with Pake Crab the star of the evening.

A nice touch, after the crab course, is to present each guest with a napkin or small towel which has been wrung out in hot water and sprayed with an inoffensive cologne. Miniature bamboo trays, such as the Japanese use for hot cloths when guests first sit down to dinner, may be used, or small plates. Try your local import outlet for the bamboo napkin baskets or trays.

A Pake treatment may be given to lobster—either eastern or the California variety which has no claws. Frozen lobster tails may also be used. The following recipe is fork food, served on steamed rice.

*PAKE LOBSTER*

4 lobster tails, about 10
  ounces each
8 anchovy strips
1¼ cups dry vermouth
¼ cup finely chopped
  dry onions
2 cloves garlic, minced
2 cubes butter
½ cup crab meat, finely
  chopped

¼ cup lobster butter
1 tablespoon A-1 sauce
¼ teaspoon Tabasco sauce
1¼ cups chicken stock
2 tablespoons cornstarch
  mixed with
¼ cup cold water

Cut each lobster tail into 8 pieces. Purée anchovy strips with vermouth and reserve. Sauté lobster with onion and garlic in butter, then add puréed anchovies, crab meat, lobster butter, seasonings and chicken stock. Bring to a boil, then cover and let simmer for 5 minutes. Thicken lightly with cornstarch mixed with cold water. Serves 4 to 6.

Sweet and sour dishes are a Chinese specialty and this is one of the best.

*SWEET AND SOUR SHRIMP*

1 pound fresh shrimp
  or prawns
4 tablespoons flour
4 tablespoons cornstarch
½ teaspoon salt

¼ teaspoon MSG
2 tablespoons water
1 egg, beaten
Oil for frying

Wash, peel and devein shrimp. Dry thoroughly in paper towels. Mix flour, cornstarch, salt, MSG and water together and add beaten egg. Mix lightly and dip shrimp in batter. Fry in safflower or peanut oil, preheated to 370°F., turning to brown on both sides. When golden brown drain on paper towels and keep warm in oven while you make the following sauce.

SWEET AND SOUR SAUCE

½ cup white vinegar
½ cup brown sugar
½ cup pineapple juice
1 teaspoon salt
¼ teaspoon pepper
4 slices canned pineapple
2 green peppers

2 fresh tomatoes, peeled
2 tablespoons cornstarch
  mixed with
¼ cup cold water
1 tablespoon chopped
  green onions

Mix vinegar, sugar, pineapple juice and seasonings in enamel or stainless steel pan and heat. Dice pineapple. Wash, remove stem fiber and seeds from green peppers and cut in inch square pieces (approximately). Halve peeled tomatoes and then cut each half in 4 wedges. Add pineapple, green peppers and tomatoes to vinegar mixture and bring to a boil. Turn heat down and let simmer 5 minutes. Stir cornstarch with water into sauce until it thickens and is clear. Add deep-fat fried shrimp, mix thoroughly and bring to a boil, then simmer 2 minutes more. Serve immediately, topped with green onions. Serves 2 to 4.

*BEAN SPROUTS WITH MUSHROOMS AND CELERY*

2 tablespoons peanut oil
3 stalks celery, sliced
1 small onion, chopped
6 mushrooms, sliced
½ cup chicken stock
1 tablespoon soy sauce

½ teaspoon salt
½ teaspoon MSG
1 pound bean sprouts
1 tablespoon cornstarch
  with
¼ cup cold water

Preheat pan and add oil; sauté celery, onion and mushrooms until onion is limp. Add chicken stock, soy sauce and seasonings. Bring to a boil and add bean sprouts. Stir-fry a few seconds, then cover and let simmer about five seconds. Thicken liquid with cornstarch mixed with cold water, adding a little at a time until it is thick enough to hold vegetables together. Serve immediately. Serves 4.

*CAULIFLOWER, WATER CHESTNUTS AND MUSHOOMS*

| | |
|---|---|
| 1 small cauliflower | 2 tablespoons soy sauce |
| 2 tablespoons oil | ½ teaspoon MSG |
| 6 mushrooms, sliced | Salt to taste |
| ¾ cup chicken broth, hot | 1 tablespoon cornstarch |
| ¼ cup sliced water | mixed with |
| chestnuts | ¼ cup cold water |

Trim cauliflower and wash; break head apart and slice large flowerlets. Preheat pan and add oil; add sliced cauliflower and sauté gently. Don't let brown. Add mushrooms and sauté with cauliflower a few seconds, then add chicken broth, water chestnuts, soy sauce and seasonings. Bring to a boil, then cover and simmer until cauliflower is done but still crunchy. Thicken with cornstarch mixture. Correct seasonings and serve immediately. Serves 4 to 5.

*ZUCCHINI WITH MUSHROOMS CHINESE STYLE*  (PLATE IX)

| | |
|---|---|
| 2 pounds small zucchini | 1 tablespoon soy sauce |
| ½ pound fresh | ½ cup chicken broth |
| mushrooms | 2 teaspoons cornstarch |
| ¼ cup oil | mixed with |
| ¼ teaspoon salt | 3 tablespoons cold water |

Wash vegetables. Trim stem ends of zucchini and slice diagonally in quarter inch slices. Trim ends of mushroom stems and slice vertically, Chinese style. Sauté mushrooms in oil for a few seconds, then add squash; stir-fry until zucchini is well coated with the oil. Add salt, soy sauce and chicken broth. Bring to a boil, cover and simmer a few seconds until zucchini is tender but still bright green and on the crisp side. Thicken quickly with cornstarch mixture and serve immediately. Serves 4 to 6.

*STRING BEANS WITH BEEF CHINESE STYLE*

½ pound tender beef
2 tablespoons soy sauce
1 tablespoon cornstarch
Oil
½ teaspoon sugar

½ teaspoon salt
¾ cup chicken broth, hot
½ pound string beans,
    Frenched or julienned

Dredge beef, thinly sliced, with mixture of soy sauce and cornstarch. Heat pan, add oil and sauté beef a few seconds, stir-frying, and add sugar and salt. Add chicken broth, then string beans. Stir and bring to a boil, then cover and let simmer a few seconds. Beans should be bright green and still crunchy. Serves 2 to 4.

One of the most popular dishes in this country is Chow Mein, which literally means fried noodles. Chow or, as it is sometimes spelled, chao, means fried and mein means noodle. Fried noodles, however, are never served alone. The name of the dish is whatever is cooked with it, i.e., Pork Chow Mein, Chicken Chow Mein, etc.

*CHICKEN CHOW MEIN*

½ pound shredded breast
    of chicken
3 tablespoons peanut oil
½ cup sliced bamboo
    shoots
⅔ cup sliced water
    chestnuts
½ cup sliced celery
1 cup sliced bok choy
2 medium-sized onions,
    thinly sliced
1 cup sliced fresh
    button mushrooms
½ teaspoon salt

¼ cup soy sauce
2 cups chicken broth,
    hot
2 cups bean sprouts
½ teaspoon MSG
2 tablespoons cornstarch
    mixed with
¼ cup cold water
4 cups cold, cooked
    noodles, fried
Shredded, cooked
    chicken for garnish
Toasted, crushed almonds

Sauté chicken in peanut oil. Add all vegetables, except the bean sprouts, and stir-fry for 10 to 15 seconds. Add salt, soy sauce and chicken broth; cover and steam for ½ minute. Add bean sprouts and steam for another ½ minute. Add MSG and thicken with cornstarch mixture. Stir a few times until liquid is uniformly thickened. Serve on bed of fried noodles (see directions below) and garnish with shredded, cooked chicken and crushed almonds. Serves 4 to 6.

FRIED NOODLES

Work ½ teaspoon salt and 1 tablespoon sesame oil into the cooked noodles. Deep-fat fry noodles until just golden.

## PORK CHOW MEIN

Substitute fresh pork for chicken. The pork, however, may be diced. Garnish with shreds of barbecued pork and/or slivers of green onion.

## PAKE NOODLES

| | |
|---|---|
| ¾ cup butter | ½ cup sesame seeds |
| 4 cups cooked fresh | 1 teaspoon MSG |
| noodles | Salt and white pepper |
| ¼ cup bread crumbs | to taste |

Melt butter in pan, add noodles and stir until well mixed with butter and heated. Add the rest of the ingredients, mix well and serve immediately. Serves 4 to 6.

## CHINESE LONG RICE

| | |
|---|---|
| 2 cups cooked Chinese | 1 tablespoon soy sauce |
| long rice, hot (cut | ½ teaspoon MSG |
| 1–2 inches in length) | ½ teaspoon salt |
| 4 cups cooked rice, hot | 2 tablespoons finely |
| 2 freshly hard-cooked | chopped chives |
| eggs, chopped | |

Combine long rice, rice and chopped eggs; add seasonings,

mix well. Serve very hot in Chinese bowls garnished with chopped chives. Serves 6 to 8.

*SHRIMP LONG RICE*

| | |
|---|---|
| 1 bundle long rice | ½ cup shredded snow |
| ½ pound shrimp | peas |
| 5 tablespoons peanut oil | 1 cup hot chicken stock |
| 1 cup diced celery | 2 tablespoons chopped |
| 1 cup chopped onion | chives |

Soak long rice in boiling water for half an hour, then drain and cut in 2 inch lengths. Clean shrimp and slice diagonally into ½ inch pieces. Marinate 20 minutes in the following sauce:

MARINADE

| | |
|---|---|
| 1 teaspoon sugar | ½ teaspoon fresh ginger |
| ½ teaspoon salt | juice |
| ⅛ teaspoon pepper | 2 tablespoons soy sauce |
| 2 cloves garlic, minced | |

Heat pan and add 2 tablespoons of the oil. Sauté celery, onions and snow peas for ½ minute. Remove and reserve. Reheat pan, add other 3 tablespoons oil and sauté the marinated shrimp. Stir in peas, celery and onions, add prepared long rice, hot stock and mix well. Cover and simmer for 5 minutes. Serve in Chinese bowls; garnish with chopped chives. Serves 6 to 8.

# Southeast Asia

OUR NEXT stop was Bangkok. Three days isn't long enough to form an opinion of any country or city, but three days is all the time we could spend there. At first glance it seemed to me that the entire city was composed of temples, called wats. You have to see it to believe it. Everywhere you see buildings and statues decorated with gold leaf, mosaics and mother-of-pearl. The temples are flanked by gigantic, elaborate statues with faces of demons. The skyline is punctured with tall gold spires, gleaming in the sunlight. Upcurved, pointed eaves, supported by colorful, grinning demons decorate the corners of temple roofs.

Thailand is Buddhist and the faithful, believing that building or beautifying a wat earns them merit in this life and the next, have contributed magnificence to the thousands of wats throughout the country. In Bangkok alone there are said to be 300 wats.

Compared to other Asian countries, Thailand is the land of plenty. At any rate, the people seem happy. Laced with klongs or canals, Bangkok is somewhat like an oriental Venice. People live in houses on stilts at the edge of the klongs, which furnish them fish for dinner, bathing facilities, water for cooking and sanitary conveniences. Transportation is by sampans, and klongs teem with activity. There are other means of transportation, of course, and roads and great highways, but the klongs capture your attention.

Thai cooking is a combination of Indian and Chinese, with emphasis on the pepper-hot features of both. Rice is the staple food of the Thais and their diet consists of fruits and vegetables aplenty, fish, beef, pork, and shrimp.

All throughout Southeast Asia you find the mixture of Indian and Chinese influence on cooking. And in all of the major cities you find a high percentage of Chinese running restaurants, and doing the business.

Singapore is an island, located at the tip of the Malay peninsula, and a free port. It is the melting pot of East and West with a population of 75 per cent Chinese and the rest Malayan, Indians, Pakistanis, Eurasian and Europeans. The name is not a Malay word but two Sanskrit words Singa Pura meaning Lion City. The Malays, before they were driven north in a senseless and bloody attack by the Javanese in about 1365 called it Tumasik. After the Javanese invasion, Singapore was abandoned and it became a pirate base until the British established a settlement there early in the nineteenth century.

The progress of the island began upon the arrival of Thomas Stamford Raffles on January 29, 1819. Impressed with the strategic position of the island, he sought to establish a new trading center for the East India Company to compete with the Dutch for the East Indies trade. It was due to his efforts and his study of Malay before undertaking to establish himself in Singapore that led to Singapore's prosperity and progress. One of the most famous hotels in the Far East, The Raffles, is named after him and a number of parks and other sites bear his name.

Singapore became a self-governing state in 1959. In 1963 it joined the Federation of Malaysia but tensions and disagreements prompted its withdrawal in August of 1965.

We didn't visit India. I'm chicken. The thought of poverty depresses me. I'll have to acquire a lot of intestinal fortitude before I make that trip. We have some very good friends there, however, who have sent us some wonderful recipes. I have included these with an assortment of Malayan and Indonesian recipes. As usual I have made some changes.

*MALAYAN LOBSTER TAILS*  (PLATE XII)

| | |
|---|---|
| 8 lobster tails, about 10 ounces | 1 teaspoon A-1 sauce |
| 1 cup melted butter | ½ cup white wine |
| 2 tablespoons chopped shallots | 2 cups cream sauce |
| 1 tablespoon curry powder | 1 cup sour cream |
| | 1 tablespoon meat sauce* |
| | ½ teaspoon white pepper |
| | Parsley or watercress |

Thaw frozen lobster tails. Dry well. Brush with melted butter and broil. Meantime, sauté shallots with remainder of melted butter, stir in curry powder and brown lightly, then add rest of ingredients. Arrange broiled lobster tails, red side up on a platter of steamed rice and pour curry sauce over top. Garnish with parsley or watercress. Serves 6 to 8.

* Use Kitchen Bouquet, Maggi, BV Meat Flavor or any beef concentrate. Add gradually, however, since different products have a different concentration and this is added primarily for color.

*MALAYAN MEAT-ON-A-STICK*

3 pounds beef, lamb
   or pork
3 tablespoons curry
   powder
½ teaspoon ground
   chilies

2 cloves garlic, minced
2 large onions, minced
1 tablespoon salt
Juice of 2 large lemons
1 tablespoon honey

Cut meat in 1½ inch cubes. Mix rest of ingredients in a large dish; add meat and rub mixture well into pieces of meat. Let stand about 10 minutes; thread on bamboo or metal skewers, allowing the bits of onion and garlic to adhere to the meat. Barbecue or broil, turning meat to brown on all sides. Serve with Peanut Sauce. Serves 6.

PEANUT SAUCE   Blend the following ingredients:

1 cup peanut butter
1 cup Coconut Cream
Juice of ½ large lemon
¼ cup soy sauce
1 tablespoon
   Worcestershire sauce

1 dash Tabasco
½ teaspoon MSG
¼ teaspoon salt

This is a noodle dish of Malayan origin. It is like some of our Western casserole dishes—a mixture determined by the inspiration of the cook and the contents of the larder. There are many recipes for Bah Mee, but you have to start somewhere, and this is a good one. After you have tried it, ad lib with cooked chicken, California or Louisiana Shrimp (small), crab meat, shredded baked or boiled ham, sautéed sliced mushrooms. All the vegetables are used uncooked.

*BAH MEE*

6 ounces white chicken meat, sliced
12 prawns, split
6 chicken livers
¼ cup peanut oil
2 cups bean sprouts
½ can water chestnuts, sliced
¼ cup shredded celery
½ cup shredded snow peas
¼ cup slivered green onions
1 pound fresh Chinese egg noodles *OR*
1 package of dry egg noodles, cooked

4 cups chicken stock
1 teaspoon Lingham's Chilly Sauce
2 tablespoons oyster sauce
1 tablespoon soya sauce
2 teaspoons MSG
Salt to taste
2 tablespoons cornstarch mixed with
¼ cup cold water
Barbecued Pork (Cha Sui)
Shredded Thin Egg Skin

Sauté chicken, prawns and chicken livers in peanut oil for 10 to 15 seconds, stirring constantly. Add all of the vegetables (all cut 2 inches long, ³⁄₁₆ inch wide and ⅛ inch thick) and stir for another 10 seconds. Add cooked noodles, chicken stock and chili sauce. Stir a few times, then cover and steam for a minute or so. Add seasonings and thickening and stir well. Serve in Chinese bowls and garnish with shredded Barbecued Pork and shredded Thin Egg Skin. Serves 4 to 6.

INDONESIAN LAMB ROAST

⅓ cup finely chopped celery
⅓ cup finely chopped onion
1 clove garlic, minced
¾ cup oil
¼ cup vinegar
2 teaspoons A-1 sauce
3 tablespoons curry powder

2 dashes Tabasco sauce
3 tablespoons honey
1 teaspoon oregano
2 bay leaves
½ cup prepared mustard
Juice and rind of 1 large lemon
6 lamp chops, or a rack trimmed of fat

Sauté celery, onions and garlic in salad oil until onion is transparent. Stir in remaining ingredients; simmer a few minutes. Chill. Marinate chops or rack in this mixture three or four hours in refrigerator, turning several times. Drain marinade from meat. Wrap bones or chops or rack of lamb with foil, leaving meaty portions exposed. Arrange in greased, shallow baking pan. Brush meat with marinade and bake at 400° F. approximately 20 minutes, or longer, depending upon thickness of meat and desired doneness. Turn meat once during the baking period and baste frequently with marinade. During the last few minutes of cooking, the meat may be placed under the broiler if further browning seems necessary. Serve remaining marinade hot, as a sauce for the meat. Serves 6.

PLATE XII. Malayan Lobster Tails, *page 157*

PLATE XIII. Mexican drinks: Sangría, *page 190;* Durango, *page 186;* Potted Parrot, *page 188;* Margarita cocktail, *page 185;* Señor Pico Tequila Daiquiri, *page 185*

*SINGAPORE NOODLES*  (PLATE IX)

2 tablespoons peanut oil
½ cup dry onions,
   thinly sliced
1 teaspoon curry powder
1 cup bok choy, sliced
2 cups bean sprouts
1 cup chicken stock
½ cup julienne
   Barbecued Pork
½ cup small shrimp

½ cup shredded Thin
   Egg Skins
2 tablespoons soy sauce
Salt, pepper and MSG
2 cups cooked fine rice
   noodles
½ teaspoon sesame seeds
1 tablespoon sliced green
   onions

Preheat wok, add oil and sauté onions with curry powder.
Add bok choy, bean sprouts and chicken stock. Cover and bring
to a boil. Add pork, shrimp, shredded Thin Egg Skins, soy
sauce and season to taste. Meantime, pan-fry noodles lightly.
Add noodles to mixture in wok; mix well and serve in serving
bowl. Garnish with sesame seeds and green onions. Serves 2 to
4.

*INDONESIAN PORK KABOBS*

| | |
|---|---|
| 2 pounds lean pork | ½ teaspoon chili powder |
| ¼ cup peanut butter | 1 clove garlic, peeled |
| 3 tablespoons soy sauce | and crushed |
| 2 tablespoons ground | 1 tablespoon lemon juice |
| coriander | |
| 1 tablespoon ground | |
| cumin | |

Cut meat in 1 inch cubes. Make a paste of the peanut butter, soy sauce, spices, garlic and lemon juice in a bowl. Add cubes of meat and rub the peanut butter paste in well. Let marinate half an hour. Thread cubes of meat on skewers and broil slowly 20 to 30 minutes, six inches from the heat. Turn to brown all sides. Serves 6. Serve with rice and the following sauce:

| | |
|---|---|
| 1 cup soy sauce | ¼ cup sherry |
| 2 tablespoons pineapple | ¼ teaspoon salt |
| juice | ½ teaspoon minced fresh |
| 1 clove garlic, crushed | gingerroot |

Mix soy sauce with rest of ingredients and bring to a boil. Let cool and strain before serving. Use as a dip or pass as a sauce.

A refreshing and colorful accompaniment to this or any other highly seasoned dish is a mathematical mixture of tomato, green pepper and onion, called a Beirut Salad. Mix and chill 2 parts chopped tomato to 1 part chopped green pepper and 1 part chopped Spanish onion. Just that. No dressing, No seasoning. Serve in small individual bowls.

## ABOUT CURRIES

There has probably been more flap about curries than any other form of cooking in the whole world. You hear all kinds of theories, some nonsensical, others quite true. Here are a few essentials to remember in making curried dishes.

1. In India, ghee is used in curry-making. This is clarified butter. While you can use butter, margarine or oil, clarified butter has certain advantages in that it doesn't burn and it doesn't spatter no matter how hot it gets. There is no mystery about it, and it is nice to have on hand. To prepare clarified butter put half or a pound of butter in a saucepan and place over moderate heat. Remove scum as it rises to the surface. When the butter is clear and the solids have settled to the bottom funnel off the clear butter into another container. Or you can let it cool in the saucepan, cover and store in the refrigerator for use as needed. The important thing is not to dig down to the salt and milk solids.

2. Onions and garlic should be as finely chopped as possible. They should be sautéed in butter or oil but should never be allowed to brown.

3. The spices for curries, or the curry powder, should be lightly fried in butter or oil for several minutes to eliminate the raw taste. The spice mix is usually added shortly after the onions and garlic have started to cook. If you are using an inferior curry mix it will show up at this time. If the curry has been adulterated with any kind of flour the curry powder will stick to the bottom of the pan.

4. Acidity is often added to curries. In the curry countries, limes or tamarind are used. Unsweetened tamarind is packed in glass jars and is available at gourmet food shops. Otherwise, we can settle for limes, lemons or even a bit of vinegar.

5. While Coconut Milk is used extensively in Indian curries,

curds, fresh or sour milk is also used. Yogurt may be used instead of curds.

6. Curry sauces or gravies are not thickened by flour or corn-starch in South Asia countries. Instead, the lid is removed and the gravy permitted to thicken by reduction.

Curries are seasoned by various combinations of cumin, cori-ander, fenugreek, ginger, dill, black pepper, cayenne pepper, mace, cardamon, cloves. Turmeric adds flavor as well as color. There is no reason why you can't use a good prepared curry powder. If you want to try your hand at blending your own there are two ways to do it. You can do it the hard way, with a mortar and pestle or you can buy a spice mill which resembles a coffee mill.

Turmeric and coriander seem to be the basis for most curry mixes. For example, here is a formula for a fairly hot curry mix which can be blended and put away in screw-top jars:

| | |
|---|---|
| ½ cup turmeric | 1 tablespoon red pepper |
| ½ cup coriander | 1 tablespoon ginger |
| 4 tablespoons black pepper | 1 tablespoon cumin |
| 2 tablespoons cardamon | ½ teaspoon cayenne pepper |

A curry paste may be prepared ahead of time and used as needed. The following spices, with the exception of the pepper, are ground and blended over low heat with 2 tablespoons clarified butter. Let cook about 4 minutes, and let cool. Stir in pepper and store in a small jar.

| | |
|---|---|
| 2 teaspoons coriander | ½ teaspoon cardamon |
| 1 teaspoon turmeric | ½ teaspoon chilies |
| ½ teaspoon cumin | ¼ teaspoon cracked black pepper |
| ½ teaspoon ginger | |
| ½ teaspoon cinnamon | |

*SHRIMP AND EGG CURRY*

1 pound cooked shrimp
4 hard-cooked eggs
2 tablespoons finely
  chopped onion
1 clove garlic, finely
  minced
¼ cup butter or oil
½ teaspoon ground chilies
1 tablespoon curry
  powder

1 tablespoon tomato
  paste
½ cup chicken broth
½ cup thick Coconut
  Milk
Salt to taste
Juice of ½ lemon

Shell and devein shrimp and cut eggs lengthwise in half.

Sauté onions and garlic in butter or oil; add chilies and curry powder and let cook, stirring to keep from sticking, until onions are limp but not browned. Add tomato paste and blend well; then thin mixture by gradually adding the chicken stock. Simmer gently, then add the Coconut Milk. Salt to taste, then add lemon juice, shrimp and egg halves, spooning the sauce over them until they are heated through. The gravy should be thick and cling to the eggs. Serve over rice. Serves 4.

While Indian curries are thickened by reduction with lid removed, there are some delightful cream curry sauces which we thicken with flour or cornstarch with apologies to no one. The flavor is the thing and curry powder can add zing to many a sauce or dressing.

Here is a light curry sauce, quickly made and best served with cooked chicken or seafood over rice.

*SUSU CURRY SAUCE*

1 onion, minced
2 stalks celery, chopped
½ cup sliced mushrooms
1 cooking apple, peeled and diced
2 tablespoons butter
1 tablespoon curry powder

½ cup chicken stock
1 quart half and half
2 tablespoons cornstarch mixed with
¼ cup cold water
Salt to taste

Sauté vegetables and apple in butter until onion is transparent and mushrooms have lost their opaque appearance. Stir in curry powder and keep stirring until curry powder is lightly browned. Add chicken stock, cover and let simmer a few minutes, then stir in half and half. Add cornstarch and water mixture to sauce, stirring until desired consistency has been reached. Season and add cooked chicken or seafood; let simmer gently until heated through. Serve over rice. Makes about 6 cups of sauce.

*CALCUTTA CURRY SAUCE*

This is a little more robust but still good with chicken or seafood.

1 onion, chopped
1 large clove garlic, minced
2 tablespoons butter
3 tablespoons curry powder
1 large green cooking apple, chopped

2 tablespoons chopped cucumber
2 tablespoons chopped pimiento
2 large carrots, chopped
2 cups chicken stock
½ cup Coconut Milk

Sauté onion and garlic in butter until onion is limp, then stir in curry powder until lightly browned. Add apple and stir in a few seconds, then add cucumber, pimiento and carrots. Add chicken stock and let cook until vegetables are cooked; then purée in food mill or blender. Reheat and add Coconut Milk. Season to taste. Add chicken or seafood and bring to a boil. Serve with a hard-cooked egg, rice, Lingham's Chilly Sauce and assorted sambals. Sauce serves 4.

*INDIAN LAMB CURRY*

2 pounds lamb
¼ cup oil
2 tablespoons ground coriander
1 tablespoon ground turmeric
1 teaspoon ground cumin
1 teaspoon ground pepper
2 teaspoons minced gingerroot

4 fresh or pickled chilies, minced
½ cup butter or oil
2 large onions, minced
2 cloves garlic, minced
4 cups water or chicken stock
1 cup thick Coconut Milk
Salt to taste

Cut lamb in small chunks, as for stew. Mix oil and ground

spices in a bowl; add meat to spice mixture and rub it in well. Let stand 10 to 15 minutes. Preheat heavy kettle and add ½ cup butter or oil. Sauté onion and garlic until onion is soft but not browned; add meat and spiced marinade mixture; cook over low heat for several minutes, stirring occasionally, until meat is well sautéed. Stir in water or stock; cover and simmer gently about an hour, or until meat is tender. Ten minutes before serving, stir in Coconut Milk. Salt to taste before serving. Serve over rice with chutney and sambals. Serves 4 to 6.

*LAMB CURRY WITH YOGURT*

4 fresh or pickled chilies, chopped
1 tablespoon minced gingerroot
2 cloves garlic, minced
1 large onion, minced
2 tablespoons ground coriander
2 teaspoons ground turmeric
1 teaspoon ground cumin
1 teaspoon ground cinnamon
1 teaspoon ground mustard
4 cups yogurt
2 pounds lamb, cubed
Large onion
2 tablespoons oil
Salt to taste

Blend chilies, ginger, garlic, minced onion and spices with yogurt, pounding or using blender; mix with lamb and let marinate 2 or 3 hours. At the end of that time, sauté the sliced onion in the oil in a heavy kettle but do not brown. Add the meat and the yogurt marinade and mix well. Cover and let simmer until meat is tender—about an hour. Salt to taste. Serves 4 to 6.

Lamb cheeks are the best part of the lamb for stew or curries. You won't find them, ordinarily, in retail markets but ask your butcher to order some for you. If he can't, use just any good cut of lamb.

*CURRIED LAMB CHEEKS*  (PLATE XI)

1½ pounds lamb cheeks
¼ cup oil
1 large onion, chopped
1 clove garlic, minced
2 tablespoons butter
6 large mushrooms,
  sliced
3 tablespoons curry
  powder

1 cup chicken or soup
  stock
2 large carrots, chopped
2 stalks celery, sliced
½ cup dry white wine
Salt to taste

Trim fat from lamb cheeks and brown in heated oil in large kettle. In a frying pan, sauté onion and garlic in the 2 tablespoons butter until the onion is transparent. Add mushrooms and sauté until they have lost their whiteness and are coated with butter. Add curry powder and stir until it is nicely browned. Be careful not to burn. Add stock and swish around to rinse pan and pour over browned lamb. Add carrots, celery and wine and mix well. Cover and simmer 2 to 2½ hours, or until lamb is tender. Add more stock if necessary. Stir occasionally to prevent sticking to bottom of kettle. Salt to taste. Serve over rice. Serves 4 to 5.

*INDIAN CURRIED CHICKEN*

1 chicken, about 3½
  pounds
1 onion, finely minced
1 clove garlic, minced
2 cardamon seeds
2 cloves
1 tablespoon ground
  coriander
1 teaspoon ground
  turmeric
½ teaspoon ground ginger

½ teaspoon ground cumin
½ teaspoon ground chilies
¼ teaspoon ground
  fenugreek
¼ teaspoon ground
  cinnamon
¼ cup butter or oil
½ cup chicken broth
Juice of ½ lemon
Salt to taste

Clean and disjoint chicken. Sauté onion, garlic and spices in butter until onion is soft but not browned. Mix well and cook over a slow heat for 4 to 5 minutes. Then add the chicken pieces and let fry in the curry mixture, turning and stirring so that the spice mixture does not stick. Add chicken stock and mix well; cover and simmer until chicken is tender, about an hour. Before serving, add lemon juice and salt to taste. Serve with rice, chutney and sambals. Serves 4 to 5.

Stick curries are a novel departure from the usual curries. Cut 2 pounds of lamb or tender beef in inch cubes and skewer on 5 inch skewers, alternating with thin slices of green ginger and tiny button onions. Make a curry sauce as follows:

*STICK CURRY SAUCE*

¼ cup chopped onion
2 cloves garlic, minced
½ cup clarified butter
3 tablespoons curry powder
2 fresh or pickled chilies, chopped

2 tablespoons tomato paste
1½ cups chicken stock
Lemon juice and salt to taste

Sauté onion and garlic in butter, add curry powder and cook until onions are soft but not browned, stirring constantly. Add chilies and tomato paste, then stir in chicken stock to thin down to a fairly thickish gravy. Pack the skewered meat in this gravy. Cover and simmer gently until meat is tender, about an hour. Check occasionally and add more stock if necessary. Season to taste with lemon juice and salt and serve with rice, chutney and sambals. Serves 4 to 5.

*MURGAI CURRIED CHICKEN*

2 frying chickens, about 2½ pounds each
2 teaspoons salt
½ teaspoon turmeric
1 cup oil
2 large onions, sliced

1 bay leaf, crumbled
2 medium-sized potatoes, peeled and diced
2 large carrots, scrubbed and sliced

Cut chicken into serving pieces and rub with salt and turmeric.

Heat shortening in heavy kettle and sauté onions, which have been separated into rings, bay leaf, diced potatoes and sliced carrots. Stir and let cook until onions are clear. Remove vegetables and reserve. Add the chicken and sauté until skin becomes golden brown. Place chicken and vegetables in casserole or baking dish and cover. Bake in moderate oven while you make the sauce.

CURRY SAUCE FOR MURGAI CURRIED CHICKEN

| | |
|---|---|
| 1 tablespoon butter | Dash of ground cloves |
| 2 teaspoons curry powder | 2 cups water |
| ½ teaspoon chili powder | ½ teaspoon turmeric |
| ¼ teaspoon cinnamon | 1 teaspoon salt |
| ⅛ teaspoon ginger | 2 medium-sized tomatoes, |
| Dash of cardamon | peeled and chopped |

In separate pan, melt butter and stir in spices except turmeric; stir and cook until spice mixture turns to a deep brown—about 5 minutes. Add water, turmeric and salt and let simmer a few seconds, then add tomatoes and let simmer another 5 minutes. Pour over chicken; cover and bake for 20 minutes in moderate oven, or until chicken and vegetables are tender. Remove cover and let cook until liquid is reduced and sauce thickened. Serves 4 to 6.

*TANDOORI CHICKEN*

| | |
|---|---|
| 1 chicken, about 3 pounds | 1 teaspoon ground cumin |
| ½ papaya, seeded and peeled | 2 teaspoons salt |
| 2 tablespoons minced gingerroot | ¼ teaspoon pepper |
| 2 teaspoons minced garlic | Juice of 2 lemons |
| 2 tablespoons ground chilies | 2 tablespoons oil |
| | 8 ounces yogurt |
| | ½ cup melted butter |

Dress and wash chicken inside and out; wipe dry inside and

out. Grind papaya, ginger, garlic, chilies and seasonings to-gether—you can use mortar and pestle, or blender—then com-bine with lemon juice, oil and yogurt. Rub the inside of the chicken with the yogurt paste, then cover outside of the chicken with the rest of the mixture and let stand one hour, piercing the chicken with a sharp knife strategically to permit the marinade to soak into the fowl. This chicken is best roasted in a rotisserie so that it turns and browns evenly. Apply melted butter every 15 minutes or so, with a brush. Cooking time 40 to 50 minutes, until tender. Serves 4 to 5.

## CURRY ACCOMPANIMENTS

Accompaniments for curry are chutney, sambals and rice. There are many different kinds of chutneys, both cooked and uncooked. You can serve as many sambals as you want, such as:

Shredded coconut
Chopped bananas
Raisins or currants
Pine nuts
Slivered almonds
Chopped cashews
Chopped cucumber or
    fingers of cucumber

Tomato and onion,
    chopped and mixed
Chopped green pepper
Crisp fried bacon,
    chopped

In India, Bombay ducks, a herring-like fish caught off the west coast of India, are dried. These are fried and crumbled over curries.

Here is a mouth-cooling curry accompaniment, called Riata, which is delightful with the hottest of curries. It can be made ahead of time and refrigerated.

*RIATA*

| | |
|---|---|
| 1 large cucumber, peeled and grated | 1 teaspoon salt |
| 3 cups yogurt | 1 teaspoon toasted cumin seeds |
| 1 tablespoon minced onion | |

Grate cucumber into yogurt, add onion and salt and chill. To toast cumin seeds, place in heavy saucepan; heat until seeds start jumping. Then crush with mortar and pestle. Just before serving, add to yogurt. Serves 8.

*TOMATO CHUTNEY*

| | |
|---|---|
| 1 tablespoon oil | ½ lemon |
| 1 whole red chili pepper | ⅓ cup raisins |
| ½ teaspoon cumin seeds | ½ cup sugar |
| ¼ teaspoon nutmeg | ½ teaspoon salt |
| ¼ teaspoon mustard seeds | |
| 4 medium-sized tomatoes, peeled | |

Heat oil in saucepan and add the crumbled chili pepper and spices. When seeds start to jump, add the tomatoes, which have been thinly sliced. Quarter lemon half and place on top. Simmer, stirring frequently, for 15 minutes. Stir in the raisins, sugar and salt. Simmer, stirring frequently, until thickened, about half an hour. Makes 2 half pints. Pack in sterilized jars and seal or cool and keep in refrigerator to use as needed. Bring to room temperature before serving.

### UNCOOKED APPLE CHUTNEY

3 green cooking apples
½ cup lime juice
3 stalks celery, thinly
   sliced
2 tablespoons preserved
   ginger

1 tablespoon chopped
   chives
1 tablespoon Lingham's
   Chilly Sauce
½ cup seeded raisins
¼ cup honey

Wash, core and chop tart green cooking apples and add ½ cup lime juice immediately. Add rest of ingredients and chill before serving. Will keep a week in the refrigerator. Makes 2 pints.

### DRIED FRUIT CHUTNEY

½ pound dried apples
½ pound dried apricots
1 quart cider vinegar
3 cups brown sugar,
   firmly packed
1 seeded chopped lemon
1 cup coarsely chopped
   onion
,2 cloves garlic, minced
2 tablespoons
   Worcestershire sauce

½ cup chopped fresh
   ginger or 2 ounces
   preserved ginger
3 chili peppers, chopped
1 teaspoon ground cloves
1 teaspoon cinnamon
½ teaspoon nutmeg
1 cup raisins
Salt to taste

Soak apples and apricots in vinegar in enamel or stainless steel kettle and let soften. Remove, leaving vinegar in kettle, and chop coarsely. Heat vinegar with brown sugar and let dissolve, then add lemon, onion, garlic and rest of seasonings and bring to a boil. Add apples, apricots and raisins and simmer until thick. Add salt to taste. Pour into sterilized jars, seal and store in cool place. Makes about 6 pints.

*FRESH PRUNE CHUTNEY*

| | |
|---|---|
| 1 cup white sugar | 2 cloves garlic, minced |
| 1 cup brown sugar, firmly packed | 2 teaspoons mustard seed |
| ¾ cup cider vinegar | 2 teaspoons salt |
| 1 cup raisins | 1½ teaspoons crushed red peppers |
| ½ cup preserved ginger, finely sliced | 3½ cups halved, seeded Italian prunes |
| ¼ cup chopped onion | |

Dissolve sugar in vinegar, bring to a boil and add rest of ingredients. Simmer until mixture thickens, 50 to 60 minutes. Pour into hot, sterilized jars. Seal and store in cool, dark place. Makes 4 pints.

Pilafs or palaus have come to mean cooked rice with any number of different ingredients. Originally, the rice was sautéed in butter or oil, seasonings added, then liquid. It was covered and allowed to cook without stirring for 20 to 25 minutes. But we now take shortcuts. Here are a couple.

*RICE PILAF – I*

| | |
|---|---|
| 3 cups cooked rice | 1½ cups finely chopped carrots |
| 4 tablespoons butter | 2 tablespoons finely chopped chives |
| ½ teaspoon salt | |
| ¼ teaspoon white pepper | |
| 1½ cups finely chopped celery | |

Sauté cooked rice lightly in butter and add seasonings. When rice is hot fold in the chopped vegetables. These should be chopped to the consistency of coffee grounds. Serve immediately. Serves 4 to 6.

*RICE PILAF – II*

3 cups cooked long
    grain rice
½ cup butter
1 teaspoon salt
½ teaspoon white pepper
½ cup finely minced
    carrot
½ cup finely chopped
    celery

3 cups bean
    sprouts
2 tablespoons chopped
    pimiento
2 tablespoons chopped
    chives

Sauté rice in butter and add seasonings. When rice is hot add carrots, celery and bean sprouts. Mix thoroughly. Stir-fry a few seconds then stir in pimiento and chives. Serve immediately. Serves 6 to 8.

# Mexico

OUR NEIGHBORS to the south of us have developed a delightful cuisine, a blending of the primitive foods of the Mexican Indian with the foods and recipes brought from Spain by the conquistadores. It may vary from one state to another and certain areas, exposed to later cultures, often show a slight influence of the French, the Austrians or the Italians but, basically, Mexican food has not changed.

Like the Polynesians, the Mexicans love food, fun and flowers. They have the same love of music, dancing and a bit of imbibing to keep a party at the proper pitch. But where the Polynesians use any excuse for a party, the Mexican's expression of music, singing, dancing and artistry is more apt to be involved with his religion and linked up with a fiesta or carnival of which there are hundreds throughout the rural districts of Mexico.

There is a certain similarity between native Mexican and Polynesian ways of cooking. For instance, both cook fish in banana leaves; both have forms of underground cooking. While Tahitians and Hawaiians cook pigs, chickens, sweet potatoes and vegetables in banana and ti leaves underground, the Mexicans cook lamb in maguey leaves and suckling pigs in banana leaves in big pots lowered into barbecue pits heated with stones.

The Hawaiians have their lomi lomi, the Tahitians their poisson cru, and the Mexicans have their ceviche, which is also fish "cooked" in fresh lime juice. The seasonings may vary but the principle is the same and all are delicious to the initiated. In this country we eat raw oysters and cherrystone or littleneck clams on the half shell. The Japanese eat sashimi. So eating fish marinated in lime juice isn't as outlandish as it sounds.

The Mexicans use Spanish mackerel or corbina for their ceviche. The following recipe is basic but it can be varied with your own seasonings once you have made it and know what to expect. Green pepper may be added or wine vinegar and a little olive oil. A pinch of oregano would do the dish no harm.

*CEVICHE*

| | |
|---|---|
| 1 pound mahimahi, diced | 1 teaspoon white pepper |
| 1 teaspoon sugar | 4 dashes Tabasco sauce |
| 2 teaspoons salt | 2 tablespoons finely chopped onion |
| 1 teaspoon MSG | Juice of four large limes |
| 1 pinch oregano (optional) | 2 cups diced tomatoes |

Marinate raw, diced fish with seasonings and onion in lime juice for 3 to 4 hours. Add tomatoes and chill thoroughly before serving. This may be served with cocktails in small dishes with cocktail forks or as an opening course. If mahimahi is unavailable, any fine textured white fish may be used. Serves 8 as an opening course.

When the first Spaniards arrived in Mexico they found the natives wearing clothes woven of cotton or maguey fibers, living in stone or wooden houses with thatched roofs and worshiping in temples whose long robed priests offered human sacrifices to their gods. The natives lived on corn and beans which they cultivated, fish which they caught and bananas and papaya which grew wild. They had already discovered how to make an intoxicating drink known as pulque, made from the sap of the maguey plant. And they had already developed the tortilla, made from corn, and cooked their frijoles (beans) seasoned with chilies. It was the Spanish who brought the onion and garlic to Mexico. While the natives occasionally dined on quail and other native birds, they were mainly vegetarians.

The Spanish settlers had horses, cattle, pigs and chickens brought over from Spain. It was they who planted sugar cane,

rice, onions and garlic along with the Indians' corn and beans. Today, bananas, papayas, pineapples, sweet potatoes, squash, avocados, tomatoes, onions, rice, beans, fish, scallops, pork, chicken, beef, lamb and various kinds of peppers and chilies are the important ingredients in Mexican cooking.

On our first trip to Mexico, my wife and I, combining business with pleasure, spent a few days fishing and resting at Las Cruces in Baja California, and then went on to other parts of Mexico looking for interesting decorations and materials for a Mexican restaurant which I had simmering on the back of the stove.

Guadalajara, the second city of Mexico, is a manufacturing center, and a wonderful, modern, thriving community. It was a pleasure to see what a change in the political regime had accomplished in so short a time. Their museums, opera house and public libraries are outstanding.

We stayed at the Camino Real, a very modern hotel on the outskirts of the city, well operated with good food. Immediately adjoining Guadalajara, or a part of it, is Tlaquepaque (pronounced slockypocky), where all the crafts are centered. Here glassblowers, silversmiths, potters, weavers and all sorts of artisans gather and produce their wares. There are some outstanding weavers in Guadalajara and we bought some delightful cottons. There are a few nice stores where you can buy all kinds of gimcracks, glassware and decorations which you can use in your home if it has a Mexican slant.

By all means, spend an hour or two at the Mercado Libertad, the free market in Guadalajara. I wouldn't miss it for anything in the world. The first floor is made up of product stands selling all of the unusual vegetables and fruits available in Mexico, fish markets by the dozen selling oysters, all kinds of fish and odd little products of the sea which you never see anywhere else. There were a couple of sugar stands—sticky, lumpy, dark brown, light brown—all kinds of candies, guava paste and little doodads that looked real good. I wanted to sample a few of the things I saw but my better judgment said I shouldn't.

Then there was the bean man. He sold all kinds of beans, edible grain and rice—with or without rat poo. There were big beans, black beans, small beans, pink beans, red beans and speckled beans. He'd sell you two or three cents' worth or a sackful.

On the second floor are the cooked foods, prepared in stalls no larger than your dining room table. In one stall a little woman had a charcoal broiler made from a 5 gallon oil can. There was a variety of tired little pieces of meat which she broiled or stewed in all manner of funny little sauces. The aroma made us want to taste some of her wares but we didn't dare.

In another stall, a Mexican woman had a great pile of dough so high she could scarcely see over it. Three or four native women helped her pat the dough into tortillas, which she fried over a grill. Then there was the fellow who barbecued a pig and all of its insides. It had a golden brown color and he sold every bit of that pig but the squeal.

There were countless stalls where oysters on the half shell, from Mazatlán, and Gulf shrimp with odd sauces were sold. Another stall had dried possum and what looked like dried armadillos. There were strange little bunches of dried herbs, tied with string. The Mexicans, like the Chinese, are great for drying foods.

Everywhere there were baskets—broad baskets, bread baskets, big baskets, tiny baskets—baskets for every conceivable purpose. I bought some to use for light fixtures.

At the Mercado Libertad you can find anything you want. They have clothes, shoes, guns, knives—just anything you can imagine. If you go to Mexico, don't miss it.

In downtown Guadalajara, one floor up, overlooking the street, is a charming little restaurant called "Copa de Leche" (which means cup of milk). It is a good place for lunch. I had an excellent boiled beef tongue served with a sauce flavored with chocolate. They use a lot of chocolate in Guadalajara. I had it in enchiladas and with chicken.

There I also enjoyed Escabeche, a delicious mixture of fish, seasonings and vegetables. It is sort of a Mexican antipasto.

*FISH IN ESCABECHE SAUCE*

2 pounds small whole
  fish
Oil for deep-frying
2 cloves garlic
2 large onions
½ small can jalapeño
  chilies
½ cup olive oil
2 green peppers,
  chopped

¼ teaspoon cumin seed
½ teaspoon oregano
½ teaspoon peppercorns,
  crushed
2 teaspoons salt
2 bay leaves
1½ cups white wine
  vinegar
Pimiento
Ripe olives

Wash and clean small whole fish, such as sardines, smelts, mullet, etc. Leave heads and tails intact; roll in flour and fry in hot oil 5 to 10 seconds until lightly browned. Remove and arrange in earthenware or Pyrex casserole. Peel and mince garlic; peel and slice onions very thin; chop chilies. In a skillet heat olive oil and sauté garlic and onions until soft. Add peppers, seasonings and wine vinegar. Bring to a boil then simmer for 10 minutes. Pour over fish. Let cool, then cover and refrigerate 24 hours. To serve, garnish with pimiento and ripe olives. Serves 4 to 6.

The same sauce may be used for poached or baked fish fillets or steaks. It may also be used as a sauce, reducing the olive oil, for chicken and meat.

After we left Guadalajara we flew to Mexico City, which we made our headquarters for the rest of our trip. What I enjoy most in Mexico is the cultural background and the people in general. They are delightful and they are striding ahead after 400 years of political and religious oppression. In my opinion, and this is 1968, there is every indication that Mexico, twenty-five years from now, will be one of the great nations of the world.

Mexico City is a little Paris. The Museum of Modern Art there is superior to the ones in New York or San Francisco. The Folklore Ballet is simply beautiful. The Museum of National History is fabulous. We have nothing to compare with it.

We took numerous trips by car, most of them just for a day. Toluca we found to be an individual city with tremendous charm. The market is worth seeing. If you go there you will appreciate the everyday life and charm of the community. San Miguel and Guanajuato are worth seeing and by all means go south to Oaxaca which has a culture of Mixtec and Zapotec. This is where the fantastic black pottery and ceramics are made.

I wasn't very enthusiastic about Puerto Vallarta on my first visit. We stayed overnight in a place called Casa Barbara, up on a hill overlooking Puerto Vallarta, right in back of the old cathedral. We must have passed two dozen pigs on the way up.

There is nothing like waking up in the morning to the smell of pigs wafting in through the window.

There is a little beach where Mr. and Mrs. Wulff have a clothing shop. Nelly Wulff creates delightful cotton casuals and interesting accessories which are sold in the best shops throughout the United States. The Oceana Hotel, where you can breakfast and dine in the patio, was where all the social life in Puerto Vallarta took place. That was before the filming of *The Night of the Iguana.*

On our next trip, there was a whole new feeling in the town. It was well on its way to becoming one of the great places where people will make their summer homes. I saw about fifty or sixty homes under construction, along a beautiful shoreline, unequaled to anything in the North American continent. These homes ranged from 35,000 dollars to 150,000 dollars. Puerto Vallarta is going to be a great place for those who want to live a nice quiet existence.

Being an old-time saloonkeeper from way back, I am always curious, wherever I go, as to what the local people drink. I was particularly curious about the use of tequila in Mexico and I discovered a strange thing. While tequila is made in Mexico you just don't find many drinks made with it in Mexico. You may find a passable Margarita occasionally, or a Tequila Sunrise, but nowhere in Mexico do you find many tequila drinks worth drinking.

In these hot countries people drink tall gin drinks with lime and sugar. Occasionally you find tequila served with lime, sugar and soda, or it is just taken straight. In fact, you find more rum drinks than tequila drinks in Mexico City.

Aside from the Margarita, we have invented our own drinks and we sell more tequila in our Señor Pico restaurant in San Francisco than any restaurant in the world, including Mexico. We have some special rum drinks, too. Here are a few libations which you may enjoy:

*MARGARITA COCKTAIL* (PLATE XIII)

In a mixing glass with cracked ice:

Juice or ½ lime
½ ounce Triple Sec
1 ounce tequila

Shake and strain into a chilled champagne glass which has been edged with salt. To do this, rub the rim of the glass with a piece of lime, then dip the rim into a saucer of salt.

The Mexicans call their champagne glasses champañeros. We bought some amber-colored ones in Mexico—Mexican bubble glass. It was fun for a while serving cocktails in these glasses, which came in all sizes and heights and sometimes a little lop-sided—no two are ever alike—but it was so much trouble to import them and they broke at such a fantastic rate that we finally had to have them made for us in this country. I still think the Mexican glass has more charm but they just aren't practical for restaurant use.

*SEÑOR PICO TEQUILA DAIQUIRI* (PLATE XIII)

In a blender with 4 ounces of crushed ice:

Juice of ½ fresh lime                1 ounce Señor Pico
¼ ounce Triple Sec                      Tequila
1 level teaspoon bar
   sugar (fine)

Blend and strain into chilled cocktail glass with salt en-crusted rim.

*DURANGO*  (PLATE XIII)

In a double old-fashioned glass filled with cracked ice:

| | |
|---|---|
| 1½ ounces undiluted frozen grapefruit juice | Calistoga Natural Alkaline Water |
| 1½ ounces tequila | Mint |
| 1 teaspoon orgeat syrup | |

Shake grapefruit juice, tequila and orgeat syrup; fill glass with Calistoga water. Serve with a sprig of mint and a malt straw.

*EL DIABLO*

In a 10 ounce glass with cracked ice:

| | |
|---|---|
| Juice of ½ lime; drop shell in glass | ½ ounce crème de cassis |
| 1 ounce tequila | Ginger ale |

Squeeze lime and drop shell in glass. Add tequila and crème de cassis. Stir and fill glass with ginger ale. Serve with a malt straw.

*MARIA THERESA*

In mixing glass with cracked ice:

Juice of ½ lime
¾ ounce Ocean Spray "Cranberry House Mix."
1 ounce tequila

Shake thoroughly and strain into chilled cocktail glass.

*TEQUILA SUNRISE*

In a double old-fashioned glass with cracked ice:

| | |
|---|---|
| Juice of ½ lime; drop shell in glass | 1½ ounces tequila |
| 1 teaspoon grenadine | Sparkling water |
| ⅓ teaspoon crème de cassis | |

Squeeze lime and drop shell in glass. Add grenadine and crème de cassis and tequila. Stir and fill glass with sparkling water.

*SINALOA SCREWDRIVER*

In 10 ounce goblet with cracked ice:

| | |
|---|---|
| 3 ounces diluted frozen tangerine juice | 1½ ounces tequila |
| 1 bar spoon Triple Sec | 1 strip lemon peel |

Stir tangerine juice with Triple Sec and tequila. Add more ice to fill glass if necessary. Twist peel and drop in glass.

*SPANISH MOSS*

In cocktail shaker with cracked ice:

1 ounce Kahlua
1 ounce tequila
½ teaspoon green crème de menthe

Shake and strain into chilled bowl-shaped wine goblet. Serve with 1 cube of ice.

*BRAVE BULL*

In an old-fashioned glass with cracked ice:

1 ounce tequila
1 ounce Kahlua
1 strip lemon peel

Stir and twist lemon peel over drink; drop in glass.

*TEQUILA GIMLET*

In an old-fashioned glass with cracked ice:

½ ounce Rose's Lime Juice
1½ ounce tequila

Stir and serve.

*Variation:* Add 1 scant bar spoon green creme de menthe.


This drink got its name from the bleary-eyed parrot which seemingly perches on the edge of the glass. He's yours to take home at Señor Pico and customers walk out with handfuls of parrots. We serve the Potted Parrots in what we call a Ten Pin Pilsener, which holds around a pint of liquid. A double old-fashioned holds about the same, between 15 to 16 ounces. If you have neither, shake the drink in a cocktail shaker and pour into two regular old-fashioned or any 8 ounce glass. The drink won't have as much eye appeal but it will taste as good.

*POTTED PARROT* (PLATE XIII)

In a double old-fashioned glass full of shaved ice:

2 ounces orange juice
1 ounce lemon juice
¼ ounce orgeat syrup
¼ ounce rock candy
   syrup

½ ounce orange curaçao
2 ounces light rum

Hand shake and pour into a 16 ounce glass. Decorate with fresh mint and serve with a 12 inch straw.

## PINA FRIA

In blender glass with 1 scoop of shaved ice:

| | |
|---|---|
| 2 ounces unsweetened pineapple juice | 1 ounce lemon juice |
| 2 slices pineapple | 1 ounce light rum |

Blend thoroughly and serve in a 12 ounce glass with sprig of fresh mint and long malt straw.

## MEXICAN PRESIDENTE

In cocktail shaker with cracked ice:

| | |
|---|---|
| Juice of ½ lime | 1 ounce light rum |
| 1 dash curaçao | 1 strip orange peel |
| 1 dash grenadine | |
| ½ ounce French vermouth | |

Shake and strain into chilled cocktail glass. Add a twist of orange peel.

## COPA DE ORO

In blender glass with 1 scoop of shaved ice:

| | |
|---|---|
| Juice of 1 whole lime | 1 ounce gold rum |
| 1 teaspoon bar sugar | |
| 1 dash Maraschino liqueur | |

Blend and strain through medium mesh kitchen strainer into a large glass compote or champagne goblet. Top with a dash of Pernod (imported) or Herbsaint (domestic). Serve with cut straws.

One of Mexico's nice customs is the doctoring and chilling

of red wine. They call it Sangría and here is the Señor Pico version, very popular with everyone who tries it. It is served in a Mexican face pitcher.

## SANGRÍA  (PLATE XIII)

In a large pitcher with cracked ice:

1 fifth burgundy wine
3 ounces orange juice
2 ounces lemon juice
2 ounces rock candy
   syrup

1 small bottle sparkling
   water

Pour wine and juices over ice, add rock candy syrup and stir well or swizzle. Just before serving, give it another good stir and pour in the sparkling water, but don't stir it. Serve in large wine goblets.

# Texas

WHILE the customs and foods of Mexico are deeply rooted in all of the border states this is especially true of Texas, where Mexican vaqueros and their families work on the big ranches. Along with my quest for decorations and materials for my Mexican restaurant I sought food ideas and recipes. After much traveling, tasting and comparing, I finally came to the conclusion that Texas and New Mexico were my best sources.

Some of the Mexican recipes in this book have been adapted to American tastes. Others are authentic enough to satisfy the most confirmed seeker of authenticity. Many of these recipes have been given to me by Texans whose forebears settled in Texas long before it became the twenty-eighth state of the Union in 1845. What is most important, however, is that these recipes are good, as a thousand customers a day at Señor Pico in San Francisco have confirmed. I hope you enjoy them.

First of all, here are a few tidbits to accompany cocktails. My favorite, at the moment, anyhow, is Chile Con Queso, for which I designed a special container and little warming unit. You

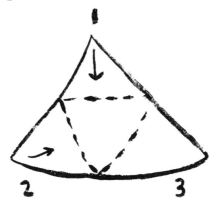

can use a fondue pot. Tostadas are simply deep fried triangles of tortillas which are used in many recipes and for dips. You can make your own or buy packaged tortilla chips under many brand names.

## RECIPES FROM TEXAS
## AND BORDER STATES

*CHILI CON QUESO* (*Chili with Cheese*)

3 cups half and half
¼ pound New York
   Cheddar, grated
½ pound Monterey Jack,
   grated
2 tablespoons minced
   onion
1 small clove garlic,
   minced
1 tablespoon butter

6 tablespoons white wine
¼ cup cornstarch mixed
   with
¼ cup cold water
¼ cup chopped jalapeño
   chilies
Salt, MSG and coarsely
   ground white pepper
   to taste

In the upper half of a double boiler heat the half and half; add grated cheese and set over low fire to melt. In a pan sauté the onion and garlic in the butter until onions are transparent. Add half of the wine to the garlic and onion pan, swish around and pour into the cheese mixture stirring well. (Meantime put hot water in bottom of double boiler and set over fire.) Thicken the cheese mixture with cornstarch and water, stirring constantly. Add chopped chilies, seasonings and rest of wine and mix thoroughly. Set over hot water until ready to use. Serve with tostada chips in fondue pot with cocktails. Makes 4½ cups dip.

While we use Guacamole primarily as a dip with tostadas or Fritos, it has many other delectable uses. For one, it makes a delicious molded salad, the recipe for which is given later. It makes a wonderful dressing for a platter of sliced tomatoes, Bermuda onions and cucumbers, and can be added to egg yolks for a distinguished stuffed egg. Be sure and keep the seed and

PLATE XIV. Mexican Chalupa Compuesta (luncheon salad), *page 205*

PLATE XV. Green Enchiladas with Sour Cream, *page 208*

PLATE XVI. Texan Sonofabitch Stew, *page 233*

bury it in the mix until serving time. This prevents the mixture from turning dark. At least it is supposed to. Sometimes a few traces escape its magic, but just stir it up. No one will notice.

*GUACAMOLE*

2 medium-sized ripe avocados
1 large tomato
1 tablespoon chopped white onion
2 ounces French dressing
1 teaspoon finely chopped Serrano chilies
½ teaspoon coriander seed, crushed
1 dash Tabasco sauce
Juice of ½ lime
Salt, pepper and MSG to taste
Tostada Basket

Peel avocados, cut in half and remove seeds. Peel tomato and chop fine. Put all ingredients, except Tostada Basket, in a mixing bowl. Break up avocado with a fork and stir with wire whip until avocado is almost smooth but still retains some of its original consistency. Serve in a Tostada Basket with tostada chips. Serves 4.

TOSTADA BASKETS are made by placing a tortilla in hot oil and then immediately shaping it with a two piece gadget used in making potato baskets. If you can't find one at your hardware store, try putting the tortilla between two wire strainers of appropriate size. The tortilla will hold its shape when it cools.

*TAQUITOS*

Some delicious and interesting hors d'oeuvres can be made from small soft tortillas, about three inches in diameter. Taquitos, meaning little tacos, are one of them. Put one teaspoon of Picadillo filling in the center of each little tortilla, fold over and skewer together with a toothpick. Deep fry in oil gently. They shouldn't be too crisp. While the following recipe would provide the filling for 120 to 125 Taquitos, the Picadillo will keep and has other uses. You can also prepare extra Taquitos and freeze them for future use.

*PICADILLO*

¼ pound ground beef
¼ pound ground pork
2 tablespoons minced onions
1 tablespoon oil
1 cup peeled, chopped tomatoes
1 clove garlic, minced
3 tablespoons wine vinegar
1 tablespoon sugar

½ teaspoon ground cumin
½ teaspoon salt
½ teaspoon MSG
2 tablespoons seedless raisins
1 tablespoon flour
2 tablespoons blanched, slivered almonds
2 tablespoons crushed walnuts

Sauté meat and onions in a little oil until onions are transparent. Add remaining ingredients with exception of the nuts. Cover and simmer half an hour, stirring occasionally. Stir in nuts last. Taste and correct seasonings. Let cool. Makes about 2½ cups.

*CHILI CHEESE BALLS*

3 tablespoons jalapeño chilies, chopped
½ pound grated Parmesan cheese

½ pound cream cheese
2 egg yolks

Be sure to clean the jalapeños well, removing oil and seeds. Mix ingredients together until they become smooth. Form the paste into marble-sized balls, ¾ to 1 inch in diameter. Spread white bread crumbs on a pastry board, then roll cheese balls in crumbs. Refrigerate first, then deep fry in oil. Makes approximately 3 dozen cheese balls.

This next tidbit is a Mexican version of the old melted cheese and cracker bit, with a bit of jalapeño pepper.

## NACHOS

24 small tortillas, 2 inches in diameter
¼ pound Cheddar cheese, grated
1 small size can jalapeño peppers

Deep fry tortillas. This makes them tostadas. Sprinkle tostadas with grated cheese and place on cookie sheet. Slip under broiler until cheese melts. To serve, top with one slice of jalapeño pepper.

Jalapeño peppers come in various sizes. The smallest available is a 6 ounce can from Mexico. They are packed in a jar in Los Angeles, contents 8 fluid ounces.

This next hors d'oeuvre calls for Flour Tortillas cut in quarters and folded over a cheese filling. You could use regular tortillas the same way or pie pastry. This is Señor Pico's Quesadilla.

## QUESADILLAS

½ pound New York Cheddar cheese
¼ cup chopped white onions
¼ cup chopped jalapeño peppers

3 dozen Flour Tortillas–8 inches in diameter
Oil for deep frying

Mix cheese, onions and peppers to a paste. Cut tortillas in quarter segments. Place a teaspoonful of filling in the center and fold ends over as illustrated. Skewer with a toothpick. Deep fry until golden brown. Remove toothpick before serving. Makes 12 dozen Quesadillas. *Note:* Picadillo or any highly seasoned seafood filling can be used in place of the cheese mixture for variety.

You can buy Flour Tortillas as well as the regular Mexican corn tortillas from Mexican grocery stores or, sometimes, in the freezing departments of the larger markets. If you are unable to find them you can make your own. Make them in small batches at a time for easier handling.

*FLOUR TORTILLAS*

| | |
|---|---|
| 2 cups white flour | 2½ tablespoons lard |
| ½ teaspoon salt | Warm water |

Sift flour and salt together; add the lard and enough water to form a soft dough. Divide into balls about 2 inches in diameter and let rest on a floured pastry board for about 20 minutes. Roll balls out as thin as possible—about ⅛ of an inch thick— and cut in eight inch rounds. You can cut around a salad plate of suitable size. Bake on an ungreased baking sheet or griddle 2 minutes on each side, turning with a pancake turner. They should bake but not brown. Stack and wrap in a clean cloth, then put in a Pliofilm bag until ready to use. Makes 6 Tortillas.

*EMPANADAS*

| | |
|---|---|
| 2 cups flour | ⅔ cup lard |
| 1 teaspoon salt | 5   tablespoons ice water |

Sift flour and salt together into a bowl. Cut half of the shortening into the flour mixture with a pastry blender until it is like fine cornmeal. Cut the remaining half of the lard into the dough until it is about the size of peas. Add the ice water, blend lightly into the dough with a fork. Gather the dough into a ball and roll out a half at a time. Cut in 3 inch circles. Put about 2 teaspoons filling on one side of each circle of dough.

Dampen the edges and fold over. Mark with tines of a fork to seal and fry in deep fat until golden brown. Makes about 2 dozen.

FILLING FOR EMPANADAS

½ pound mahimahi or
  other white fish
2 tablespoons chopped
  onion
½ clove of garlic, minced
2 tablespoons oil
Dash of white wine
2 teaspoons flour
½ teaspoon salt

¼ teaspoon pepper
1½ tablespoons fish or
  chicken stock
2 teaspoons minced
  jalapeño pepper
2 teaspoons minced
  green onion
1 tablespoon crushed
  almonds

Chop mahimahi and sauté with onion and garlic in oil until about half cooked. Add a dash of wine, blend in flour, add salt and pepper and stir, then stir in liquid. Remove from fire and add peppers, green onions and almonds.

Empanadas, of course, may have other fillings—meat, chicken or cheese with nuts, onions, and chopped chili peppers. They can even be baked instead of fried in deep fat. After all, they are just little Mexican turnovers.

Refried beans make a wonderful cocktail dip. Leftover refried beans can be frozen and used for bean dips at a later date. Canned refried beans are now on the market and they are excellent for this purpose.

REFRIED BEAN DIP

1 can refried beans
½ teaspoon chili powder
3 dashes Tabasco sauce
2 tablespoons finely
  chopped onion

2 heaping tablespoons
  sour cream
Salt to taste

Mix ingredients well in a bowl and refrigerate at least one hour before serving. Serve with tostadas or corn chips.

You can experiment with the seasonings of the bean dip with

chopped jalapeño peppers instead or in addition to the chili powder. Taste as you go so you don't get it too pepper hot.

There are many variations for Gazpacho, the cold soup of Mexico, including the addition of diced avocado, a mixture of chopped fresh herbs, or a dollop of sour cream. These are refinements to be explored. This is a basic recipe.

*GAZPACHO SOUP*

| | |
|---|---|
| 1 clove garlic, cut | 2 tablespoons olive oil |
| 3 cups peeled, seeded, finely chopped tomatoes | 2 teaspoons lemon juice |
| | 1 teaspoon salt |
| 1 cucumber, peeled, seeded and chopped | ¼ teaspoon white pepper |
| | 1 dash Tabasco sauce |
| 4 tablespoons minced green pepper | 1 cup chilled tomato juice |
| ½ cup chopped Bermuda onions | ¼ cup chopped parsley |

Rub mixing bowl with garlic, add tomatoes, cucumbers, green pepper and onion and mix well. Add olive oil, lemon juice and seasonings. Stir well, cover and chill for at least 4 hours. Before serving, add the chilled tomato juice and mix thoroughly. Serve in chilled bowls with 2 ice cubes in each. Top with chopped parsley. Makes 5 to 5½ cups.

Albondiga means meatball in Mexico. This is a soup made with meatballs, wonderful for lunch with a green salad and French bread, and plenty of red wine.

*ALBONDIGA SOUP*

SOUP

| | |
|---|---|
| ½ cup finely chopped onion | ⅔ cup peeled, chopped tomatoes |
| 1 clove garlic, minced | 2 quarts beef consommé |
| 2 tablespoons oil | Meatballs |
| 1 teaspoon chili powder | |

Sauté onions and garlic in oil until limp and transparent. Add chili and chopped tomatoes and let cook a few moments with the onions and garlic. Add consommé and bring to a boil. Let simmer while you prepare the little albondigas.

MEATBALLS (ALBONDIGAS)

½ pound ground beef
½ pound ground pork
½ cup cooked rice
1 tablespoon cornstarch
⅛ teaspoon garlic
 powder

¼ teaspoon oregano
1 teaspoon salt
¼ teaspoon pepper
1 egg
¼ cup chopped cilantro
 (Chinese parsley)

Mix meat and rice in mixing bowl. Add cornstarch, seasonings and slightly beaten egg. Mix thoroughly by hand and shape into balls about the size of a walnut. Bring broth to a boil; drop balls into boiling broth. Cover and cook about 30 minutes. Serves 6 to 8. To serve pour into Mexican pottery bowl and ladle out into individual pottery bowls, putting several meatballs in each bowl, and sprinkle with a little chopped cilantro.

*AZTEC SOUP*

½ cup chopped onion
Butter for sautéeing
½ cup chopped okra
4 tablespoons chopped
 celery leaves
2 teaspoons crushed
 basil leaves
3 quarts chicken stock
1 tablespoon tomato
 paste

Salt and pepper to taste
½ cup sherry
½ cup cooked, diced
 calf brains
Tostada slices
Avocado
Pasilla chili

Sauté onions and okra in butter until onions are limp but not browned. Stir in celery leaves and basil for a second or two, then add chicken stock mixed with the tomato paste. Add salt and pepper and bring to a boil. Let simmer half an hour. Add sherry, calf brains and let simmer until ready to serve. Correct seasonings and ladle soup into bowls over 1 tablespoon tostada slices, and 1 tablespoon diced avocado. Sprinkle lightly with Pasilla chili. Makes about 14 cups of soup.

*VERA CRUZ FISH SOUP*

FISH STOCK

| | |
|---|---|
| 2 pounds fish heads, tails and bones | 1 cup chopped celery |
| 4 quarts water | 2 teaspoons salt |
| 1 bay leaf | ½ teaspoon pepper |
| ½ teaspoon oregano | 2 teaspoons MSG |
| 1 cup chopped onions | 1 cup white wine |

Place fish heads, tails and bones in a soup kettle. Add cold water and rest of ingredients except wine. Bring to a boil. Add wine and continue to cook for an hour. Discard bones. Lay a cloth in a colander over another pot and strain, mashing onions and celery to a dry pulp.

FINISHED SOUP

| | |
|---|---|
| Strained soup stock (about 8 cups) | 4 tablespoons chopped celery leaves |
| 1 cup chopped tomatoes | Salt, pepper to taste |
| 2 tablespoons flour | |
| 2 cups diced mahimahi or halibut | |

Bring fish stock to a boil; add chopped tomatoes and thicken slightly with flour mixed with a little cold water. Add the diced fish and celery leaves. Bring to a boil and simmer 20 minutes, or until fish is done. Correct seasonings. Makes about 11 cups.

Rice is served in Mexico almost as often as refried beans. No matter what else is served, it is always—or nearly always—accompanied by rice. Enchiladas, tacos, tamales, meat always seem to be flanked by the inevitable beans and rice.

*MEXICAN RICE*

| | |
|---|---|
| 2 cups long grain rice | 3–3¼ cups hot chicken |
| ¼ cup butter | stock |
| ½ cup chopped onions | 1 teaspoon salt |
| 1 clove garlic, minced | ½ teaspoon MSG |
| 2 tablespoons chopped | ¼ teaspoon white pepper |
| green pepper | |
| 1 can tomato sauce—✳300 | |

Sauté rice in butter until thoroughly coated. Add onion, garlic and green pepper and sauté until onion is transparent. Keep stirring to let rice turn color evenly. Add tomato sauce and cook until heated, then add chicken stock. Cover and cook over low heat for 20 minutes. Season to taste. Serves 6.

Refried beans is one of the national dishes of Mexico. No matter where you go, or what hour of the day, refried beans will turn up—at breakfast with your eggs, at the bullfights tucked into a tortilla, at luncheon or dinner. They are mashed cooked beans, but only certain beans are suitable. Pinto or Mexican red beans are the best. As the name implies, they may be refrigerated and reheated as required.

*SENOR PICO'S REFRIED BEANS*

| | |
|---|---|
| 1 pound pinto beans | Salt to taste |
| ¼ pound salt pork, diced | ½ cup lard for frying |
| 2 cloves garlic, chopped | (or bacon fat) |
| 1 large onion, chopped | Cheddar cheese |
| Boiling chicken stock to | |
| cover | |

Soak beans in water overnight. In the morning drain water off beans. In a large cooking pot, sauté the salt pork, add the garlic and onions; stir constantly until garlic is golden and the onions are transparent. Add drained beans to pork mixture and stir to coat the beans with the fat. Add boiling chicken stock to cover beans, stir once more and bring to a boil. Cover and simmer, stirring from time to time to be sure beans won't stick to the bottom of the pot. Simmer for 4 hours, stirring occasionally. When done, season with salt to taste and let cook 10 minutes more. Drain beans, saving the liquid.

Heat a large skillet or heavy kettle and add lard or bacon fat. Add some of the beans to the hot fat and mash thoroughly. Keep adding more beans and mashing, then add some of the liquid and more beans until all of the beans and liquid are used. Keep stirring and cooking until mashed bean mixture is thick. To serve, top with grated Cheddar cheese. Serves 6.

Tacos are one of Mexico's most delightful between meal snacks, found at bus stops, lunch counters and roadside stands throughout the country. A taco is a tortilla folded and fried crisp and filled with meat or chicken, garnished with sauce, shredded lettuce, sliced radishes and grated sharp cheese. The Mexicans sometimes fill their tacos and then fry them but I think this makes them too greasy. I like the tortillas fried crisp into a proper shape, drained on paper towels and then filled. You can stand the taco shells in a pan in the oven to keep warm and use as needed. If you want to prepare tacos for luncheon or an afternoon snack provide bowls of the garnishes and sauce and let guests finish their own tacos. They're great with cold beer. While the fillings most often used are beef or chicken, you can use refried beans with onions, Picadillo or enchilada fillings if they are a little on the dry side.

*BEEF TACOS*

| | |
|---|---|
| 2 chorizos (Mexican sausage) | 2 tablespoons white vinegar |
| 1 large onion, chopped | 1 teaspoon salt |
| 3 tablespoons oil | ¼ teaspoon pepper |
| 1 pound ground beef | 2 cups enchilada sauce |
| 1 teaspoon chili powder | 12 tortillas |

Peel and crumble chorizos. Sauté onion in oil until limp, add chorizos and beef and sauté until beef is crumbly and has lost its redness. Add chili powder, vinegar, salt and pepper. Stir well and let simmer for a few minutes. Add enchilada sauce, mix well, cover and let simmer for about 1 hour. Meanwhile fry the tortillas in oil and quickly fold together. Dip in hot oil again, holding the tortilla with tongs. Remove and let cool. As they cool they should become crisp. When meat mixture has simmered for an hour, remove cover and let cook until almost dry. Fill fried tacos and let individuals apply garnishes. Allow 2 per person. Serves 6.

GARNISHES FOR 12 TACOS

1½ cups shredded lettuce
1 cup grated Wisconsin
   Cheddar cheese

1 cup Salsa
½ cup sliced radishes

*CHICKEN TACOS*

1 large onion, chopped
   fine
2 tablespoons oil
2 cups coarsely chopped
   cooked chicken

1 cup Red Enchilada
   Sauce
½ teaspoon salt
12 tortillas, fried and
   shaped

Sauté onions in oil until limp; add chopped chicken and mix well. Add Enchilada Sauce, and salt; let simmer until mixture is almost dry. Fill prepared tacos and garnish. Serve 2 tacos per person. Serves 6.

*SALSA*

2 large tomatoes,
   chopped
3 canned California
   chilies, chopped
1 large onion, finely
   chopped

1 tablespoon chopped
   fresh coriander
1 teaspoon minced garlic
1 teaspoon salt
½ teaspoon pepper
Juice of 1 lemon

Combine all ingredients. A tablespoon of olive oil may be added. This will keep in a jar in the refrigerator a couple of days.

*TOMATO TABLE SAUCE*

10 small fresh green
   chilies
1 medium-sized white
   onion
2 cloves garlic
1 tablespoon chopped
   cilantro

10 peeled tomatoes,
   chopped
2 tablespoons vinegar
2 tablespoons olive oil
½ teaspoon Tabasco sauce
Salt to taste

Clean chilies and mince; chop onion very fine; mince garlic. Combine chilies, onion and garlic and add cilantro (Chinese parsley). Add tomatoes and remaining ingredients. Mix and store in covered glass containers in refrigerator.

A chalupa is Mexico's answer to the open-faced sandwich, built on a crisp fried tortilla. When made on 3 inch tortillas it is more like a canapé and serves about the same purpose. It can be any size, any shape and made from refried beans, Picadillo, chorizos and grated cheese, chopped pork or chicken or a combination of any of these goodies, to achieve a sort of Mexican Dagwood.

Here is a luncheon salad built on a fried tortilla. In case you are wondering, compuesta means composed. With it serve cold Mexican beer with a simple dessert like Flan or coffee ice cream sprinkled with grated bittersweet chocolate.

*CHALUPA COMPUESTA SALAD*   (PLATE XIV)

| | |
|---|---|
| Lettuce leaves | 1½ cups Guacamole |
| 6 cups shredded lettuce | 6 green pepper rings |
| 6 tortillas, fried crisp | 18 thinly sliced onion |
| 3 cups refried beans | rings |
| ¾ cup grated Cheddar | 6 ripe olives, pitted |
| cheese | 6 small ripe tomatoes, |
| 1½ cups shredded, cooked | quartered |
| white chicken meat *OR* | |
| 1½ cups cooked, peeled | |
| and deveined shrimp | |

Cover bottom of 6 dinner-sized plates with lettuce leaves and ½ cup each of shredded lettuce. Place tortillas on cookie sheet and cover each with ½ cup refried beans. On top of the beans sprinkle 2 tablespoons grated Cheddar cheese; slip cookie sheet under broiler until cheese melts. Place a tortilla with beans and cheese on top of shredded lettuce on each plate. Sprinkle each with another ½ cup of shredded lettuce, then add ¼ cup shredded chicken or shrimp. Top each salad with ¼ cup Guacamole; garnish with green pepper ring and 3 onion rings; top with ripe olive. Arrange 4 tomato quarters around base of each salad. Serve with Salsa (red tomato sauce) on the side. Serves 6.

Enchiladas are tortillas with meat, cheese or chicken fillings. They are rolled and baked until hot, then served with various highly seasoned sauces. The sauces are either made with a tomato base and red chilies, or made with Mexican green tomatoes and green chilies. First fry the tortillas in oil until soft and pliable—not crisp. Drain and dip into the sauce, coating both sides completely. Place the filling in the center of the tortilla, then roll and place in a greased baking dish, with the overlapped edges down. Heat in a moderate oven, 375° F. When heated through, pour hot enchilada sauce over them and top with grated Wisconsin Cheddar cheese.

*RED ENCHILADA SAUCE*

| | |
|---|---|
| 1 cup chopped onions | 1 cup flour |
| 2 teaspoons garlic | ¼ cup salt |
| 2 tablespoons oil | 2 tablespoons MSG |
| 2½ quarts boiling broth | ¼ cup oil |
| 6 tablespoons Gebhardt's Chili Powder | 2 small cans Las Palmas Chili Sauce |

Sauté onions and garlic together in 2 tablespoons oil. When onions are transparent, add to boiling broth. Mix all other ingredients with the Las Palmas Chili Sauce to make a heavy paste. Reduce with some of the broth to pouring consistency, to avoid the possibility of lumping, and gradually stir into the hot broth. Stir for five minutes, then let simmer for another 10 minutes. Makes about 4 quarts of sauce.

*FILLING FOR CHICKEN ENCHILADAS*

| | |
|---|---|
| 4½ cups cooked chicken, coarsely chopped | 1 cup enchilada sauce |
| ½ cup cooked chopped onions | 2 teaspoons salt |
| | 2 teaspoons MSG |
| ¼ cup chopped ripe olives | 1½ cups grated Cheddar cheese |
| | 12 tortillas |

Mix all ingredients. Put about half a cup of filling in each tortilla (fried soft), roll and place overlapped side down in greased baking dish. Bake in a moderately hot oven, 375° F. until heated through. Meanwhile, reheat sauce. When enchiladas are hot, spoon sauce over them and sprinkle each with 2 tablespoons grated cheddar cheese. Allow 2 enchiladas per person.

To make beef enchiladas, simply substitute coarsely chopped cooked beef for the chopped chicken. However, if you are inspired to make enchiladas on a sudden impulse and have no cooked beef on hand, here is a recipe using ground beef.

*GROUND BEEF ENCHILADAS*

| | |
|---|---|
| 1½ pounds ground beef | 2 teaspoons MSG |
| ¾ cup chopped onions | 12 tortillas |
| 3 tablespoons oil | ¼ cup chopped ripe |
| 3 cups Red Enchilada | olives |
| Sauce, heated | 1½ cups grated Cheddar |
| Pinch of cumin seed | cheese |
| 2 teaspoons salt | |

Sauté meat and onions in oil until meat is crumbly and the onions are limp; add 1½ cups of the enchilada sauce, the cumin, salt and MSG and let simmer ½ an hour. Meanwhile, fry tortillas until they are soft and pliable; dip fried tortillas in the other 1½ cups of enchilada sauce. Back to the meat mixture, add the ripe olives, then divide mixture among the 12 tortillas. Roll and place overlapped sides down in greased baking dish. Spoon the balance of the enchilada sauce over the enchiladas and bake in moderate oven 375° F. for 20 minutes. Remove from oven and sprinkle with grated cheese. Serve with refried beans. Allow 2 enchiladas per person. Serves 6.

A Mexican-style meal can be put together in minutes if you keep tortillas in the freezer, sauce in the refrigerator at all times and instant rice on the shelves. The fillings can be varied, such as cream cheese, chopped Poblano chilies, chopped black olives and chopped canned chicken. Pork can be used in place of chicken or beef. Avocados, shrimp, onions and chili powder, or Guacamole with chicken or shrimp can be used for fillings. Experiment. Try something different!

*CHEESE ENCHILADAS*   (PLATE XV)

| | |
|---|---|
| 2 cups cottage cheese | 2 tablespoons chopped |
| 1 pound New York white | jalapeño chilies |
| Cheddar, shredded | 1 teaspoon salt |
| ¼ cup chopped cooked | 1 teaspoon MSG |
| onions | 12 tortillas |
| ¼ cup crushed tostadas | Red or Green Enchilada |
| 2 tablespoons chopped | Sauce |
| olives | Oil |

Mix cheeses, onions, tostadas, olives and chilies; add seasonings. Fry tortillas in oil until soft and pliable—not crisp. Drain and dip into whichever sauce is being used, coating both sides completely. Place filling in center of prepared tortillas and roll. Place in greased baking dish with overlapped edges down.

If you are using Red Enchilada Sauce, pour hot sauce over enchiladas and top with grated Wisconsin Cheddar cheese. Bake in moderate oven, 350° F., until thoroughly heated and cheese has melted. Serves 6, allowing 2 per person.

If you are using Green Enchilada Sauce, pour sauce over rolled cheese enchiladas and bake in moderate oven until piping hot—*without* cheese. Top with sour cream AFTER removing enchiladas from oven.

*GREEN ENCHILADA SAUCE*   (PLATE XV)

| | |
|---|---|
| 2 cans cream of | 1 can chicken broth |
| mushroom soup | ½ cup raw puréed |
| (Campbell's) | spinach |
| 1 small can Ortega | ½ teaspoon salt |
| chilies (3½ ounces) | 1 teaspoon MSG |
| 1 large onion, chopped | 2 tablespoons flour |
| 1 clove garlic, minced | ½ pint sour cream |

Purée mushroom soup, chilies, onion and garlic in blender. Add to chicken broth and bring to a boil. Add puréed spinach and seasonings and let simmer 10 to 15 minutes. Thicken with flour mixed with a little cold water. Stir into sauce and bring to a boil. Reduce heat and stir constantly to avoid lumping. Correct seasonings and pour over basic Cheese Enchiladas and bake in moderate oven. Top with sour cream before serving.

Tamales are probably best known of all Mexican dishes. If you live where you can buy the prepared masa, corn husks and other Mexican specialties, there is no reason why you can't have fun making your own. And you might as well make a quantity of them, if you have a freezer. They can be frozen and steamed as needed.

The procedure is to buy the coarse prepared tamale masa and prepare it for lining the corn husks. Then the filling is put in the center of each husk, the husks are rolled firmly and tied. Here are the ingredients and instructions for 35 medium-sized tamales.

### SEÑOR PICO'S TAMALES

MASA

| | |
|---|---|
| 2–2¼ pounds corn husks | 1 tablespoon Gebhardt's |
| 1 pound lard | Chili Powder |
| 7 pounds coarse tamale | 1 cup Las Palmas Chili |
| masa | Sauce |
| 3 tablespoons salt | 1 cup chicken broth |
| 2 tablespoons MSG | |

Separate and clean any stray corn silk from husks. Soak in warm water for 15 minutes. Place lard in mixing bowl and whip at high speed; gradually add the prepared masa, then salt, MSG, chili powder, chili sauce and chicken broth. Beat to the consistency of whipped cream. Test masa by placing a spoonful in cold water. If it floats to the surface, it is ready for the tamale preparation. Lay husks, according to size, tip to base and base to tip, reversing them as needed. Spread masa to a thickness of approximately ⅛ thick and 3 inches long, leaving the tip and base bare. Place filling in center of husks, then roll together firmly. Tie ends securely with raffia or string. Cut off excess husks to make a neat tamale.

At Señor Pico we have a "tying jig" that facilitates the tying of the tamales. If you become a tamale buff it would be easy to have one made out of wood.

*TAMALE FILLING*

½ pound ground pork
¼ cup oil
1 clove garlic, minced
¼ cup finely chopped onions
1 cup chicken stock
1 small can tomato paste
2 teaspoons salt
2 teaspoons MSG

2 teaspoons Gebhardt's Chili Powder
1 can Las Palmas Chili Sauce (10 ounces)
½ cup masa
¼ cup flour
2 cups diced boiled beef or other meat
Salt cured black olives

Sauté pork in oil, add garlic and onion and cook until transparent and limp. In saucepan heat chicken stock, add pork and onion mixture, tomato paste, seasonings and chili sauce. Let simmer 15 to 20 minutes to develop flavor. Thicken with masa and the flour, mixed with cold water, stirring constantly to make a smooth, thick sauce. Add beef and then let cool. Put 2 heaping spoonfuls of meat and sauce on prepared husks, add 2 salt cured black olives, roll tamale and tie. Steam above boiling water in tightly closed steamer for 1 hour. Note: Diced cooked turkey or chicken or a mixture of both, or veal may be substituted for the beef. Picadillo may also be used. Enough filling for 35 medium-sized tamales.

*TAMALITOS*

Should you have more filling than you need, make tiny tamales, using small husks, prepared the same way as for the large ones. Spread masa on husks, add filling and roll together firmly. Tie ends with raffia or string. These may be steamed for immediate use or frozen until needed. To serve, steam for half an hour, snip off one end and serve hot with cocktails. Guests take a bite and scrape the filling into their mouths, something like eating an artichoke leaf.

In Mexico, chili rellenos, or stuffed chili peppers, are made with Poblano chilies. Here in the United States you can buy canned Poblano chilies from Mexican grocery stores. If unavailable in your area, you can substitute bell peppers or canned green peppers.

Standard procedure for Chili Rellenos is to stuff the pepper, dredge it with flour, dip it in batter and deep-fry in oil. After eating hundreds of Chili Rellenos from here to Mexico, I decided that there must be a better way to do it, so we experimented. We bake our Chili Rellenos at Señor Pico. The restaurant process is too complicated for home use and requires special equipment, but you can try it using individual baking dishes for each Chili Relleno.

*CHILI RELLENOS CON QUESO*

| | |
|---|---|
| 6 canned Poblano chilies | Flour |
| 6 pieces of Monterey Jack cheese, ½″×½″× 2″ | 1 cup egg whites (about 8) |
| 6 pieces of New York Cheddar cheese, ½″×½″×2″ | ½ cup egg yolks (about 6) |
| | 4 tablespoons melted butter |

Drain chilies thoroughly. Put a piece of Jack cheese and a piece of cheddar in each pepper. Dust with flour. Preheat oven to 375° F. Beat egg whites until stiff. Beat egg yolks and then combine the two. Just before you are ready to coat the stuffed peppers, add melted butter to egg mixture. Be sure it is just melted, not hot. Meanwhile, oil 6 individual baking dishes. Pour a thick coating of batter into the baking dishes, lay the stuffed peppers in the batter, then spoon the rest of the batter on top. Bake for 15 minutes. Serves 6.

To serve, remove Chili Relleno from baking dish with spatula to plate and top with Chili Relleno sauce. Serve with an enchilada or tamale (or both) and refried beans and rice.

### SAUCE FOR CHILI RELLENOS

½ cup chopped onions
1 clove garlic, minced
1 tablespoon oil
2 tablespoons tomato
   paste
1 cup chopped tomatoes

1 can beef broth (1⅓ cups)
1 teaspoon sugar
½ teaspoon salt
1 teaspoon vinegar
1 tablespoon flour

Sauté onions and garlic in oil until onions are transparent; add tomato paste and chopped tomatoes and let simmer a few moments. Add broth, sugar, salt and vinegar. Let simmer until tomatoes have disintegrated, then put through food mill or in blender. Reheat and thicken lightly with flour mixed with a little cold water. Stir and bring to a boil. Serve over Chili Rellenos.

In case you prefer to deep-fry your Chili Rellenos, here is a Mexican recipe. The filling may be meat or cheese. The procedure is the same.

## MEXICAN CHILI RELLENOS

FILLING

2 onions, chopped
2 tablespoons oil
½ pound ground beef
½ pound ground pork
1 cup chopped tomatoes
1 teaspoon salt
½ teaspoon pepper
½ teaspoon ground
   cinnamon

½ teaspoon chopped
   candied citron
2 tablespoons vinegar
2 tablespoons chopped
   blanched almonds
2 tablespoons chopped
   pine nuts

Sauté onions in oil until transparent, then add ground meat. Stir until meat is crumbly and cooked, then add chopped tomatoes, seasonings, citron, vinegar and nuts. Let simmer over low heat until thick.

PREPARATION OF CHILIES

4 eggs
12 canned Poblano chilies

½ cup flour
Oil for frying

Beat egg whites until stiff; beat egg yolks and combine the two. Stuff Poblanos with meat filling. Cover them well with flour, and then roll in egg batter and fry in deep fat at 375° F. until golden brown. Remove, drain on paper towels and place in sauce. Boil up and serve.

SAUCE

1 onion, chopped
1 tablespoon oil
1½ pounds chopped
   tomatoes
1 piece stick cinnamon
1 cup beef stock or
   consommé

1 teaspoon salt
¼ teaspoon pepper
3 tablespoons chopped
   parsley

Sauté onion in oil until transparent, add chopped tomatoes

and cinnamon and let simmer until tomatoes are mushy. Remove cinnamon and purée. Reheat, add beef stock, salt and pepper. Simmer until thickened. Add fried chilies, boil up once and serve. Garnish with chopped parsley.

## CHILI RELLENOS WITH REFRIED BEANS

| | |
|---|---|
| 2 tablespoons finely chopped onion | 3 dashes Tabasco sauce |
| 2 tablespoons tomato paste | Salt and pepper to taste |
| 1 tablespoon oil | 6 canned Poblano chilies |
| ½ teaspoon oregano | Egg batter and flour |
| 2 cups refried beans | ½ cup sour cream |
| | 4 ounces grated Cheddar cheese |

Sauté chopped onions and tomato paste in oil, add oregano and let cook a few seconds, then add beans and seasonings. Blend and let cook a few minutes. Stuff chilies with bean mixture. Flour well and roll in egg batter (see previous recipe for instructions). Deep-fry in oil until golden brown. Remove and drain on paper towels. Arrange in greased baking dish. Cover with sour cream and grated cheese. Bake in 350° F. oven until lightly browned. Serves 6.

Tortillas are the staff of life throughout Mexico so you have tortillas with your breakfast eggs. This dish is said to have originated on the cattle ranches of Durango. Nice way to start the day anywhere.

## HUEVOS RANCHEROS

| | |
|---|---|
| 12 eggs | 1¾ cups Ranchero Sauce |
| Butter for frying | Salt and pepper |
| 6 tortillas | |

Fry eggs in frying pan in butter. Heat tortillas on griddle or in skillet but don't let them get crisp. Put one on each heated breakfast plate. Heat sauce, if it has been made ahead of time. Pour sauce over eggs and let cook a few seconds, then lift eggs onto tortillas and spoon some of the sauce over them. Allow two eggs per serving. Eggs may be poached in the sauce and served the same way. Crisp fried bacon or small fried sausages may be served on the side or you can do it the Mexican way and serve rice and refried beans with the eggs. Serves 6.

*RANCHERO SAUCE*

| | |
|---|---|
| 1 clove garlic, minced | 1 can Spanish-style |
| 1 tablespoon oil | tomato sauce (1¾ |
| 1 small green chili, | cups) |
| chopped | Salt and pepper to taste |

Sauté garlic in oil and add chopped chili (canned is easiest). Add tomato sauce and let simmer. Season with salt and pepper.

*SEÑOR PICO CHICKEN*

| | |
|---|---|
| 2 young chickens, 2–2¼ | Bread crumbs |
| pounds each | Oil |
| Salt, pepper and MSG | 2 carrots, finely diced |
| 4 slices capocollo, ⅟₁₆″ | 2 stalks celery, chopped |
| thick | ½ cup chopped onions |
| 2 pieces Monterey Jack, | ½ cup white wine |
| 2½″×1½″×½″ | ½ cup chicken stock |
| Flour for coating | |
| 2 eggs beaten with | |
| ¼ cup water | |

Split chickens, crack backbone. Remove ribs. Season with

salt, pepper and MSG. Place one piece of capocollo and one piece of Monterey Jack cheese on one half of each chicken half and fold over. Skewer or tie together with string. Dust with flour, dip in egg wash and then in crumbs. Sauté in hot oil in large skillet, turning frequently so the pieces brown evenly. When browned, remove to roasting pan or large casserole. In same skillet, sauté carrots, celery and onions until tender. Add to chicken in roasting pan. Wash out skillet with wine and add to chicken. Cover and let cook 30 minutes or until tender. Remove chicken to heated serving platter and keep warm in oven. Make sauce in roasting pan, using drippings and vegetables. Serves 4.

SAUCE FOR SEÑOR PICO CHICKEN

| | |
|---|---|
| 1 tablespoon Dijon mustard | ½ cup white wine |
| 1 small can tomato sauce | Chicken broth |
| ½ teaspoon MSG | 2 tablespoons cornstarch |
| ½ teaspoon salt | mixed with |
| ¼ teaspoon pepper | ¼ cup cold water |
| ½ teaspoon Worcestershire sauce | |

Sieve vegetables in roasting pan, then return to make sauce. Add mustard, tomato sauce, MSG, salt, pepper, Worcestershire sauce and wine. Stir well and add chicken broth to make 4 cups of liquid. Thicken with cornstarch mixture. Simmer a few moments, stirring constantly, and pour over chicken.

*MEXICAN BROILED CHICKEN*

| | |
|---|---|
| 3 chickens, 2¼ pounds each | ½ cup leaf oregano |
| ½ teaspoon Gebhardt's Chili Powder | 4 tablespoons salt |
| | 4 tablespoons MSG |
| | 1 quart oil |

Clean and split chickens. Mix chili powder, oregano, salt, MSG and oil in enamel or glass pan. Arrange 6 chicken halves in pan and let marinate 12 hours, turning occasionally. When ready to cook, place on broiler, skin side down. Broil 15 minutes, basting occasionally with marinade. Turn chickens and broil 5 to 10 minutes more, brushing the skin with the marinade until chickens are brown. Serves 6.

## MEXICAN MEAT ON A SWORD

2 pounds top round steak
Flour
Oil
Salt, pepper and MSG
6 tablespoons chopped
   onion

6 tablespoons julienned
   Poblano peppers
4 metal skewers

Cut steak into 4 servings and pound with a meat mallet. Dust steak with flour and fry in oil in *hot* skillet. Turn and season. Meanwhile, in a separate pan, sauté onions and Poblano peppers together. Let cook and stir until onions are transparent and soft. When steak is done, place 3 tablespoons of the onion and pepper mixture on each steak and roll. Secure with skewer and serve with Mexican Rice and refried beans. Serves 4.

## RABBIT MEXICAN STYLE

2 rabbits, 1–1½ pounds
   each
½ cup peanut oil

2 small chili peppers
2 garlic cloves, crushed
Flour

Cut legs from rabbits and cut backs in three pieces. Preheat heavy kettle, add oil and heat. Drop in chili peppers and let them fry until brown, pressing them occasionally with a fork to extract the pepper juice, then discard. Rub each piece of rabbit with the crushed garlic and then flour lightly. Sauté pieces in the chili-flavored oil. When golden brown, remove from kettle and put into casserole or covered baking dish. Put in oven turned low to keep warm while the sauce is being prepared.

SAUCE FOR MEXICAN RABBIT

2 tablespoons butter
1 large carrot, finely diced
½ cup finely chopped onion
3 tablespoons chopped green pepper
1 cup chopped mushrooms
1 tablespoon flour
2 cups chicken broth
Juice of 1 small orange

1 heaping tablespoon peanut butter
½ teaspoon cumin seeds
1 tablespoon toasted sesame seeds
3 cloves
3 slices orange peel
Dash of nutmeg
Salt and pepper to taste
1 tablespoon chopped parsley

Pour off the oil in which the rabbit was cooked and add the butter. When hot, add carrot, onion, green pepper and mushrooms. Cook over a slow fire until almost done. Keep stirring and be careful not to let brown. Add the flour and mix well with the vegetables, then add the broth and stir until slightly thickened. Add all of the rest of the ingredients except the parsley. Let mixture simmer until thoroughly blended, about 10 minutes. Salt the rabbit in the casserole and pour over it the cooked sauce. Sprinkle with parsley, cover and bake in a moderate oven for one hour, or until meat is tender. Baked potatoes go well with this dish. Serves 6.

This recipe came to me labeled "Tamale Pie" but it really is an Americanized version of "Chilaquiles," a true Mexican dish made up of alternating layers of pieces of tortillas, a sauce consisting of serrano chilies, green tomatoes, coriander and white onions, and layers of grated cheese. Frankly, I like this one better but I am going to change the name.

*CHILAQUILE PIE*

¼ cup oil
1 large onion, chopped
1 green pepper, chopped
2 pounds ground beef
2 teaspoons chili powder
½ teaspoon oregano
¼ teaspoon garlic powder
2 teaspoons salt
¼ teaspoon black pepper
1 ⚹2½ can Las Palmas
  Red Chili Sauce

1 ⚹2 can whole kernel
  corn
1 small can pitted black
  olives, or more
10 soft tortillas
1 pound Tillamook
  cheese, grated
Chopped green onions
Coriander sprigs
Sliced radishes

Preheat large skillet, add oil, onion and green pepper and sauté until onion is transparent. Add beef and stir-fry until meat is crumbly and has lost its red color. Add seasonings and let simmer for a few seconds to develop flavor, then add chili sauce, corn and olives. Cover and simmer 30 minutes. Meantime, cut up the tortillas, or tear them, and fry but do not brown, then drain. When meat mixture is ready, start with a double layer of tortilla pieces in the bottom of a large, well-greased casserole and alternate layers of tortillas, meat mixture and grated cheese, ending with cheese on top. Bake uncovered in 350° F. oven for 45 minutes. Garnish with chopped green onions, sprigs of coriander and sliced radishes. Serves 8 to 10.

*Rajas* is the Mexican word given to strips of green Poblano chilies and *pollo* means chicken. Put them together and you have a delicious concoction that is particularly good for buffet suppers. If canned Poblano chilies are not available you can substitute bell peppers. Parboil and then julienne them. Keep the rest of the menu light. A good cold California Gewürztraminer would go well with this.

*RAJAS CON POLLO*

| | |
|---|---|
| 1 capon, 5 pounds | 6 corn tortillas made |
| 2 teaspoons salt | into tostadas |
| 1 teaspoon MSG | ½ pound Poblano chilies, |
| 1 cup finely chopped | julienned |
| onion | Oil |
| 1 cup melted butter | ½ pound Cheddar |
| 1 cup flour | cheese, grated |
| 1 quart whipping cream | |

Simmer capon in boiling water until tender, adding salt and MSG when about half done. Cool, skin and bone. Cut meat into ¾ inch chunks. In a heavy saucepan, sauté the chopped onion in melted butter until it is limp and transparent. Add flour and stir thoroughly, then gradually stir in the whipping cream. Keep stirring until mixture comes to a boil and is smooth. Reduce heat and let simmer gently, stirring now and then to prevent scorching. If mixture seems too thick it can be thinned with a little of the chicken broth. Meanwhile, cut tortillas into triangles and fry in oil to a golden brown. Add chicken meat to cream sauce and stir in chili strips; mix thoroughly. Oil a 3½ to 4 quart casserole and in it arrange alternate layers of tostadas, chicken and cheese, saving enough cheese for a thick layer on top. Put in oven preheated to 375° F. for 30 to 45 minutes, or until bubbling and cheese has melted. Serves 6.

*Puchero,* a Spanish word for cooking pot, is the Mexican answer to a cross between our New England boiled dinner and a Hawaiian luau. It starts out calmly something like a cassoulet and all of a sudden you get the feeling, as you read down the list of ingredients, that the cook had been nipping on the cooking sherry and suddenly decided to clean house. For example, here are the ingredients of one recipe: beef, lamb, ham, chicken, marrow bone, cabbage, zucchini, sweet and white potatoes, bananas, avocados, chick peas, pears, turnips, carrots, onions, garlic, tomatoes, peppercorns, lard, coriander and lemons. If you get the impression that you can put just about anything you want in a Puchero you are right. All you need is a big enough pot.

In all fairness, the sweet potatoes and fruit are cooked separately. The white potatoes are sliced and fried in lard, and so are the bananas. The broth from the Puchero is strained and served as a first course with chopped coriander, diced avocado and wedges of lemon or lime. The main course consists of the meat on a huge platter surrounded by cooked fruits and vegetables. A big bowl of Guacamole accompanies the feast.

The following recipe is fairly basic. You can use any or all of the foregoing ideas. Get cozy with the kitchen sherry and let your fancy take flight.

*PUCHERO*

1 cup garbanzo beans
4 quarts water
2 pounds boiling beef
1 small ham hock
1 chicken, disjointed
1 beef marrow bone
2 cloves of garlic, minced
2 large onions, sliced
4 leeks, cleaned and cut up
2 tablespoons tomato paste
1 teaspoon crushed peppercorns
1 tablespoon salt
8 small or new potatoes
8 small white onions
4 stalks celery cut in ½ inch pieces
4 turnips, peeled and halved
4 carrots, scrubbed and halved
8 small zucchini, halved lengthwise
1 can whole kernel corn
1 small head of cabbage, cut in 8 wedges

Soak beans overnight. Next day remove skins and put to cook in a large kettle with 4 quarts of water. Add beef, ham hock, chicken, marrow bone, garlic, onion, leeks, tomato paste and crushed peppercorns. Bring to a boil, cover and simmer for an hour, then add salt and simmer 2 hours longer. When meat is tender, add all vegetables except the cabbage. When vegetables are almost done, add the cabbage. Cover and cook 10 to 15 minutes longer or until cabbage is tender but still somewhat crisp. Arrange meat and chicken pieces on a large platter surrounded by the vegetables. Or you can serve the meat and chicken on one platter and the vegetables on another. Strain the broth, correct seasonings and serve as a first course with chopped coriander, diced avocado and wedges of lime, which may be passed separately. If there is not enough liquid, add canned chicken broth. Serves 8 hungry people.

Some of the desserts of Mexico are pretty much like desserts anywhere. The old-fashioned desserts were mainly various types of custards, rice and bread puddings with various combinations of coconut, almonds, sherry, spices, raisins and pine nuts. Sponge cakes and ladyfingers were gussied up with custard, whipped cream and sherry. Fruit and nut fillings are tucked into pastry and deep-fried. Cakes are baked for fiestas, holy days and other special occasions. Fruits are often served for desserts.

*BANANAS WITH RUM*

| | |
|---|---|
| 2 cups water | 1 teaspoon rum extract |
| ½ cup white sugar | 6 large ripe bananas |
| ½ cup brown sugar | ¼ cup butter |
| 2 slices lemon with rind, halved | 2 ounces Jamaica rum |
| 4 slices orange with rind, halved | |

Boil water with sugars and fruit until a syrup forms, one that will glaze a spoon. Add extract. Split bananas in half lengthwise and sauté in butter. Spoon sauce over bananas and sprinkle a teaspoon of rum over each half of banana. Serves 6.

Here is another more elaborate banana and rum dessert.

*BAKED BANANAS WITH RUM SAUCE*

RUM SAUCE

| | |
|---|---|
| 2 egg yolks | ¼ teaspoon salt |
| ½ cup sifted powdered sugar | 1 ounce Jamaica rum |
| ¼ cup half and half | 2 egg whites |

Beat egg yolks until thick and lemon-colored; add sugar and half and half and salt and mix thoroughly. Place in top of double boiler over hot water and beat until mixture thickens, about 5 minutes. Stir in rum gradually and continue beating until smooth. Chill. Just before serving, beat egg whites until stiff and fold into sauce.

| | |
|---|---|
| 8 bananas | ¼ teaspoon ground cloves |
| 2 tablespoons melted butter | 2 tablespoons grated orange rind |
| ½ cup brown sugar | 1 cup orange juice |

Peel bananas and place in shallow baking dish. Brush with melted butter and bake in 350° F. oven for 10 minutes. Meanwhile, mix brown sugar, cloves, grated orange rind and orange juice. Spoon mixture over bananas and return to oven for 15 minutes. Serve hot with chilled Rum Sauce. Serves 8.

One of the most popular of Mexican desserts is Flan, a smooth custard baked in caramelized sugar.

*FLAN*

| | |
|---|---|
| 1 cup sugar for caramelizing | 4 cups milk |
| 3 egg whites | 1 cup sugar |
| 8 egg yolks | ¼ teaspoon salt |
| | 2 teaspoons vanilla |

In a baking dish or pan put the first cup of sugar and place over heat. Stir constantly until the sugar melts and turns golden. Remove pan from heat and tip it back and forth and sideways until the inside is entirely coated with the caramel. Let cool. Beat egg whites and egg yolks together, then beat in a little of the milk. Add sugar and beat until sugar is dissolved. Add rest of milk, salt and vanilla. Strain into caramel-coated pan. Place in pan with about an inch of hot—not boiling—water. Bake at 325° F. for an hour or more or until a silver knife inserted in the center comes out clean. While the pudding is still hot invert a round platter on top of the baking dish. Reverse quickly and pudding will slip out. It may be served as is or flamed with brandy. Serve immediately. Serves 8.

Several years ago, before I got the bug to open a Mexican restaurant, a group of us flew down to Tamuin in Mexico, for a dove shoot. Tamuin is about fifty miles from Tampico, on the eastern coastal plain, and slightly inland. Few maps show it. We were all staying at the Tamuin Hotel and each morning we'd leave for our dove shoot returning at dinner time.

One evening we asked the Mexican maitre d', a nice guy by the name of Carlos, who had been most attentive, if we could have a Mexican dinner. "Why certainly, I'll be happy to arrange one for you. You shall have a Huacotica dinner." When I asked him what kind of a dinner that was, his reply threw me. "It's a giant tamale cooked underground." That sounded great. We all agreed we had to have that.

The next night we returned to the hotel quite late. By the time we entered the dining room, around 9 P.M., everybody else had left. We sat down to a delicious salad of tomatoes, green Jalapeño peppers and tiny shrimp.

PLATE XVII. Mexican party table, *page 230*

PLATE XVIII. Presidio Chili from Texas, *page 232*

*TAMUIN SALAD*

4 cups small shrimp
½ cup French dressing
4 ripe but firm avocados
8 small peeled, ripe
   tomatoes
8 green pickled jalapeño
   peppers*
¼ cup finely chopped
   onion
½ cup finely chopped
   celery
½ teaspoon freshly
   ground pepper

1 tablespoon salt
2 teaspoons MSG
Juice of 1 lemon
24 lettuce leaves
4 cups shredded lettuce
32 chilled asparagus
   spears for garnish
2 hard-cooked eggs and
   4 pitted olives
   for garnish
2 lemons, quartered

Marinate shrimp in French dressing. Peel and dice avocado, dice tomatoes and combine in bowl. Add jalapeño peppers, which have been drained and minced, the onion, celery and seasoning, including lemon juice. Mix thoroughly but lightly. On chilled large salad plates arrange three lettuce leaves to form cup. Place ½ cup shredded lettuce in bottom of each cup. In the bottom of an 8 ounce soup or cereal bowl, place ½ cup of marinated shrimp and an eighth of the salad mixture. Unmold on shredded lettuce. Do this for the other seven salad plates. Garnish each salad with 4 spears of asparagus. Top with a slice of hard-cooked egg and a slice of ripe olive. Serve a wedge of lemon with each salad. Extra dressing may be passed. Serves 8.

After the salad we were served Escabeche. There was an excellent fish course, and then Carlos brought in the biggest tamale I've ever seen in my life. It was two feet long and about eighteen inches thick. He brought it to the table in a big

* "Jalapeño Peppers en Escabeche" can be secured from Mexican food supply houses or grocers. Ask for green pickled jalapeño peppers (hot) packed with "oil, vinegar, salt, sugar, garlic, onions, carrots and spices."

wooden trough-like bowl. The outer leaves were banana leaves, brown from baking, and inside there were ti leaves. There were big knots at each end where the leaves had been tied together. Carlos slit the top open with a big knife and the most wonderful savory tamale smell steamed out. The masa was nice and firm and underneath the thick sauce were big pieces of turkey, chicken, pork, corn and big black olives. It had a great flavor— not too pepper hot—just good. We went to work on that tamale with gusto and gallons of Mexican beer.

I've never forgotten that big tamale. It kept popping into my mind until one day I tried to make one at the restaurant for a group of friends. I had too many helpers, however. This was really the case of too many cooks, and every one of them must have salted that tamale. It looked all right and it smelled good but it was so salty no one could eat it.

The big tamale idea was still on my mind when we opened Señor Pico, and we finally did it. Underground cooking was out, so we rigged up a clay jacket and baked it in the oven. There is a muslin liner and lots of banana and ti leaves to protect the tamale from any flavor of clay. It is almost as impressive as the tamale I had in Tamuin and everyone seems to like it. Ours serves about eight persons and we have to have two days' notice.

This might be fun for a Mexican patio party instead of individual tamales. If you want to dig a hole in the back yard, you can steam your tamale underground, luau style. You'll need plenty of banana and ti leaves for this. The Mexicans put the food to be steamed in an earthenware casserole. A fire is built over stones in the pit, then a grate is laid over the stones and casserole set on the grate. After all the food and meat is in the pot, it is covered with a lid and then covered with a thick pad of leaves. Maguey leaves are used in Mexico but any large leaves and wet gunny sacks can be substituted. The pit is then sealed with mud and a fire built on top of the pit which burns from 5 to 6 hours.

Of course, you really don't have to go to all this fuss for

a Mexican party. You can make Presidio Chili and serve it in a big olla or you can buy some awfully good chili beans frozen, or canned. With a little judicious seasoning and some canned corn you can turn out a pretty good dish fast.

Suppose you want to make Green Enchiladas. With some canned products you can do it in 20 minutes. Serve them attractively with some sour cream and you have a makings of a party.

The decorations for a Mexican party are easy. Mexican pottery is not expensive and can be found all over the country in import outlets. Many of your own serving trays and platters can be covered with ti leaves to fit into the decor. Our Mexican party photograph (PLATE XVII) shows Empanadas and Quesadillas in Mexican face food warmers, kept hot with warming candles. There is a big bowl of individual tamales, a molded Guacamole Salad with shrimp and sour cream dressing, surrounded by tacos. The centerpiece is one of the planters we bought in Oaxaca. This is the place where the black pottery comes from. There's a shop there called Yalalag, run by a nice guy by the name of Enrique, who just knocks himself out to be nice to you. We buy all kinds of stuff from him—belts, rebozas and pottery of all kinds. The front of his shop is just jammed with planters and chimneys with faces. The chimneys are portable fireplaces, wonderful for taking the chill off the night air on a deck or patio. They're an attractive addition to the patio at any time.

The planters are pretty cute, sprouting marguerites, petunias or Mexican paper flowers like those shown in the photograph. It was these planters that inspired the little Mexican face food warmers which we had made for Señor Pico.

Getting back to the Mexican party, you can simplify this menu with gussied-up chili beans poured over broiled hamburgers on buns. Top them with slices of cheese and slip them under the broiler to melt the cheese. Have a tub of beer on ice or get one of those aluminum kegs of draft beer. The salad can be made the day before. In other words, you are having a

Mexican party, American style. It has the feeling and flavor of Mexico but it is done the American way. You don't have to knock yourself out. And don't forget, you can buy frozen tortillas, if there isn't a Mexican food shop in your area.

*MOLDED GUACAMOLE RING WITH SHRIMP*

| | |
|---|---|
| 2 packages celery Jell-O | 1 cup finely chopped |
| 2 cups boiling water | tomatoes |
| 2 cups cold water | 2 pounds cooked, shelled |
| 3 cups Guacamole | shrimp |

Dissolve gelatin in boiling water; add cold water and let chill until partially congealed. Add Guacamole and chopped tomato, folding in until well mixed. Pour into oiled ring mold and let chill until firm, at least 4 hours. Unmold, just before serving, on round platter. Fill center and garnish sides with chilled, deveined shrimp. Serve with Francia Dressing. Serves 8 to 12.

This same gelatin mixture may be molded individually and served with cottage cheese and fruit for a luncheon salad.

*FRANCIA SALAD*

| | |
|---|---|
| 1 package celery Jell-O | Shredded lettuce |
| 1 cup boiling water | 6 slices canned pineapple |
| 1 cup cold water | 3 cups cottage cheese |
| 1½ cup Guacamole | 6 ripe bananas |
| ½ cup finely chopped | Lemon juice |
| tomato | 1 large can mangoes |
| Lettuce cups | |

Dissolve gelatin in boiling water; add cold water and let chill until partially congealed, or follow directions on package (if you are in a hurry) and use ice cubes in dissolved gelatin. When partially congealed, fold in Guacamole and chopped tomatoes; pour into 6 oiled individual molds, and chill until firm. To serve, arrange lettuce cups on large salad plates and add shredded lettuce. On bed of shredded lettuce place slice of pineapple; add ½ cup cottage cheese and top with molded

Guacamole. Peel and quarter bananas and soak in lemon juice to keep them from discoloring. Garnish salad with well-drained mango slices and banana quarters. Top salad with a little Francia Sour Cream Dressing and pass additional dressing. Serves 6.

*FRANCIA SOUR CREAM DRESSING*

1 cup sour cream, whipped
1 cup mayonnaise
1 tablespoon chopped carrots from jalapeño Peppers en Escabeche*

1 tablespoon finely chopped serrano chili
Juice of 1 lemon
Salt and white pepper to taste

Combine sour cream and mayonnaise and fold in carrots, chili and lemon juice. Season to taste.

* If the carrots from the jalapeños are not handy, substitute pimiento which has first been soaked in the liquid from the serrano chili and then finely chopped.

## BROWNSVILLE

I'll never forget a Mexican party we attended on one of those big Texas ranches, just north of Brownsville. Cocktails were served in the lovely old ancestral home, originally built by Spanish ancestors, and then we were driven to an oak forest close by.

Now an oak forest in Texas is different from anywhere else. The trees are smaller in diameter, they are not very high and the tops come together to form a natural arbor. A Mexican brush fence had been made to encircle a group of some of the oaks, which gave the area a feeling of intimacy and charm. Under one tree was the women's primping place. A mirror hung from the branches and on a table were such feminine necessities as Kleenex, combs, cosmetics, etc. There were hammocks to relax in, chairs to lounge in with tables scattered about conveniently. A Mexican orchestra from Matamoros, across the border, provided music.

At one end of the enclosure was the dining area with long tables and benches for about fifty people. Directly behind the dining area was the cooking area. There was a stone fireplace and oven with a grating on which large Mexican earthenware pots and bowls simmered and bubbled. There were tables where Mexican women in colorful, starched dresses patted tortillas and peeled and chopped onions, tomatoes and peppers. Old men toted wood. There was a sort of playpen where the tiny babies played good-naturedly while their mothers prepared dinner. Well-behaved older children played and ran about but kept to themselves. It was a wonderful, relaxed family scene— no strain, no tension—everyone happy and gay.

The food was fabulous. There were Chile Rellenos, refried beans, tacos made with some wonderful but strange ingredients. Beef and chicken were cooked in several ways. There was

Civeche, piping hot tortillas, pastries and Mexican candy. We ate, drank beer or wine and someone started singing Mexican folk songs and some of the old Texas songs. It was just a helluva nice party. I've never been to a luau or any other kind of a party that compared with it. One of the reasons it was so wonderful, of course, was because it wasn't dreamed up on impulse or planned with the idea of being unusual or different. This was something that had been going on for years and guests felt happy to be a part of it.

Over the years I have made quite a few trips to various parts of Texas, sometimes to hunt, other times to attend a cattle roundup or a cattle sale. Sometimes we just stopped to visit, en route to Mexico. I am always impressed by the casual but extremely efficient way that everything is done. And if a primitive way of doing something gets the job done, no one is about to bring around any highfalutin improvements. Cooking in sand is just one such primitive practice. I saw it done at a roundup in Texas and I saw it done throughout Mexico.

You get one of those big old Mexican clay pots, called an olla, which will break if you look at it, so don't look at it too hard. You fill it with whatever you want to cook, and you put it on a thick bed of sand—not dirt. Then you build a fire of oak or any wood, except boxwood, and get it going good. Make a circle of burning embers about 3 inches high and 4 inches wide around the pot, about an inch or two away from the base. Don't push it against the pot or you'll either break it or burn the food.

You can boil water quickly, keep coffee hot, and really cook this way. But my idea is to precook anything that takes a long time and take it to the barbecue or picnic in the olla and just build the fire around it to keep the food hot.

Let's say you are going to have a party for 75 or 100 people. Make a stand of bricks and put the sand on top. Just keep these little fires going around the required number of ollas and the food will stay piping hot.

Take tamales, for instance. These must be steamed, so put some stones in the bottom of the pot and then enough water so the tamales will be above water but the water will boil and the steam will keep the tamales hot. It makes a nice show. When you lift the lid the steam billows out and it looks like you are actually cooking food.

Beans can be served this way, too, as shown in PLATE XVII, which gives you an idea of what you can do in your own back yard.

Everyone has a special recipe for chili beans or chili con carne. There must be a thousand different recipes. Here is one that legend says was created by a jailer with culinary talents somewhere west of the Pecos. We tried it, liked it, dubbed it Jailhouse Chili and put it on the menu at Señor Pico's in San Francisco. About a year after we opened I received a letter from a California food manufacturing company stating that they canned a product called Jailhouse Chili and that the name was copyrighted.

Now, I've had enough experience with people trying to horn in on our products and the name Trader Vic's or Señor Pico to appreciate how they felt about it, so now we call it

*PRESIDIO CHILI*  (PLATE XVIII)

1 pound kidney beans
  (1½ cups)
½ pound ground beef
½ pound diced pork
1 large onion, chopped
1 fat clove of garlic,
  minced
½ cup oil
1 bay leaf
2 tablespoons Gebhardt's
  Chili Powder

½ teaspoon oregano
1½ cups Las Palmas Chili
  Sauce
1 red California chili,
  chopped
1 teaspoon MSG
2 teaspoons salt
1 cup whole kernel corn

Wash and pick over beans and put to soak in cold water overnight. Next day, sauté beef, pork, onions and garlic in oil, in large heavy pot. Add all ingredients except salt and corn. Add beans and enough water to cover, 3 inches above beans. Cover and let simmer until beans are done, stirring occasionally, about an hour and a half. Add salt the last half hour of cooking. Add corn just before serving. Serves about 8.

*SONOFABITCH STEW*   (PLATE XVI)

The original "Sonofabitch Stew" was a ranch hand recipe, cooked out on the range. Here is a recipe, however, which can be prepared at home by a simple expedition to your nearest butcher shop. You might be wise to order the beef cheeks ahead of time. If unavailable you can substitute other cuts of beef, but it is the gelatinous quality of the cheeks that make this dish outstanding. It is great for an outdoor gathering. You can keep it hot in an olla set in sand with a ring of burning embers around it.

5 pounds beef cheeks, cut in inch pieces
½ cup oil
3 cups chopped onion
3 cloves of garlic, minced
½ cup flour
1 quart chicken stock
1 cup white wine
1 ⚹2 can solid pack tomatoes

1 small can tomato paste
1 tablespoon crushed cumin seeds
1 tablespoon each salt and MSG
1 teaspoon pepper
1 beef tongue, under 3 pounds
1 pound tripe, partially cooked

Brown cheeks in oil, in large heavy pot. Add onions and garlic, and sauté until limp and yellow. Stir in flour thoroughly, then add chicken stock, wine, tomatoes and tomato paste. Add seasonings, cover and simmer until beef cheeks are tender, about 3 hours. Add more stock or water if necessary. Meantime, scrub the tongue thoroughly. Put in kettle with tripe, add:

2 medium-sized onions
1 large carrot
3 outer stalks of celery with leaves

8 crushed peppercorns

Add boiling water, barely covering, and simmer, uncovered, until tongue and tripe are tender, about 3 hours. When done drain, skin and trim tongue. Dice tongue and tripe and add to beef cheeks. It is possible to buy partially cooked tripe from your butcher. If not, it is a 12-hour process and should be cooked ahead of time. Serves 15 to 18.

On one of my frequent trips to Brownsville, my interest in Mexican recipes prompted a friend to give me a little cookbook entitled *Good Eating*, published by the Women of The Church of the Advent, Espiscopal, as a fund-raising project for the church.

It contained some terrific recipes, so when I started working on this book I asked if I might include some of the recipes. Permission was graciously given me by Reverend J. Rufus Stewart and Mrs. M. P. McNair, president of the women's organization.

*CHICKEN ENCHILADAS WITH SOUR CREAM*

4 cups diced cooked
   chicken
½ pound grated Cheddar
   cheese

1 pint sour cream
12 tortillas

Combine chicken meat, grated cheese and sour cream. Fry tortillas in deep fat, one at a time, until soft, then dip in the following chili sauce mixture. Fill with chicken mixture and roll. Place rolls close together in flat greased casserole, and pour sauce over them. Bake in 350° F. oven for 10 or 15 minutes, or until thoroughly heated. Serves 6 or 12.

SAUCE

2 onions, finely chopped
1 clove garlic, minced
2 tablespoons oil
1½ cups canned green
   chilies, chopped

5 ripe tomatoes, peeled
   and chopped
Pinch of oregano
1 teaspoon salt
¼ teaspoon pepper

Fry onion and garlic in oil until transparent and limp. Add chopped chilies and tomatoes, oregano, salt and pepper. Cook until mixture thickens.

*CHICKEN MOLE*

1 fat hen, 4 pounds
1 teaspoon salt
¼ teaspoon pepper
½ cup raisins
½ cup pecans
½ cup peanuts

2 squares cinnamon-
   flavored Mexican
   chocolate
1 small can Mexican
   mole powder

Cut up hen as for frying. Put in stewing kettle and add just enough water to cover. Bring to a boil, skim, reduce heat and let simmer. After about an hour's time add salt and pepper. Turn off fire, and let chicken stand in liquid. In a little of the chicken broth, simmer raisins and nuts and mash to pulp. Add chocolate, grated, and the mole powder, and enough chicken broth to make a paste. Pour this mixture into the pot with the chicken and broth and cook all together, slowly, until chicken is done and sauce is thick. Total cooking time 2½ to 3 hours. Add more salt and pepper if needed and serve with Mexican Rice. Serves 4.

*TEXAS CHILI*

| | |
|---|---|
| 1 large onion, chopped | 1 teaspoon crushed |
| 1 clove garlic, minced | cumin seed |
| 3 tablespoons oil | 4 cups beef stock |
| 1 pound ground beef | Salt to taste |
| 3 tablespoons chili | |
| powder | |

Fry onion and garlic in oil until limp and transparent. Remove from fat and reserve. Fry meat in same oil until browned and crumbly. Return onion and garlic to meat pan, add chili powder, cumin seed and beef stock. Cover and simmer about an hour, stirring occasionally. When about half cooked, add salt to taste. Serves 4.

*TEXAS ENVUELTOS*

The difference between enchiladas and envueltos seems to be a technicality.

FILLING

| | |
|---|---|
| 1 pound ground beef | 1 teaspoon salt |
| 2 tablespoons oil | ¼ teaspoon pepper |
| 1 clove garlic, minced | 24 tortillas, fried soft |
| ½ teaspoon crushed | ½ cup shredded Cheddar |
| cumin seed | cheese |

Brown meat in oil with garlic, add cumin seed, salt and pepper and cook until done. Put cooked meat mixture in center of soft-fried tortillas and roll tightly. Place in greased casserole. Pour sauce over rolled tortillas, cover and bake for 30 minutes in moderate oven 350° F. To serve, sprinkle with grated Cheddar cheese. Serves 12, allowing 2 envueltos per person.

SAUCE

1 onion, chopped
½ large green pepper, chopped
2 stalks celery, chopped
2 tablespoons oil
1 ⋕2 can solid pack tomatoes

1 large bottle stuffed green olives
2 canned pimientos
¼ teaspoon pepper

Fry onion, green pepper and celery in oil. Add tomatoes, chopped up, and cook until tomatoes have disintegrated. Chop and add olives, pimientos and pepper. Let mixture cook 15 minutes, then pour over rolled tortillas.

*TEXAS CHILAQUILES*

1 onion, chopped
1 clove garlic, minced
2 tablespoons oil
2 cups canned tomatoes
1 teaspoon salt
¼ teaspoon pepper
1 can Ortega peppers (3½ ounces)

1 package tortillas
Oil for frying
1 pound grated Cheddar cheese
½ pint sour cream

Sauté onion and garlic in oil until transparent; add tomatoes, salt and pepper and simmer until tomatoes are cooked. Add chili peppers, cut in strips. Let simmer while you prepare tortillas. Cut tortillas into triangles and fry in hot oil. Remove immediately. Arrange layers of fried tortillas (tostadas) in well-greased casserole, then a layer of the sauce and a thick layer of grated cheese. Continue in this manner until dish is filled, ending with grated cheese. Bake in medium oven, 350° F., half an hour. Just before serving cover top with sour cream and bake until sour cream is heated. Serves 6 to 8.

*PARSLEY CHEESE NOODLES*

½ pound noodles
1 cup cream-style cottage
  cheese
¼ cup chopped parsley
⅛ teaspoon garlic powder
¼ cup melted butter
¼ cup crumbled blue
  cheese

¼ cup grated onion
¼ teaspoon white pepper
1 teaspoon salt
3 eggs, well beaten
Paprika

Cook noodles in salted water and drain. Combine noodles with cheese and rest of ingredients except eggs. Toss lightly and stir in beaten eggs. Pour into well-greased casserole and bake at 350° F. for 30 minutes. Sprinkle lightly with paprika before serving. Serves 6.

*BROWNSVILLE MEATBALLS*

2 pounds ground beef
2 eggs, beaten
1 cup unsweetened
  applesauce
1 cup dry bread crumbs
2 teaspoons salt

1 tablespoon grated
  onion
¼ teaspoon freshly
  ground pepper
¼ cup cooking oil

Mix meat with ingredients and seasonings. Shape into meatballs. Brown in cooking oil. Remove, keep warm in oven while making the following sauce, in the same skillet.

SAUCE FOR BROWNSVILLE MEATBALLS

¼ cup chopped celery
¼ cup sliced carrots
2 tablespoons chopped
  green pepper
1 clove garlic, peeled
  and minced

Oil
2 tablespoons flour
2 cups tomato juice
¼ teaspoon salt
2 teaspoons sugar

Sauté vegetables in oil until tender. Stir in flour, then add tomato juice, stirring until thickened. Add seasonings and pour over meatballs in a casserole. Cover and bake in 325° F. oven 50 to 60 minutes, or until tender. Serves 8 to 10.

## BROWNSVILLE BEEFBURGERS STROGANOFF

| | |
|---|---|
| 1½ pounds ground beef | 1 cup cream of |
| 3 slices of bacon, diced | mushroom soup |
| ½ cup chopped onion | 1 cup dairy sour cream |
| 1½ tablespoons flour | 1 ounce white wine |
| ¼ teaspoon paprika | 8–10 hamburger buns |
| 1 teaspoon salt | Butter |

Brown ground meat and bacon, add onions and cook until onion is tender but not browned. Drain off excess fat. Blend flour and seasonings into meat mixture, stir in soup. Cook slowly uncovered 20 minutes, stirring frequently. Add sour cream and wine and heat through. Meanwhile, split hamburger buns, toast and butter them. Serve meat mixture on two halves of buns. Serves 8 to 10.

## CHICKEN RING

| | |
|---|---|
| 2½ cups diced cooked chicken | 1 teaspoon paprika |
| | ¼ teaspoon white pepper |
| 3 cups cooked rice | ¼ cup chopped pimiento |
| 1 cup bread crumbs | 4 eggs, beaten |
| 2½ cups milk | ¼ cup butter |
| 1 teaspoon salt | |

Combine all ingredients in order given and mix thoroughly. Pack into large well-buttered ring mold and bake in a pan of hot water in a slow over 325° F. from 45 to 60 minutes. Allow chicken ring to rest in a warm place for 10 minutes or so before turning onto large platter. Fill center with the following mushroom sauce. Serves 10 to 12.

*MUSHROOM SAUCE*

¼ cup butter
¼ pound fresh
  mushrooms, sliced
¼ cup flour
2 cups chicken stock,
  heated
2 egg yolks, beaten

¼ cup cream
¼ teaspoon salt
¼ teaspoon paprika
1 teaspoon chopped
  parsley
1 teaspoon lemon juice

Melt half of the butter in a frying pan and add mushrooms. Stir and cook gently for 5 minutes. Place remaining butter in the upper part of a double boiler, add flour and rub to a smooth paste. Stir in gradually the hot chicken stock and cook until thick and creamy. Add egg yolks beaten with the cream and season with salt and paprika, stirring until thick and smooth. Add mushrooms, parsley and lemon juice. Keep hot over boiling water until ready to serve.

*CHICKEN WITH WINE*

2 frying chickens
½ cup oil or butter
3 yellow squash, sliced
1 large onion, sliced
½ clove garlic, minced
3 tomatoes, sliced
1 teaspoon salt
¼ teaspoon ground
  pepper

1 bay leaf
¼ teaspoon fines herbes
1 small piece stick
  cinnamon
3 whole cloves
1 cup chicken broth
1 cup red wine
1 large can whole kernel
  corn

Clean and disjoint chickens and brown in oil. Place chicken in Dutch oven or baking dish. Sauté squash and set aside, then sauté onions and garlic until limp. Add tomatoes and cook until mushy. Add seasonings, chicken broth and wine and bring to a boil. Add squash and pour entire mixture over chicken. Pour drained corn over the top. Cover and bake in medium oven about 1½ hours or until chicken is tender. Baste occasionally with liquid. Add more chicken broth if necessary. Remove cinnamon, cloves and bay leaf before serving. Serve with steamed rice. Serves 4 to 5, depending upon size of chickens.

## CHICKEN BONNE FEMME

½ cup flour
2 teaspoons salt
½ teaspoon pepper
1 plump pullet, 3 pounds
¼ cup butter
2 cups fresh sliced mushrooms

1 cup heavy cream, scalded
2 egg yolks, beaten
½ cup chopped ripe olives
½ cup sherry

Shake flour, salt and pepper in a paper bag. Disjoint chicken and add to paper bag. Shake thoroughly. Melt butter in heavy skillet and brown chicken. Remove chicken to greased casserole. Brown mushrooms in butter and add to casserole. Cover and bake in moderate oven, 350° F., until tender, about 45 minutes. Remove from oven and drain off liquid and fat into skillet in which chicken was browned. Discard all but ¼ cup of the fat, add cream, beaten egg yolks and chopped olives. Stir over medium heat until thickened. Add sherry. Taste and correct seasonings. Pour over chicken and serve with rice or buttered noodles. Serves 4 to 6.

## GULF SHRIMP DEVINE

⅔ cup olive oil
⅓ cup lemon juice
½ teaspoon salt
⅛ teaspoon pepper
2 pounds raw shrimp, shelled and deveined

3 tablespoons butter
1 clove garlic, crushed
1 cup blanched, slivered almonds
Dash Tabasco sauce
½ cup dry vermouth

Make marinade of olive oil, lemon juice and seasonings.

Marinate shrimp in this for at least 2 hours. Overnight will do no harm. Melt butter in large skillet; add garlic and shrimp, reserving marinade for later use. Stir-fry shrimp over medium heat until they are pink. Discard garlic and remove shrimp to a hot platter. Sauté slivered almonds in butter until golden, then add the marinade, Tabasco and vermouth. When well blended, pour this sauce over the shrimp. Serve with saffron rice mixed with chopped chives or finely chopped green onions. Serves 4.

*MOLDED AVOCADO RING WITH*
*SOUR CREAM SHRIMP DRESSING*

| | |
|---|---|
| 4 cups mashed avocado | 3 tablespoons onion juice |
| 4 tablespoons lemon juice | 3 tablespoons gelatin |
| 2 teaspoons salt | ½ cup cold water |
| ⅛ teaspoon cayenne pepper | 1¼ cups boiling water |
| 1 teaspoon sugar | Few drops green coloring |
| | 1 cup mayonnaise |

To mash avocado, cut in half, peel and sprinkle with lemon juice. Press through ricer, then through sieve. Add seasonings, sugar and onion juice. Soak gelatin in cold water, add boiling water and stir until dissolved. Chill until it begins to congeal. Blend avocado mixture with gelatin. Set in refrigerator until mixture begins to congeal. Add coloring and beat for 3 minutes with rotary beater, then fold in mayonnaise and stir until completely blended. Add more coloring if it is too light. Taste and correct seasonings. Pour into large greased ring mold and let set overnight in refrigerator. Serve with the following dressing.

## SOUR CREAM SHRIMP DRESSING

| | |
|---|---|
| 1 clove garlic | 2 tablespoons |
| 1 pint heavy sour cream | horseradish |
| 1½ cups catsup | 1 teaspoon paprika |
| 2 tablespoons | 1 tablespoon lemon juice |
| Worcestershire sauce | ¼ teaspoon dry mustard |
| 1½ tablespoons grated | ½ pound cooked, shelled |
| onion | and deveined shrimp, |
| 1 teaspoon salt | cut in pieces |

Rub mixing bowl with cut garlic and pour in sour cream. Add rest of ingredients except shrimp and stir well, but do not beat, until blended. Fold in cut up shrimp and refrigerate until ready for use the next day.

## SOUR CREAM CHOCOLATE CAKE

| | |
|---|---|
| 1 cup sour cream | 1 cup sugar |
| 2 eggs, beaten | 1 teaspoon soda |
| 1¼ cup flour | 1 teaspoon salt |
| 2 tablespoons cocoa | 1 teaspoon vanilla |

Mix sour cream with eggs. Sift flour, measure and sift again with dry ingredients. Add to sour cream and egg mixture, folding the mixture together. Add vanilla. Bake in two Teflon or greased 8 inch layer tins 3 minutes at 325° F. and an additional 9 minutes at 300° F. Test with toothpick. Bake longer if necessary. Put together with mint-flavored whipped cream. Frost top with some of the flavored whipped cream and sprinkle with shaved chocolate or chocolate shot.

*FLAN TEXAS STYLE*

| | |
|---|---|
| 12 egg yolks | 1 teaspoon vanilla |
| 1 cup sugar | 3 tablespoons sugar |
| 1 cup milk | |

Beat egg yolks with fork. Add sugar gradually, beating until all lumps have disappeared. Add milk and vanilla. Brown 3 tablespoons sugar in top of double boiler over flame. When brown, remove from fire and turn top of double boiler until sides and bottom are coated. Pour egg mixture into coated top and set over bottom of double boiler containing boiling water. Cook for 1 hour. When done, turn out on plate immediately. Serves 6.

*HALFWAY COOKIES*

| | |
|---|---|
| 1 cup shortening | ½ teaspoon salt |
| ½ cup brown sugar | 1 package semisweet |
| ½ cup white sugar | chocolate bits |
| 2 egg yolks | 1 cup chopped black |
| 1 tablespoon water | walnuts |
| 2 teaspoon vanilla | 2 egg whites |
| 2 cups sifted flour | 1 cup brown sugar |
| ¼ teaspoon soda | |

Cream shortening and sugars, add beaten egg yolks, water and vanilla. Sift flour with soda and salt and add to shortening and egg mixture. Spread on cookie sheet with sides to less than ½ inch thickness. Press the chocolate bits over the cookie mixture, then spread black walnuts over all. Beat egg whites and fold in brown sugar. Spread over cookie mixture. Bake in preheated oven at 300° F. for 25 to 30 minutes. Cool. Cut into squares and top with vanilla ice cream. Makes about 50 cookies.

# Home Port

SAN FRANCISCO, the end of a cook's tour, where everyone seems to be interested in food and its preparation. This probably accounts for the hundreds of restaurants here where the adventurous can dine on foods from all over the world. The homesick traveler or immigrant can always find a small restaurant somewhere which offers the dishes of his homeland.

Since her bawdy beginning, San Francisco has been the Mecca of gourmets, the paradise of the bon vivant. The land of gold and sunshine attracted people from every walk of life, from every country, and San Francisco has been the gateway.

The early California dishes were mostly transplants—either the dishes of Spain or those brought over the plains from the East. A few, like Hangtown Fry or Oyster Loaf, were locally concocted to filch gold from prospectors in town on a spree, when eggs were selling for a dollar apiece.

The recipes in this concluding chapter are an assortment of early California dishes, recipes everyone seems to enjoy and some I have enjoyed that just didn't seem to fit in anywhere else. I hope you enjoy them too.

# EARLY CALIFORNIA FAVORITES

*SAN FRANCISCO OYSTER LOAF*

| | |
|---|---|
| 1 loaf sour dough French bread | Fine dry bread crumbs |
| 1 cup melted butter | 3 eggs, slightly beaten |
| 2 dozen medium-sized oysters | Salt and pepper |
| | Sliced lemon |
| | ¼ cup chopped parsley |

Remove top from round or oval loaf of French bread and save. Hollow out the loaf, then brush inside of loaf and lid liberally with some of the melted butter. Bake in hot oven, 400° F., until very hot and toasted. While loaf is heating, roll oysters first in bread crumbs, then in beaten eggs and again in bread crumbs. Fry in the rest of the melted butter in a heated heavy frying pan. Season oysters, as they cook, with salt and pepper. Fry on both sides but be careful not to over-cook; 4 to 5 minutes is enough to brown them. Fill the hot, crusty loaf with the fried oysters; pour a little of the butter in which the oysters cooked over them; cover with thin slices of lemon and sprinkle with chopped parsley. Place toasted lid on loaf and serve. Serve 6 oysters to a person, then slice the bread case and pass. Serve with chili sauce or catsup. Serves 4.

*HANGTOWN FRY*

| | |
|---|---|
| 8 medium-sized oysters | ½ cup butter |
| Fine dry bread crumbs | ¼ cup milk |
| 4 eggs beaten | Salt and pepper |

Roll oysters in bread crumbs, then beaten eggs, and again in bread crumbs. Melt butter in frying pan (omelet pan) and brown oysters on one side in hot butter. Meantime, add rest of beaten eggs to milk, salt and pepper, and mix well. Turn oysters and let cook a few seconds, then add egg and milk mixture to oysters and cook like an omelet, lifting the cooked portion of the egg to let the uncooked part run down onto the hot frying pan. When lightly browned underneath, fold and serve with crisp bacon or fried sausages on warm plates. Serves 2.

## DUPONT STREET CASSOULET

| | |
|---|---|
| 2 lamb chops, 6 ounces each OR 1 lamb shank, 10 ounces | 1 carrot, finely chopped |
| | 1 medium-sized onion, chopped |
| 1½ pounds raw turkey meat (second joints and drums) cut into bite-sized pieces | 2 whole tomatoes, peeled and chopped |
| | 2½ quarts lamb or chicken broth |
| 3 tablespoons flour | 1 pound white navy beans |
| ⅓ cup oil | |
| 1 stalk celery, finely chopped | 5 garlic sausages (French or Italian) |

Dust lamb chops or lamb shank and turkey pieces with flour. Place meat in a 6 quart cooking pot and sauté in oil until browned. Tie celery, carrot and onion in cheesecloth for a "bouquet garni" and place on meat. Add tomatoes and broth; bring to a boil and add beans. Let simmer or gently roll for ½ hour. Add 3 of the garlic sausages sliced in ⅛ inch slices and continue to simmer for another 2 hours, or until beans are done. Remove and bone the lamb. Dice the meat into bite-sized pieces and return to beans. Remove "bouquet garni." Slice remaining two garlic sausages lengthwise into ¼ inch slices and fry until brown. Just before serving decorate top of cassoulet with garlic sausage slices. Serves about 8.

*RABBIT STEW*

| | |
|---|---|
| 2 young rabbits, about 1½ pounds each (save livers and hearts) | Flour |
| | Salt, pepper and MSG |
| | ½ cup oil or clarified butter |
| 1 quart red wine | |
| 4 carrots, diced | 2 cups consommé |
| 3 onions, chopped | ½ cup currant jelly |
| 2 cups chopped celery | ½ pound mushrooms, sliced |
| ½ teaspoon juniper berries | |
| 1 bay leaf | 4 tablespoons butter |
| 4 ounces cognac | |

Cut rabbits into 7 pieces each (3 from back and 4 legs). Pour wine into crock, add pieces of rabbit and chopped vegetables, juniper berries and bay leaf. Marinate livers and hearts in cognac. Let rabbit marinate for 2 days. Keep under refrigeration. Drain rabbit and vegetables in colander. Let dry and save wine marinade. Flour rabbit, season with salt and pepper and MSG, and sauté in oil or clarified butter in Dutch oven or heavy baking pan until golden brown on all sides. Set aside.

Sauté drained vegetables, add a pint of the marinade and 2 cups consommé and bring to a boil. Reduce heat, cover and let simmer half an hour or until vegetables are tender. Put through food mill or mash. Add browned rabbit; cover and bake in preheated 350° F. oven 40 to 45 minutes. Remove from oven, stir in the currant jelly until melted. Add more of the marinade if necessary. Cover and return to oven to bake until rabbit is tender.

Sauté mushrooms in butter in a skillet until they have lost their whiteness and are tender; remove and add to rabbit. Remove hearts and livers from cognac and chop; sauté in same pan that mushrooms were cooked, then add cognac in which they were marinated and flambé. When rabbit is done, remove pieces from pan and place in serving dish. Add chopped liver and hearts to sauce and bring to a boil; pour over rabbit and serve. Serves 4 to 6.

*HAM HOCKS AND LIMA BEANS*

1 pound large dried lima beans
2 large onions, chopped
2 cloves garlic, minced
3 tablespoons butter
1 cup chopped celery
2 large tomatoes, chopped

3 ham hocks, cracked
2 teaspoons celery seed
3 red peppers, tied in cheesecloth
¼ teaspoon pepper
1 teaspoon salt
½ cup dry red wine

Wash, sort and put beans to soak overnight in a large kettle, using 3 to 4 times as much water as beans. Next day bring beans to a boil in the water in which they were soaked. In a skillet, sauté onions and garlic in butter until onions are limp; add celery and tomatoes and let simmer a few minutes until thoroughly blended. Add to lima beans. Add ham hocks, celery seed and peppers. Cover and let simmer about an hour. Add salt and wine, cover and bake in preheated 350° F. oven 30 to 45 minutes or until beans and ham hocks are tender. Remove peppers tied in cheesecloth. Serves 4 to 6.

*LAMB SHANKS WITH NAVY BEANS*

| | |
|---|---|
| 1 pound white navy beans | 1 cup chopped celery |
| 6 lamb shanks | ½ cup chopped carrot |
| Salt, pepper and MSG | 1 ※2 can solid pack tomatoes (which equals |
| Flour | about 2½ cups) |
| ¼ cup oil | ½ teaspoon pepper |
| 2 garlic sausages, sliced | 2 teaspoons salt |
| ½ cup chopped onion | 1 cup dry white wine |

Soak beans overnight. Season shanks with salt, pepper and MSG and dust with flour. Heat oil in heavy kettle or Dutch oven and brown lamb shanks. Set aside. Fry garlic sausages and set aside. Sauté onion, celery and carrot until onion is limp. Add tomatoes, drained beans and pepper. Add boiling water to cover and return lamb shanks to pot. Cover and bake in preheated 325° F. oven for about an hour. Add salt and wine. Cover again and bake another 30 to 45 minutes, or until lamb shanks and beans are tender. If beans are soupy, remove lid and cook until liquid is sufficiently reduced. Vegetables should be completely disintegrated in the gravy. Serves 6.

*APPLE BETTY*

| | |
|---|---|
| ¾ cup brown sugar | 1½ cups fine bread crumbs |
| ½ teaspoon cinnamon | |
| ¼ teaspoon nutmeg | ¼ cup melted butter |
| ¼ teaspoon cloves | 3 cups peeled, sliced raw green apples |
| ¼ teaspoon salt | |
| Grated rind of ½ lemon | ½ cup water |
| 1 tablespoon lemon juice | |

Sift together the brown sugar, spices and salt. Add the grated lemon peel and lemon juice. Mix bread crumbs with melted butter. Spread ⅓ of the bread crumb mixture on the bottom of a buttered baking dish. Arrange half of the apples on the crumbs, then sprinkle with half of the spiced sugar mixture. Over this spread another ½ cup of the bread crumbs. Add the rest of the apples. Add the water, then top with remainder of the bread crumbs and spiced sugar mixture. Bake the pudding, covered, in a preheated 350° F. oven for about 40 minutes, or until the apples are almost tender, then remove cover and bake for 15 minutes until the top is golden brown and the juice is reduced. Serve hot with sweetened whipped cream or ice cream. Serves 6 to 8.

*RICE PUDDING*

| | |
|---|---|
| ⅓ cup rice | 2 eggs |
| 3 cups scalded milk | ¼ cup sherry |
| ½ teaspoon salt | 1 banana, peeled |
| ½ cup sugar | ¼ cup orange |
| 1 tablespoon gelatin | marmalade |
| ½ cup cold water | 1 cup crushed pineapple |
| 1 teaspoon vanilla | 1 small can mandarin |
| ¼ cup raisins | oranges |

Wash rice and cook with scalded milk, salt and sugar in upper part of double boiler until rice is done. Stir in gelatin, which has been dissolved in cold water, and add vanilla. Meanwhile, place raisins, eggs and sherry in a blender and blend until raisins are coarsely chopped. Add cut up banana and orange marmalade and blend a second or two more. Combine mixture from blender with pineapple and add to rice. Mix thoroughly. Drain mandarin oranges and arrange sections in bottom of well-oiled pudding mold. Spoon rice mixture over oranges. Chill. Unmold and serve with the following sauce. Serves 8.

2 egg yolks
1 cup sifted
  confectioners' sugar

⅛ teaspoon salt
6 tablespoons curaçao
1 cup whipping cream

Beat egg yolks, add sugar and salt and beat until sugar is dissolved. Slowly beat in the curaçao. Whip cream until stiff. Fold egg mixture into the whipped cream. Chill.

### GINGERBREAD

1 cup sugar
1 scant cup oil (remove
  1 tablespoon)
1 cup molasses
1 cup boiling water
2½ cups sifted flour
1 teaspoon soda

1½ teaspoons baking
  powder
½ teaspoon salt
1 teaspoon ginger
½ teaspoon cinnamon
½ teaspoon cloves
2 eggs, beaten

In mixing bowl, mix sugar, oil, molasses and boiling water, using the same cup for each. Sift flour with soda, baking powder, salt and spices. Mix with molasses and water mixture and add beaten eggs. Bake in a well-greased square pan in moderate preheated 350° F. oven, 40 minutes. Serves 12 to 16. Delicious served hot, topped with vanilla ice cream or whipped cream.

## SAN FRANCISCO FAVORITES

### LIZ'S CHEESE PUFFS

4 ounces sharp Cheddar
  cheese
¼ cup melted butter
½ teaspoon Dijon mustard
Dash Worcestershire
  sauce

¾ cup flour, sifted
⅛ teaspoon salt
Pinch of white pepper
1 tablespoon poppy
  seeds (or sesame
  seeds)

Grate cheese and mix with melted butter, mustard and Worcestershire sauce. Combine with flour and seasonings. Form into a ball and refrigerate for half an hour. Then form into marble-sized balls. Pour poppy or sesame seeds in a saucer and dip each cheese ball into the seeds and then place, seed side up, on a cookie sheet. Bake at 375° F. for 10 minutes. Makes about 30 cheese puffs. *Note:* These can be frozen and baked as needed.

*CALVES LIVER STROGANOFF*

1½ pounds thinly sliced
  calves liver
Salt and pepper
Flour
3 slices bacon
¼ cup melted butter
¼ cup chopped onion
1 cup chopped fresh
  mushrooms

½ cup white wine
1 cup sour cream
½ teaspoon salt
¼ teaspoon white pepper
Dash Worcestershire
  sauce

Season liver with salt and pepper and dredge in flour. Chop bacon and fry in skillet until crisp. Discard fat and drain bacon on paper towel. Add butter to skillet and sauté liver quickly until browned on both sides. Remove to heated serving platter to keep warm in oven. Sauté onions and mushrooms, adding additional butter if necessary, until onions are limp and mushrooms cooked. Add wine and bring to a boil; reduce heat and add sour cream, seasonings and Worcestershire sauce. Blend and heat; taste and correct seasonings; stir in crisp bacon and spoon over fried liver. Serves 6.

*BROILED LAMB CHOPS WITH CURRIED RICE* (PLATE XIX)

8 small loin lamb chops,
  1¾–2 inches thick
2 large cloves garlic
Salt and pepper

½ pound large
  mushrooms
¼ cup butter
Parsley or watercress

Rub lamb chops with cut garlic on both sides. Preheat broiler and place chops about 4 inches from element. Cooking time will depend on thickness, 15 to 20 minutes. Wash and slice mushrooms vertically, Chinese style. Sauté in butter. Arrange chops on either side of curried rice, if a rectangular platter is used, or around the mound of rice if a chop plate is used. Overlap sliced mushrooms on rice. Garnish platter with parsley or watercress. Serves 8.

*CURRIED RICE*

½ teaspoon salt
3 cups boiling water
2 cups quick cooking
   brown rice
¼ cup finely chopped
   onions
½ cup chopped celery
½ cup chopped
   mushrooms

½ cup butter
1 tablespoon curry
   powder
½ cup Trader Vic's
   chutney
½ cup pine nuts

Add salt to boiling water, stir in rice; reduce heat to low. Cover tightly and steam for 15 minutes. Meanwhile, sauté onions, celery and mushrooms in butter until onions are limp. Stir in curry powder and continue stirring for several seconds until curry is nicely browned. Chop chutney and add to curry mixture, then stir entire mixture into rice. Add pine nuts last, just before serving. Serves 8, allowing ¾ cup per person.

A nice accompaniment to Broiled Lamb Chops with Curried Rice are Pake Brussels Sprouts, cooked Chinese style and served with Parmesan cheese.

*BAKED GREEN BEANS*

1 pound green beans
3 slices bacon
1 large onion, peeled
   and chopped

1 cup sliced fresh
   mushrooms
1 can chicken broth
Salt, pepper, MSG

Wash beans and snip off ends. Arrange lengthwise in rectangular or oval baking dish with a cover. Chop bacon and sauté in skillet; add onion and sauté until limp. Add sliced mushrooms and stir-fry a few seconds until limp but not browned. Add chicken broth to skillet and bring to a boil. Pour broth, bacon and vegetables over beans; add seasonings, cover and bake in moderate 350° F. oven until tender but not overcooked, about 20 minutes. Broth may be thickened with a little cornstarch mixed with cold water, or saved for soup. Serves 4.

*BAKED LAMB CHOPS*

8 double loin lamb chops, well trimmed
¼ cup flour
1 teaspoon salt
½ teaspoon pepper
¼ cup butter
½ pound fresh mushrooms, sliced
½ cup chopped onions
1 clove garlic, minced
1 cup celery, sliced
¼ cup chopped parsley
¼ teaspoon oregano
½ cup chicken broth
½ cup white wine
8 small carrots
1 can whole white onions (8 ounces)
½ can pitted black olives (8 ounces)
1 package frozen peas
2 teaspoons lemon juice

Rub chops with flour mixed with salt and pepper. Heat skillet with butter and brown chops well. Remove to large earthenware casserole or baking dish which can be used for serving. In same skillet, sauté mushrooms, onions and garlic until onions are limp. Add celery and parsley and sauté for a few seconds, then stir in oregano; add broth and wine, mix well and bring to a boil. Pour over lamb chops; cover and bake in a moderate 350° F. oven for 20 minutes. Add carrots and bake 15 minutes, then add drained onions and olives, and peas. Continue cooking until lamb is tender. Stir in lemon juice before serving and correct seasonings. Serve with steamed rice, buttered noodles or mashed potatoes. Serves 8.

## VEAL ROSEMARY

| | |
|---|---|
| 2 pounds veal cutlet | 1 large onion, chopped |
| ¾ cup flour | very fine |
| 1 teaspoon salt | 2 tablespoons olive oil |
| 1 tablespoon paprika | ½ teaspoon rosemary |
| 1 teaspoon MSG | 1 cup sour cream |
| ¼ teaspoon pepper | |

Cut veal in serving portions and pound well. Combine flour, salt, paprika, MSG and pepper. Dredge veal in this mixture, rubbing in thoroughly. Sauté onions in oil, add veal and brown on both sides. Remove to baking dish. Sprinkle with the rosemary, add the sour cream. Cover and bake in 350° F. oven for 1 hour. Serve 4 to 6. Serve with rice.

## SICILIAN MEATBALLS

| | |
|---|---|
| 4 slices bread | 1 large onion, chopped |
| 1 pound ground round | 1 clove garlic, minced |
| ½ pound ground pork | ½ pound fresh |
| 3 eggs | mushrooms, sliced |
| ¼ cup finely chopped | 1 cup tomato hot sauce |
| parsley | (small can) |
| ¼ cup Parmesan cheese | 1 cup Italian mushroom |
| 1 teaspoon salt | sauce (small can) |
| ½ teaspoon pepper | ½ cup red wine |
| ¼ cup olive oil | ½ cup consommé |

Soak the bread in water; squeeze thoroughly and mix with the meat. Add eggs, parsley, Parmesan cheese, salt and pepper. Mix thoroughly and make into small balls about 1½ inch in diameter. Preheat heavy kettle or Dutch oven, add oil and brown the meatballs. Set aside. Sauté onions, garlic and mushrooms in the oil in which the meatballs were browned, until onions are limp. Add hot sauce, mushroom sauce, wine and consommé and bring to a boil, then reduce heat, cover and let simmer half

PLATE XIX. Home Port Broiled Lamb Chops with Curried Rice, *page 253*

PLATE XX. Tropical drinks: Rum Mint Squash, *page 271;* Babalu, *page 266;* Tonga Punch, *page 270;* Rangoon Ruby, *page 269;* Tortuga, *page 271*

an hour. Return the meatballs to the sauce; cover and simmer another 30 to 40 minutes. Serves 6. Serve with egg noodles or spaghetti.

*POACHED SALMON WITH RED CAVIAR*

6 salmon steaks, 5–6 ounces each

1½ cups white wine

Red caviar

2 tablespoons flour and butter roux

6 tablespoons hollandaise sauce

6 tablespoons whipped cream

¼ teaspoon lemon juice

Poach salmon steaks in wine gently. When done, remove to warm platter; reserve liquid. Spread each salmon steak with 1 to 1½ tablespoons red caviar. Stir the roux into the wine in which the salmon was poached and stir over heat until it thickens, then gently stir in the hollandaise sauce, whipped cream and lemon juice. Pour wine sauce over the steaks and garnish platter with parsley. Top each steak with a slice of lemon topped with a bit of red caviar—about ½ teaspoon. Serves 6. *Note:* Salmon fillets may be used and other types of fish may be substituted for the salmon.

*POACHED SALMON WITH SOUR CREAM SAUCE*

4 salmon fillets or steaks
½ cup white wine
½ cup chicken broth
1½ tablespoons flour and butter roux
½ cup whipped sour cream
½ teaspoon salt
⅛ teaspoon white pepper
¼ teaspoon dried dill weed
Dash Worcestershire sauce
Lemon wedges
2 teaspoons chopped parsley
Paprika

Poach salmon gently in white wine and chicken broth. When done remove fish to warm platter. Thicken poaching liquid with the roux and fold in the sour cream. Season, add Worcestershire sauce and pour over salmon steaks. Garnish platter with wedges of lemon, parsley and top each fillet or steak with ½ teaspoon chopped parsley and a flick of paprika. Serves 4.

*DEVILED CHICKEN*

1 tablespoon dry mustard
1 tablespoon paprika
2 teaspoons salt
½ cup white wine
1 roasting chicken, about 3 pounds
1 cube butter
1 cup bread crumbs

Make a paste of the mustard, paprika, salt and wine. Cut chicken into serving pieces and coat with the paste. Melt butter in a roasting pan with a tight-fitting cover. Turn the chicken in the butter then sprinkle with bread crumbs. Place cover on pan and place in 325° F. oven and bake for an hour or so. This is a good dish when dinner is apt to be delayed. You can turn the oven down to 200° and it will keep hot without damage. Serves 4.

*BEEF AND BEANS*

2½ pounds beef for stew
½ cup oil
2 large onions, chopped
1 clove garlic, minced
3 cups red beans
9 cups boiling water
2 teaspoons dried
  rosemary

3 chili tepines or small
  red peppers
½ teaspoon cumin
1 teaspoon celery seed
½ teaspoon pepper
1 small can tomato hot
  sauce
2 teaspoons salt

Brown meat in oil; sauté onions and garlic until transparent. Add beans and boiling water. Tie rosemary and chili tepines or small red peppers in a muslin bag; add to meat with cumin, celery seed and pepper. Cover and let simmer slowly for about three hours, stirring occasionally. Add tomato sauce after beans have begun to swell. Add more water if necessary so there is plenty of gravy. Add salt the last half hour of cooking so the beans are not toughened. Remove muslin bag before serving. Serves 8 to 10.

*CHICKEN FRICASSEE*

1 five pound, dark
  feathered hen, cut into
  serving pieces
1 large clove garlic,
  minced
1 large onion, chopped
½ pound mushrooms,
  sliced
¼ cup flour
3 cups chicken broth

1 cup chopped celery
½ cup chopped carrot
½ teaspoon rubbed sage
¼ teaspoon thyme
¼ teaspoon marjoram
⅛ teaspoon nutmeg
1 tablespoon chopped
  parsley
¼ teaspoon white pepper
Salt to taste

Try out fat from hen in Dutch oven or heavy stewing kettle. Add butter if additional fat is needed. Sauté chicken pieces, browning lightly and reserve. Sauté garlic and onions until limp and transparent; add mushrooms and sauté until they lose their opaqueness. Stir in flour until it has absorbed all of the fat, then stir in the chicken broth, and continue to stir until the gravy boils and thickens. Add more broth or hot water if necessary. Add remaining ingredients and mix thoroughly, then return chicken to gravy. Simmer about 2½ to 3 hours, or until meat is tender. Remove neck and back pieces—serve only the meaty pieces of chicken. Serves 4 to 5.

## CORNMEAL DUMPLINGS

| | |
|---|---|
| 1½ cups sifted flour | ⅔ cup milk |
| ½ cup yellow cornmeal | 3 tablespoons melted |
| 4 teaspoons baking | butter |
| powder | 1 well-beaten egg white |
| 1 teaspoon salt | |

Sift flour, cornmeal, baking powder and salt together into a bowl. Add milk and melted butter and stir just enough to mix into a stiff batter. Fold in the beaten egg white and drop by spoonfuls on top of the fricasseed chicken—not into the gravy. Cover tightly and let steam for 15 minutes. Cornmeal dumplings take a little longer than plain flour dumplings.

## CHICKEN PIE

Follow directions for Fricassee Chicken but let cool until the meat can be removed from the bones. (Throw the bones, back and neck into a kettle for soup). Mix the chicken meat, keeping it in as large pieces as possible, with the gravy and reheat. Add a cup of freshly cooked peas and diced carrots and pour into an oiled baking pan or large shallow casserole. Top with the following batter:

| | |
|---|---|
| ½ cup yellow cornmeal | ½ cup prepared biscuit |
| 1 teaspoon salt | mix |
| ½ cup boiling water | ½ cup milk |
| ¼ cup melted butter | 1 egg white, beaten |
| 1 egg yolk, beaten | |

Mix cornmeal and salt with boiling water and add butter. When cool stir in the beaten egg yolk and biscuit mix; add milk and fold in beaten egg white last. Pour over hot chicken mixture and bake at 375° F. for about 25 minutes or until top is done and golden brown. Serves 4 to 5.

# Drink Recipes

## SAN FRANCISCO FAVORITES

Since the Gold Rush days San Francisco has been known as a city of two-fisted drinkers. Martinis, highballs, and Scotch on the rocks outsell anything else, but quite a few discerning people like something that tastes good. Here are a few of the favorites.

### RHUM COSMO

In mixing glass with 1 scoop shaved ice:

| | |
|---|---|
| Juice of ½ lime | 1½ ounce Rhum |
| Dash of rock candy | Barbancourt |
| syrup | ½ slice pineapple |
| 1 ounce pineapple juice | |

Shake drink and pour into a 10 ounce goblet. Decorate with half a slice of pineapple and mint. Serve with straws.

Here are a pair of noggins dedicated to the Sunday sailors of San Francisco Bay.

### PORT LIGHT

In blender with 1 scoop shaved ice:

| | |
|---|---|
| 2 teaspoons honey | 1 egg white |
| 1 ounce lemon juice | 2 ounces Bourbon |
| ½ ounce Mynor's Passion | |
| Fruit Nectar | |

Blend and pour into Port Light glass, or a red tumbler with cracked ice. Decorate with fresh mint.

*STARBOARD LIGHT*

In blender with 1 scoop shaved ice:

2 teaspoons honey

1 ounce lemon juice

½ ounce Mynor's Passion
  Fruit Nectar

1 egg white

2 ounces Scotch

Blend and serve in Starboard Light or green tumbler with cracked ice. Decorate with fresh mint.

This is a pretty drink for the girls. Not too strong but it has authority.

*WHITE WITCH*

In sling glass with cracked ice:

Juice of half lime—save
  shell

½ ounce white crème de
  cacao

½ ounce Cointreau

1 ounce Trader Vic's
  White Jamaica Rum

Stir and fill with sparkling water; stir once. Decorate with lime shell and fresh mint which has been dampened and dusted with powdered sugar.

This is a home remedy for butterflies.

## MOOLEY COW

In 10 ounce goblet or tumbler with cracked ice:

½ ounce white crème de cacao
1 ounce vodka
Milk

Stir and fill glass with milk. Dust with nutmeg unless someone objects.

A drink that seems to have caught on for late evening drinking is a combination of Scotch and Drambuie on the rocks.

## RUSTY NAIL

In old-fashioned glass with cracked ice:

1 ounce Scotch
½ ounce Drambuie

Stir and serve.

Every guy thinks he has the one and only gin fizz recipe but this old-timer is way out in front of anything made with gin that I've ever tasted. Good for Sunday morning get-togethers.

## SILVER STALLION

In blender with ½ scoop shaved ice:

Juice of ½ lemon          2 ounces gin
2 ounces vanilla ice      1 egg white
  cream

Blend and pour into chilled goblet or fizz glass. Fill with seltzer and top with a dash of nutmeg or grated orange peel.

This next one is a Reno import, strictly for home consumption. It sounds crazy but it makes a delicious, smooth concoction with a rabbit punch.

*JACKALOPE*

In crock:

>1 bottle good Bourbon
>1 cup sugar
>1 dozen lemons

Cut lemons in half, squeeze into crock with Bourbon and sugar, and drop shells in too. Stir thoroughly. Cover and re-frigerate overnight. Remove lemon shells before using. Shake with ice like a cocktail and strain into chilled cocktail glasses. And shake like crazy—this needs the dilution.

*VELVET HAMMER*

In mixing glass with crushed ice:

>¾ ounce evaporated milk
>½ ounce white crème de cacao
>½ ounce Cointreau

Shake well and strain into chilled cocktail glass. Serve as an after dinner drink.

## TRADER VIC'S TROPICAL DRINKS

Nowhere during my travels in the past few years did I find any drinks worth remembering. So we continue to concoct our own. We must be doing something right. Here are a few of our most popular tropical drinks. (PLATE XX)

*BABALU*  (PLATE XX)

In blender with 1 scoop shaved ice:

¾ ounce pineapple-grapefruit juice
½ ounce lemon juice
2 ounces gold rum

Blend and serve in 10 ounce glass with cracked ice. Decorate with mint and fruit stick. Serve with a malt straw.

*CARIBBEAN*

In shaker with cracked ice:

1 ounce orange juice
½ ounce lemon juice
¼ ounce grenadine

¼ ounce curaçao
3 ounces light rum
3 ounces sparkling water

Shake and pour into 14 ounce chimney glass. Garnish with sliced orange and pineapple decoration. Add sprig of mint and serve with long straw.

*HONOLULU*

In blender with 3 bar scoops crushed ice:

½ slice pineapple          Dash rock candy syrup
½ ounce lemon juice        1½ ounces light rum

Blend and strain through medium mesh strainer into glass compote. Serve with cut straws.

This is purportedly from the Shepheard's Hotel in Cairo but for the life of me I can't remember who gave it to me.

*SUFFERING BASTARD*

In a double old-fashioned glass with shaved ice:

Juice of 1 whole lime—      1 dash orange curaçao
   save 1 shell             1 ounce light rum
1 dash rock candy syrup     2 ounces dark rum
1 dash orgeat syrup

Fill glass with shaved ice. Top with metal shaker and hand shake drink. Decorate with lime shell and fresh mint. Serve with a malt straw.

*HAPA TIKI*

In blender with shaved ice:

1 ounce orange juice        ¼ ounce orgeat syrup
¾ ounce lemon juice         ½ ounce brandy
1 ounce light rum

Blend and pour into double old-fashioned glass with cracked ice. Top with a gardenia, and serve with a malt straw.

*TABU*

In blender with 1 scoop shaved ice:

| | |
|---|---|
| 1½ ounces unsweetened pineapple juice | 1 dash rock candy syrup |
| | 1 ounce light rum |
| ½ ounce lemon juice | 1 ounce vodka |

Blend and pour into double old-fashioned glass. Decorate with fresh mint and fruit. Serve with a malt straw.

This is an old time Trader Vic drink but it is still a favorite.

*FOG CUTTER*

In shaker with cracked ice:

| | |
|---|---|
| 1 ounce orange juice | 1 ounce brandy |
| 2 ounces lemon juice | ½ ounce gin |
| ½ ounce orgeat syrup | Sherry float |
| 2 ounces light rum | |

Shake all ingredients except sherry float and pour into a 14 ounce chimney glass, or a bigger one if you can find it. Add ice to fill glass, and add sherry wine float. Serve with straws (and two aspirin).

*MAHUKONA*

In blender with ½ scoop shaved ice:

| | |
|---|---|
| 2 dashes Angostura bitters | ½ slice pineapple |
| | ½ ounce Triple Sec |
| 1 dash rock candy syrup | 1 ounce light rum |
| ½ ounce lemon juice | |

Blend and serve in 10 ounce Pilsener glass half full of shaved ice. Decorate with fresh mint and fruit on a stick. Serve with a straw.

*RANGOON RUBY* (PLATE XX)

In 10 ounce glass with cracked ice:

Juice of ½ lime—drop
shell in glass
1½ ounces cranberry
juice

2 ounces vodka
Sparkling water

Stir with ice. Add sparkling water. Garnish with mint and serve with a straw.

*SCORPION*

In blender with 1 scoop shaved ice:

1½ ounces lemon juice
2 ounces orange juice
½ ounce orgeat syrup

1 ounce brandy
2 ounces light rum

Blend and pour into a Grapefruit Supreme glass with cracked ice. Decorate with a gardenia and serve with cut straws.

*SHARK'S TOOTH*

In mixing glass with cracked ice:

Juice of ½ lime—save
shell
½ ounce lemon juice

½ dash rock candy syrup
1 dash grenadine
2½ ounces gold rum

Stir and serve in 10 ounce Pilsener glass with cracked ice. Fill with sparkling water. Decorate with lime shell, fresh mint and fruit. Serve with a straw.

*SINGAPORE GIN SLING*

In 14 ounce chimney glass with cracked ice:

½ lime—save the shell
1 dash Angostura bitters
1 ounce Cherry Heering

2 ounces Old Tom Gin
Ginger beer
Benedictine float

Squeeze lime juice into glass; add bitters, Cherry Heering and gin. Fill glass with ginger beer, stir and add float of Benedictine. Decorate with lime shell, fresh mint and serve with long straws.

*TONGA PUNCH*   (PLATE XX)

In blender with ½ scoop shaved ice:

| | |
|---|---|
| ½ lime | 1 dash grenadine |
| 1½ ounces orange juice | ½ ounce curaçao |
| ¾ ounce lemon juice | 2 ounces light rum |

Blend and serve in 14 ounce chimney glass. Decorate with fresh mint and serve with long straw.

*RUM EASTERN SOUR*

In 16 ounce or double old-fashioned glass with ½ scoop shaved ice:

| | |
|---|---|
| ½ orange | 1 dash rock candy syrup |
| ½ lemon | 2 ounces light rum |
| 1 dash orgeat syrup | |

Squeeze orange and lemon into glass and drop in shells. Add rest of ingredients. Fill glass with shaved ice; top with metal shaker and shake drink. Decorate with fresh mint and fruit. Serve with malt straws.

*RUM MINT SQUASH*  (PLATE XX)

In old-fashioned glass:

| | |
|---|---|
| 1 dash Peychaud bitters | 6 or 7 mint leaves |
| 1 dash rock candy syrup | 1 ounce gold rum |
| 1 ounce plain water | Twist of lemon peel |

Muddle mint leaves in bitters, syrup and water, add rum and cracked ice and stir. Serve with twist of lemon peel.


*TORTUGA*  (PLATE XX)

In blender with ½ scoop shaved ice:

| | |
|---|---|
| ½ lime—save shell | 1 dash curaçao |
| 1 ounce lemon juice | 1 ounce Italian vermouth |
| 1½ ounces orange juice | 1¼ ounces 151 proof |
| 1 dash grenadine | Demerara Rum |
| 1 dash créme de cacao | |

Blend and serve in the biggest glass you can find—a small glass vase—with cracked ice. Decorate with lime shell, fresh mint and serve with long malt straws.


*TRADER VIC'S GROG*  (PLATE XX)

In 16 ounce or double old-fashioned glass filled with shaved ice:

| | |
|---|---|
| Dash of Angostura bitters | 1 ounce unsweetened |
| 1 ounce lemon juice | pineapple juice |
| 1 ounce Mynor's Passion | 2 ounces 8-year-old |
| Fruit Nectar | Jamaica rum |

Shake and pour into old-fashioned glass. Decorate with cherry and serve with a straw. *Note:* At Trader Vic's this drink is served in a Ten Pin Pilsener glass.

# PARTY PUNCHES

I am a great advocate of the punch bowl, be it a cocktail party, a barbecue or a buffet supper. Here are a few to fit every occasion.

*TIKI PUNCH*

8 ounces Triple Sec
8 ounces gin
3 ounces fresh lime juice

2 fifths chilled champagne

Mix Triple Sec, gin and lime juice and pour over large pieces of ice in a punch bowl. Stir and let chill for half an hour. At serving time add chilled champagne. Serve in punch cups or goblets. Serves 12 to 15.

*TONGA PUNCH*

1 quart orange juice
1 pint lemon juice
Juice of 8 limes
10 ounces orange curaçao

1 quart light Puerto Rican rum
4 ounces grenadine

Mix ingredients in a gallon jug; pour into a punch bowl over chipped ice and stir thoroughly about 20 minutes before serving time. Add large pieces of ice. Float five or six gardenias. Serve in bamboo or coconut cups. Serves 16 to 20.

*FISH HOUSE PUNCH*

¾ pound sugar
1 quart fresh lemon juice
1 quart sparkling water

2 quarts Jamaica rum
1 quart brandy
4 ounces peach brandy

Dissolve the sugar in a little water; add rest of the ingredients in a large punch bowl, then add a 10 pound cake of ice. Let stand 2 hours before serving, stir occasionally. Serves 20 to 25.

*LEAMINGTON BRANDY PUNCH*

| | |
|---|---|
| 1 pound dessert sugar | 1 fifth cognac |
| 1 fifth lemon juice | 2½ fifths sauterne |

Place sugar in a gallon jug and add the lemon juice. Shake until sugar is thoroughly dissolved, then add the cognac and mix. Fill gallon jug to the top with sauterne or any good white wine (about 2½ fifths). Mix well and chill. At serving time pour over a large piece of ice in a punch bowl. Garnish with fresh mint. Serves 20 to 25.

## MEASUREMENTS, EQUIVALENTS AND HELPFUL INFORMATION

| | |
|---|---|
| 1 dash | 6 drops |
| A few grains, dash or pinch | $\frac{1}{16}$ teaspoon |
| 60 drops | 1 teaspoon |
| 1 teaspoon | $\frac{1}{3}$ tablespoon |
| 3 teaspoons | 1 tablespoon |
| 2 tablespoons | 1 fluid ounce |
| 4 tablespoons | $\frac{1}{4}$ cup or 2 fluid ounces |
| 5$\frac{1}{3}$ tablespoons | $\frac{1}{3}$ cup |
| 8 tablespoons | $\frac{1}{2}$ cup or 4 fluid ounces |
| 16 tablespoons | 1 cup |
| 1 cup | $\frac{1}{2}$ pint or 8 fluid ounces |
| 2 cups | 1 pint or 16 fluid ounces |
| 2 pints | 1 quart or 32 fluid ounces |
| 4 quarts | 1 gallon or 128 fluid ounces |

| CAN SIZES | WEIGHT | APPROXIMATE NO. CUPS |
|---|---|---|
| 8 ounce Tall or Buffet | | 1 |
| Picnic | 10$\frac{1}{2}$ ounces | 1$\frac{1}{4}$ |
| No. 1 Tall | 16 ounces | 2 |
| No. 1 Flat | | 1 |
| No. 300 | 14 to 16 ounces | 1$\frac{3}{4}$ |
| No. 303 | 16 to 17 ounces | 2 |
| No. 2 | 1 pound 4 ounces | 2$\frac{1}{2}$ |
| No. 2$\frac{1}{2}$ | 1 pound 13 ounces | 3$\frac{1}{2}$ |
| No. 3 | 2 pounds 1 ounce | 4 |
| No. 3 – Fruit Juice | 2 pounds 14 ounces | 5$\frac{3}{4}$ |
| No. 5 | 3 pounds, 8 ounces | 7 |
| No. 10 | 6 pounds, 10 to 12 ounces | 12 to 13 |

## SOURCES OF SPECIAL INGREDIENTS

Gourmet: GRM    Chinese:  CHIN
Mexican:  MEX    Japanese: JAP

Cresca Company distributes Trader Vic's Food Products throughout most of the country (or write Cresca Company, 825 E. 140th St., Bronx, N.Y. 10454).

*BOSTON:* CHIN—Sun Sun Co., 34a Oxford St.

*CHICAGO:* CHIN—Man Sun Wing Co., 229 S. Wentworth Ave.; JAP —Shiroma, 1058 W. Argyle Ave.; MEX—Supermercado La Casa Del Pueblo, 1814 S. Blue Island Ave.; Blanco Bakery & Grocery, 1540 W. 18th St.

*DALLAS:* CHIN and JAP—Jung Oriental Foods & Gifts, 2519 N. Fitz-hugh; MEX—Hernandez Finer Foods, 2120 Alamo.

*DENVER:* CHIN and JAP—Pacific Mercantile Co., 1946 Larimer St.; Granada Fish Market, 1919 Lawrence St.; MEX—John's Market, 909 15th St.; La Popular Tortilla and Tamale Shop, 1937 Larimer St.

*HOUSTON:* CHIN—Great Oriental Import and Export, 2009 Polk St.; JAP—Japanese Food Corp., 2002½ White St.; MEX—El Jalepena & Chili Supply, Navigation Blvd.

*NEW YORK:* CHIN—Eastern Trading Co., Inc., 2801 Broadway; JAP —Katagiri Co., 224 East 59th St.; MEX—Large supermarkets and department stores; GRM—Maryland Gourmet Mart, Inc., 412 Amsterdam Ave.

*SAN FRANCISCO:* CHIN—Kwong Hang (groceries), 918 Grant Ave.; Mow Fung (vegetables), 733 Washington St.; JAP—Hosada Bros., 1596 Post St.; MEX—Sanchez, 1923 Fillmore St.; Mi Rancho, 23rd and Shotwell Sts.; GRM—Simon Bros., 2829 Calif. St.; Normandy Lane, City of Paris, Geary at Stockton St.

*WASHINGTON, D.C.:* CHIN—New China Supply Co., 709 H Street, N.W.; JAP—House of Hanna, 15th & T Sts., N.W.; MEX—Mexican & Spanish Store, 1636 17th St. N.W.

# INDEX